Federal Legal Research

CAROLINA ACADEMIC PRESS
LEGAL RESEARCH SERIES

Suzanne E. Rowe, Series Editor

❧

Arizona — Tamara S. Herrera

Arkansas — Coleen M. Barger

California — Hether C. Macfarlane & Suzanne E. Rowe

Colorado — Robert Michael Linz

Connecticut — Jessica G. Hynes

Federal — Mary Garvey Algero, Spencer L. Simons, Suzanne E. Rowe, Scott Childs & Sarah E. Ricks

Florida, Third Edition — Barbara J. Busharis & Suzanne E. Rowe

Georgia — Nancy P. Johnson, Elizabeth G. Adelman & Nancy J. Adams

Idaho — Tenielle Fordyce-Ruff & Suzanne E. Rowe

Illinois, Second Edition — Mark F. Wojcik

Iowa — John D. Edwards, M. Sara Lowe, Karen L. Wallace & Melissa H. Weresh

Kansas — Joseph A. Custer & Christopher L. Steadham

Louisiana — Mary Garvey Algero

Massachusetts — E. Joan Blum

Michigan, Second Edition — Pamela Lysaght & Cristina D. Lockwood

Minnesota — Suzanne Thorpe

Missouri, Second Edition — Wanda M. Temm & Julie M. Cheslik

New York — Elizabeth G. Adelman & Suzanne E. Rowe

North Carolina — Scott Childs

Ohio — Katherine L. Hall & Sara Sampson

Oregon, Second Edition — Suzanne E. Rowe

Pennsylvania — Barbara J. Busharis & Bonny L. Tavares

Tennessee — Sibyl Marshall & Carol McCrehan Parker

Texas — Spencer L. Simons

Washington, Second Edition — Julie Heintz-Cho, Tom Cobb & Mary A. Hotchkiss

Wisconsin — Patricia Cervenka & Leslie Behroozi

❧

Federal Legal Research

Mary Garvey Algero
Spencer L. Simons
Suzanne E. Rowe
Scott Childs
Sarah E. Ricks

Suzanne E. Rowe, Series Editor

CAROLINA ACADEMIC PRESS
Durham, North Carolina

Library of Congress Cataloging-in-Publication Data

Federal legal research / Mary Garvey Algero ... [et al.].
    p. cm.
Includes index.
ISBN 978-1-61163-122-7 (alk. paper)
1. Legal research--United States. I. Algero, Mary Garvey. II. Title.

KF240.F48 2011
340.072'073--dc23

2011038237

CAROLINA ACADEMIC PRESS
700 Kent Street
Durham, North Carolina 27701
Telephone (919) 489-7486
Fax (919) 493-5668
www.cap-press.com

Printed in the United States of America.

Summary of Contents

Contents

List of Tables and Figures

Tables

Series Note

This book complements the Legal Research Series published by Carolina Academic Press, which includes titles from many states around the country. The goal of each book is to provide law students, practitioners, paralegals, college students, laypeople, and librarians with the essential elements of legal research in each state. Unlike more bibliographic texts, the Legal Research Series books seek to explain concisely both the sources of legal research and the process for conducting legal research effectively.

Preface and Acknowledgments

Federal Legal Research complements the state-specific books that comprise the Legal Research Series published by Carolina Academic Press. The book offers concise, accessible explanations of primary authority in the federal system, along with chapters on secondary sources, updating, bill tracking and legislative history, and legal ethics and court rules. Similar to other books in the series, *Federal Legal Research* takes a process-oriented approach to research, discussing strategies and techniques for conducting American legal research both online and in print. While the focus of the book is federal law, state law resources are briefly mentioned in some chapters to highlight variations and to provide connections to the other books in the series.

One challenge in writing a book for both novices and experienced researchers is when and how to introduce new terms. The novice needs background that the experienced research would probably find unnecessary. We have taken two approaches. First, the index to this book includes a "Words and Phrases" entry with subentries to basic terms and indications of where the terms are defined in the text. On the pages indicated, the terms will be italicized to help the reader find them. Second, each chapter of the book includes numerous cross-references to discussions in other chapters. While we tried to keep these cross-references to a manageable number, we decided to err on the side of inclusion to provide guidance for a novice who might be feeling overwhelmed.

In writing this book, each author took responsibility for the following chapters: Mary Algero — secondary sources, judicial systems and judicial opinions, case law research, and court rules and rules of professional responsibility; Spencer Simons — research techniques, statutory research, and bill tracking and legislative history; Suzanne

Rowe—legal authority and the research process, and citators; Scott Child—administrative law research; and Sarah Ricks—constitutional law research. As series editor, Suzanne Rowe took the lead in harmonizing the contents of the chapters and the voices of five authors.

We are grateful to many colleagues, librarians, research assistants, and professional support staff for their contributions to this work. We are especially grateful for the editorial and research assistance of Mason Whitcomb, Kimberly Trujillo, and Jamison McCune. Please note that each of the authors has published other books on related topics, and some of their earlier work is reflected here.

Federal Legal Research

Chapter 1

Legal Authority and the Research Process

I. Introduction

Legal research is the process of finding authoritative sources that address a particular legal question. The process is most successful when it is planned in advance and when the researcher takes an organized approach. This book introduces the most important sources of federal law and explains how to research those sources in a planned, organized research strategy.

II. Legal Research Documents

Legal documents are available from a plethora of sources. For most legal documents, the traditional sources have been books. Statutes and administrative regulations are published in books often called *codes* because they codify statutes and regulations by topic. Judicial opinions are published in series of books called *reporters*. Many documents are available both in print and online. Online sources include government sites that provide access to the documents for free but sometimes have limited search capacity; relatively inexpensive commercial sites that may offer more user-friendly searching; and very expensive sites like Lexis and Westlaw, which provide vast numbers of documents and advanced searching techniques. Even when a researcher is working exclusively online, the citation to a document may be to a print version. Judicial opinions, for example, are most often accessed by citation to reporters. Still other documents are available exclusively online, especially as state governments reduce their print publications.

As legal materials have become more widely available,[1] the challenge in legal research has shifted from identifying potentially relevant documents to analyzing search results. To begin to analyze the results of any search, researchers must be able to recognize documents based on their appearance, content, and citation and to understand how various documents fit in the hierarchy of legal authorities. While it is easy to recognize statutes and distinguish them from regulations when those documents appear in different books in different parts of the library, it is more difficult for the novice researcher to know when looking at a computer screen what a document is and how important it is in the hierarchy of legal authorities.

Appendix A of this chapter contains samples of some of the most common and important legal sources: a constitutional provision, a statute, an administrative regulation, a judicial opinion, and an annotation from *American Law Reports*. Appendix B provides samples of citations to those and other legal sources. The next two parts of this chapter show how those sources are classified and how they fit into the legal hierarchy.

III. Sources and Classes of Legal Authority

Law is produced by entities or individuals vested with law-making power. The federal government has three branches — the legislative, the executive, and the judicial — and each produces legal authority.

---

1. Note that the wide availability of documents does not mean that documents are always easy to find. Searching for a document in an online database can be difficult for the novice researcher, even when armed with a citation. Sometimes finding a document — including a statute or a regulation — in a print source is still easier and more efficient than finding the document online.

A. Primary vs. Secondary Authority

Speaking broadly, there are two classes of law. *Primary authority* is law produced by government bodies with law-making power. Legislatures write statutes; courts write judicial opinions; and administrative agencies write regulations. *Secondary authorities*, in contrast, are materials that are written about the law, generally by practicing attorneys, law professors, or legal editors. Secondary authorities include law practice guides, treatises, law review articles, and legal encyclopedias. These secondary sources are designed to aid researchers in understanding the law and locating primary authority.

B. Mandatory vs. Persuasive Authority

Primary authority can be either mandatory or persuasive. *Mandatory authority* is binding on the court that would decide a conflict if the situation were litigated. Mandatory authority is also called *binding authority* because parties within its jurisdiction are bound by it. In a question of federal law, mandatory or binding authority includes the United States Constitution, statutes enacted by Congress, regulations issued by federal agencies, and opinions of the United States Supreme Court. In addition, opinions of intermediate appellate courts are binding on federal trial courts.

Persuasive authority is not binding but may be followed when it is relevant and well reasoned. Authority may be merely persuasive if it is from a different jurisdiction or if it is not produced by a law-making body. In a question of federal law, examples of persuasive authority include state statutes, opinions of state courts or foreign courts, and secondary authorities ranging from law review articles to treatises. In some situations, federal judicial opinions are persuasive, not mandatory. For example, a federal trial court in the Ninth Circuit is not bound to follow the opinions of the other intermediate appellate courts.[2]

---

2. The federal court system is explained in Chapter 8.

2. Generating Search Terms

After gathering facts and determining the jurisdiction, generate a list of search terms. You will use these terms to begin research in print and online sources that use indexes and to search online through a synopsis or the full text of documents. (In online searching, the search terms are sometimes referred to as *keywords*.)

To conduct thorough research, you will need a comprehensive list of words, terms, and phrases that may lead to law on point. Organized brainstorming is the best way to compile a comprehensive list of search terms. Some researchers ask the journalistic questions: Who? What? How? Why? When? Where? Others use a mnemonic device like TARPP, which stands for Things, Actions, Remedies, People, and Places. Whether you use one of these suggestions or develop your own method, generate a broad range of search terms regarding the facts, issues, and desired solutions of your client's situation. Include in the list both specific and general words. Try to think of synonyms and antonyms for each term since at this point you are uncertain which terms an index, synopsis, or document may include. Using a legal dictionary or thesaurus may generate additional terms.[5]

In initial brainstorming, the goal is to produce as many terms as possible. But when you begin researching, use those terms that appear on the list most often or that seem most relevant. As your research progresses, you will learn new search terms to include in the list and decide to take others off. For example, a secondary source should use words and phrases that are important in analyzing a particular area of law. Reading cases should give you insights into the terms judges tend to use in discussing this topic. These words, phrases, and special terms need to be added to the list.

You should also review the list periodically to help you refine your research. If an online search produces far too many results, re-

---

5. Chapter 3 introduces legal dictionaries. Increasingly, online databases contain thesauri that suggest alternative terms.

view the list for more specific search terms. On the other hand, if the terms you use initially produce no hits, review the list for broader terms.

3. Keeping a Research Log

Keeping a research log can help you stay organized throughout the research process. Begin the log by summarizing the important facts and identifying the jurisdiction. Next, generate a list of search terms, using one of the brainstorming techniques. Then, try to write in a single sentence the issue you are researching. This exercise can crystallize your task and keep you focused as you start to search for relevant materials. (You might begin a new project unable to summarize the issue or issues succinctly; after researching secondary sources, you should be able to refine your initial statement of the issue.)

Then sketch out a list of resources you intend to check, ensuring that you will touch each step of the legal research process. Decide on an initial order for the steps of your research, recognizing that you might march through the six steps as listed or that information that you have as you begin to research might suggest you should start with enacted law, cases, or citators. As you conduct your research, keep in your log a list of the resources you actually use, the searches that you conduct, and the results. When searching in print, make notes on a legal pad or on your computer. When searching online, use database functions that allow you to save searches (e.g., "History" or "Research Trail").

As you continue your research, your log will develop. Add new search terms as you encounter them. Refine your single sentence summarizing the issue as you learn more about the law. List any factual questions that you need to confirm with the client if they affect the legal analysis. Record the most important authorities for your issue. While you will initially skim legal documents to determine whether they are relevant, you must stop at numerous points during your research and carefully read the documents that seem to be guiding your analysis. For this careful reading, many researchers find that they are more effective reading documents in print rather than online. Further, taking notes helps researchers understand complex documents more thoroughly than simply highlighting the documents does.

Ideally, you should outline the issues in detail in your log and include key statutes, cases, and other authorities next to each point in your outline. In this way, your log will turn into an outline of your analysis, with supporting authorities for each point. Cut and paste into your log the critical text from controlling primary authority, along with its citation information. If you record citation information for authorities you are certain to rely on, you will have that available when you begin writing your document without having to relocate each authority.

B. Using Secondary Sources

Beginning a new research project with a secondary source will often be more effective than beginning immediately to search for statutes or cases on point. In complex legal matters, beginning research with a secondary source is essential. A secondary source is likely to provide background information that gives context to the rest of the research. A secondary source may provide an overview of the pertinent issues, aiding in the analysis of the legal problem. The text of a secondary source will likely explain unfamiliar terminology and concepts, making it possible to develop a more effective list of search terms. Also, secondary sources often provide a shortcut to researching primary authority by including summaries of and references to statutes, regulations, and cases. Secondary sources are covered in Chapter 3.

C. Researching Enacted Law

The third step in the research process covers three types of *enacted law*: the constitution, statutes, and regulations. Researching these three types of law is intertwined. Federal statutory books include not only the text of statutes but also the text of the U.S. Constitution. These books also contain references to related regulations. Online, statutes and constitutional provisions may be provided in a combined database; regulations will typically be in different databases, but related statutes and regulations will often be hyperlinked.

The most useful sources for researching enacted law are *annotated*, meaning that they provide extensive references to related legal materials. For example, an annotated statutory code might contain references to helpful secondary sources, related regulations, and judicial opinions that cite each statute.

This book treats enacted law in four chapters: Chapter 4 addresses the U.S. Constitution, Chapter 5 covers statutes, Chapter 6 deals with the related topics of bill tracking and legislative history, and Chapter 7 explains regulations and other types of administrative law.

D. Researching Cases

A researcher following the fundamental process often arrives at the fourth step — researching judicial opinions — already knowing the names, citations, and essential legal points of a number of cases that might be relevant. References in secondary sources and annotated codes will have provided that information.

The careful researcher should take advantage of two additional research tools. The first tool is a digest. A *digest* is an extensive topical index of cases in a certain jurisdiction or subject area. Digests exist in print in multi-volume sets and online in powerful databases. The second tool is keyword searching in online databases that contain cases from the relevant jurisdiction or on the specific topic. Keyword searching is more likely to be effective after the researcher has gained considerable background in the area of law.

After finding citations to relevant cases, the researcher must read them carefully. Relying on a summary in a secondary source or a digest is dangerous and could lead to malpractice. Cases have traditionally been published first in series of books called *reporters*. Even now that much research takes place online, cases are often referenced by citation to reporters. Chapter 8 covers cases, including sections on the federal court system and the parts of a judicial opinion. Chapter 9 explores techniques for researching cases.

E. Updating Research

Before using any legal authority to analyze a problem, a researcher must know whether the document being read is the current version of the authority and how that authority has been treated by later actions of a court, legislature, or agency. A few examples show the difference between currency and subsequent treatment. Regarding currency, a statute might have been amended so recently that the one located in a code is no longer current. A case may have been reversed on appeal. Regarding subsequent treatment, a statute might have been found unconstitutional by a court. A case might have been overruled years after it was decided, or a case might have been criticized by a line of other cases over a period of years. There is an obvious overlap between currency and subsequent treatment, which is addressed next. Chapter 10 explains in detail how to use citators to determine the validity of an authority and to expand the research universe.

1. Checking Currency

Ensuring that authorities represent the current law is fairly easy when using online sources like Lexis and Westlaw. They update their databases frequently, and either provide the current language or provide links to documents that affect the currency of an authority (e.g., a recently enacted bill that repeals the statute you are researching). In print research, ensuring that authorities are current often requires checking both *pocket parts*, extra pages inserted in a slot at the back of the book, and softbound supplements. Pocket parts and supplements contain more recent information because they can be printed more quickly than hardbound volumes can be updated. Not all print sources use pocket parts and supplements. To ensure the currency of federal regulations when working in print, the researcher has to consult other publications (namely the *List of Sections Affected* and the *Federal Register*). Some secondary sources are never updated, though later editions may be published with more recent information.

2. Determining Subsequent Treatment

Determining how a particular authority has been treated by later actions of a court, legislature, or agency requires using a citator. This step has traditionally been called "Shepardizing" because the first major citators were series of books called *Shepard's Citations*.

Now there are two citators that set the gold standard for checking the subsequent treatment of authorities, although others exist.[6] Lexis provides the "Shepard's" service, while Westlaw provides "KeyCite." Each of these two citators gives the researcher extensive information about subsequent legal sources that have cited a particular authority, allowing the researcher to determine whether an authority is still valid and respected. This validation of resources is required for all research projects.

Note that citators provide overlapping but different information from sources that check the currency of authorities. A pocket part for a statute will show whether the language of the statute has been amended and may refer to recent cases that discuss the statute. A citator, in contrast, will highlight the case that found the statute unconstitutional or the line of cases that criticized the statute.

3. Expanding Research

Citators are also valuable research tools beyond their primary role of validating authorities by checking subsequent treatment. The citators' extensive lists of sources are valuable research tools because they refer to cases, statutes, and other sources that might also be relevant to a particular research project. In other words, once you have determined that a particular statute or case is relevant to your work, a list of other authorities that have cited that statute or case is a treasure trove of additional, relevant authorities.

F. Ending Research

One of the most difficult problems new researchers face is deciding when to stop researching. Occasionally, research reveals a definite answer to the problem. More often, deadlines imposed by the court or a supervisor (or, for academic writing, a publication deadline) limit the amount of time spent on a research project. In law

---

6. Other services provide useful but less extensive citators. As examples, Fastcase provides "Authority Check"; VersusLaw provides "V.Cite"; and Google Scholar provides "How cited." While these services are helpful, they are not as extensive or as sophisticated as Shepard's or KeyCite.

practice, the expense to the client is also a consideration. In projects without clear answers, you have to decide when to stop. When research in various sources leads back to the same authorities, you can be confident that you have been thorough. At that point, review the outline in your research log to ensure each point of analysis is supported as fully as possible. As a final check, review each step of the basic research process to ensure you considered each one.

If you have worked through the research process and found no legal authority, it may be that nothing relevant exists. Before reaching that conclusion, expand your search terms and look in a few more secondary sources. Consider whether other jurisdictions may have helpful persuasive authority.

Remember that the goal of legal research is to solve a client's problem. If the law does not support the solution that your client had in mind, think creatively to address the problem in a different way. While you must inform the client when a desired approach is not feasible, you need to suggest an alternate solution if possible.

Appendix A. Samples of Legal Documents

Figures 1-1 to 1-4 contain excerpts from primary federal authority. Figure 1-5 contains an excerpt from a secondary source. Additional samples of other sources appear in later chapters. Specifically, Chapter 3 has an excerpt from a treatise, Chapter 6 contains examples of legislative history documents, and Chapter 8 contains a PDF of a case in a West reporter.

Figure 1-1. Constitutional Provision

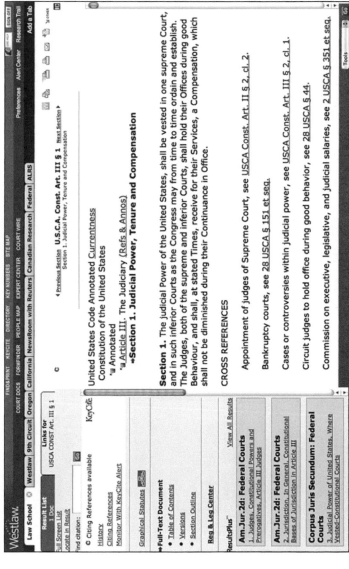

Source: Westlaw. Reprinted with permission of West, a Thomson Reuters business. This provision is referenced in Chapter 4.

Figure 1-2. Statute

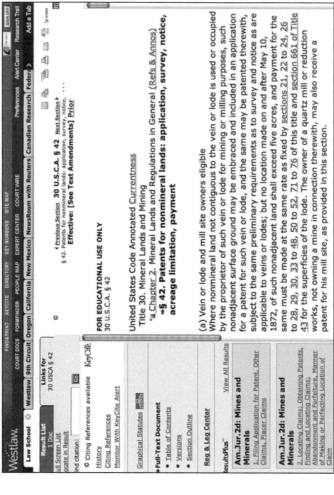

Source: Westlaw. Reprinted with permission of West, a Thomson Reuters business. Excerpts of annotations for this statute in the *United States Code Annotated* are shown in Chapter 5, in Figures 5-1 and 5-2.

Figure 1-3. Regulation

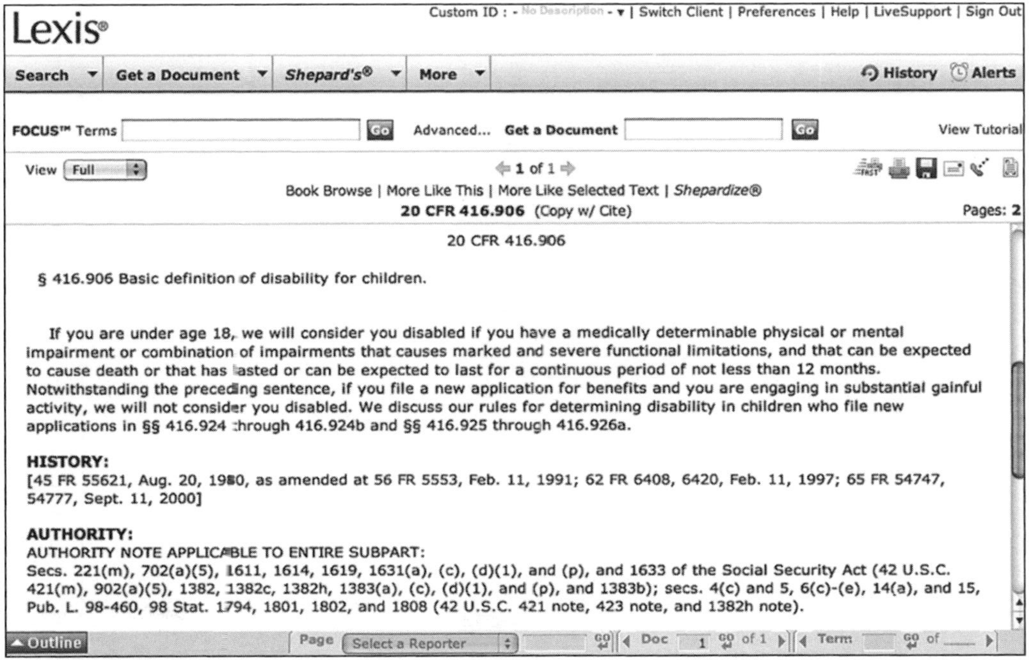

Source: Copyright 2011 LexisNexis, a division of Reed Elsevier Inc. All Rights Reserved. Lexis is a registered trademark of Reed Elsevier Properties Inc. and is used with the permission of LexisNexis. This regulation is referenced in Chapter 7.

Figure 1-4. Judicial Opinion

[PUBLISH]

IN THE UNITED STATES COURT OF APPEALS

FOR THE ELEVENTH CIRCUIT

| FILED |
| U.S. COURT OF APPEALS |
| ELEVENTH CIRCUIT |
| JANUARY 11, 2010 |
| JOHN P. LEY |
| ACTING CLERK |

No. 08-16010

D.C. Docket No. 07-00361-CR-KD

UNITED STATES OF AMERICA,

Plaintiff-Appellee,

versus

LUDIVIC WHITE, JR.

Defendant-Appellant.

Appeal from the United States District Court
for the Southern District of Alabama

(January 11, 2010)

Before DUBINA, Chief Judge, BIRCH and SILER,* Circuit Judges.

SILER, Circuit Judge:

---

* Honorable Eugene E. Siler, Jr., United States Circuit Judge for the Sixth Circuit, sitting by designation.

Source: U.S. Courts website, http://www.ca11.uscourts.gov/opinions/ops/200816010.pdf. This is the first page of the slip opinion for the case that appears in Chapter 8, Figure 8-2.

Figure 1-4. Judicial Opinion, *continued*

INTRODUCTION

Ludivic White, Jr., appeals his conviction for possession of a firearm by a person convicted of a misdemeanor crime of domestic violence, in violation of 18 U.S.C. § 911(g)(9). For the following reasons, we affirm.

I.

At around 2:00 a.m. on April 20, 2007, Police Officers Brad Latham and Otha Lee Hargrove received a complaint about loud music coming from a vehicle parked in a high-crime area of Mobile, Alabama. Upon arriving at the scene, the officers saw a vehicle that matched dispatch's description. As Officer Hargrove drove by the vehicle with his windows partially open, he smelled a "strong" odor of marijuana and heard music emanating from the car. The vehicle contained four occupants: two females in the front seat and two males in the back seat.

Latham approached the driver and asked for identification, which she was unable to provide. The officers then questioned the occupants about whether they had been smoking marijuana. The occupants denied possessing or using any drugs. Latham asked the driver to exit the vehicle and requested her name and social security number to perform a background check. Latham then requested that White step out of the car. Shortly thereafter, Hargrove, who was busy performing a background check on the other male passenger, heard Latham say "gun," at which

---

Source: U.S. Courts website, http://www.ca11.uscourts.gov/opinions/ops/ 200816010.pdf. This is the second page of the slip opinion for the case that appears in Chapter 8, Figure 8-2.

Figure 1-5. *American Law Reports* Annotation

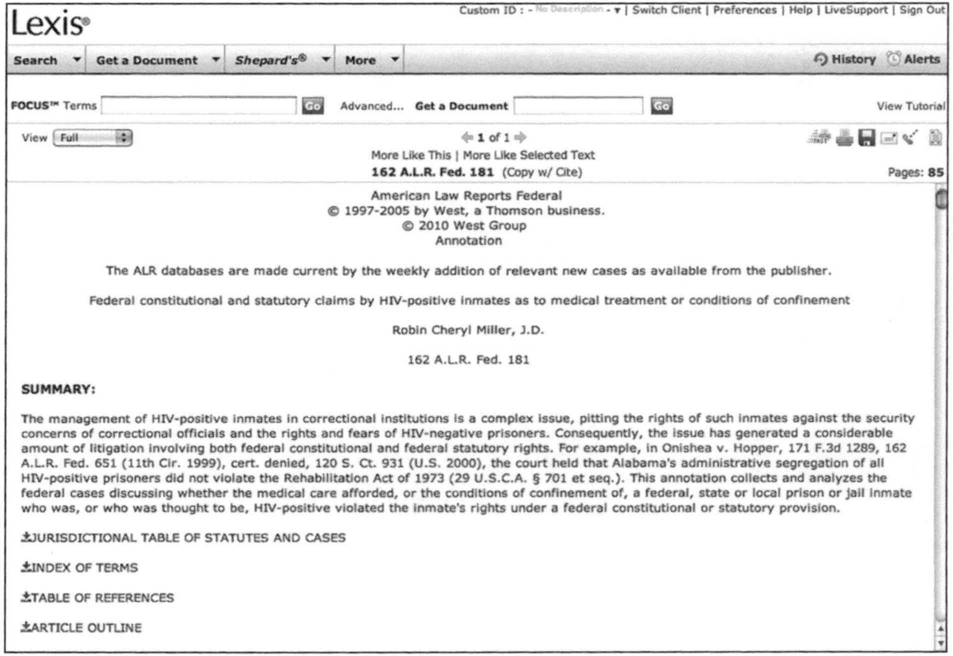

Source: LexisNexis, a division of Reed Elsevier Inc. All Rights Reserved. Lexis is a registered trademark of Reed Elsevier Properties Inc. and is used with the permission of LexisNexis. *American Law Reports* is published by West, a division of Thomson Reuters, and is used with permission. This annotation is referenced in Chapter 4.

Appendix B. Sample Citations for Legal Documents

The following citations do not conform to any particular manual's requirements. Rather, they are the types of citations a researcher is likely to encounter when searching either online or in print sources. Citations are explained in chapters that cover primary resources. Note that, even when research is conducted exclusively online, legal citations often refer to the volume, section, or page of a print volume.

Document	Citation	Comments
United States constitutional provision	U.S. Const. art. III, § 1	Provisions in the federal Constitution are arranged by articles and sections.
Federal statute	30 U.S.C. § 42	This is a citation to the official set of federal statutes, the *United States Code*. The statute is located in Title 30, Section 42.
	30 U.S.C.A. § 42	This citation is to the same statute in a series published by West called the *United States Code Annotated*.
	30 U.S.C.S. § 42	Again, this is the same statute, but it is cited to a series published by LexisNexis called the *United States Code Service*.
Senate report on a bill	Sen. Rpt. 99-146	This citation references a report published by a Senate committee in the 99th Congress.
Federal regulation	20 C.F.R. § 416.906	This is a final regulation published in the *Code of Federal Regulations*.
Case decided by the United States Supreme Court	*N.Y. Times Co. v. Sullivan*, 376 U.S. 254 (1964)	This citation is to the official reporter for Supreme Court cases, called *United States Reports*. The case appears in volume 376, beginning on page 254.
	N.Y. Times Co. v. Sullivan, 84 S. Ct. 710 (1964)	This is the same case, cited to a West publication called *Supreme Court Reporter*.
	N.Y. Times Co. v. Sullivan, 1964 U.S. LEXIS 1655	Again, this is the same case, but with a citation unique to the online service Lexis.
Law review article	106 Mich. L. Rev. 1543 (2008)	This is a citation to a law review article by Cass R. Sunstein that was published in the *Michigan Law Review*.
American Law Reports annotation	162 A.L.R. Fed. 181 (2000)	An annotation in *American Law Reports* summarizes law on specific topics. The annotations are written by staff editors and typically not cited, although they are very useful research tools.

Chapter 2

Research Techniques

Chapter 1 presents the framework in which United States legal authority is created, the various types of legal authority, and the research process that most efficiently discovers the relevant authorities in their proper relationships to each other. This chapter discusses basic principles underlying legal research, factors to consider in choosing whether to research online or in print, and techniques to add power and precision to legal research. The concepts discussed in the chapter are widely applicable and will appear in various guises in the remaining chapters of this book.

I. Basic Principles

The researcher beginning a project faces an immense body of legal authority. Fortunately, much effort has been invested by many people in organizing legal authority in order to help the researcher consistently and dependably locate authority needed for the task at hand. Keep in mind the following basic principles (summarized in Table 2 1) whenever you perform legal research.

Table 2-1. Overview of Research Principles and Techniques

Basic Principles	Examples
A. Determine the meaning of words.	• Use a legal dictionary for unfamiliar terms. • Note recurring words and phrases in a line of cases. They may have a unique meaning within a developing doctrine and might be useful terms for further searching. • Identify defined terms in statutes before reading statute sections.
B. Take advantage of the work of others.	• When researching in an unfamiliar or complex topic, start by reading commentary, such as treatises. • Use forms to aid in drafting procedural and transactional documents, saving yourself time and effort. Be sure you research and know the law before drafting.
C. Use the interconnectivity of American legal materials.	• Understand each type of legal resource and learn to use finding tools so that you can use one relevant document to find all related documents, of whatever type.

A. Determine the Meaning of Words

Every person new to the study of law is confronted with many terms of art. Keep a legal dictionary close at hand and look up all unfamiliar words and phrases.

You will encounter unfamiliar words and phrases throughout your career. In addition to terms of art, some words and phrases develop special meanings as legal doctrines evolve. These words and phrases have meanings within the context of particular lines of cases, as courts use the words or phrases repeatedly as each case builds upon previous cases concerning a legal issue. For example, the meaning of the phrase "due process of law," which appears in the Fifth Amendment of the U.S. Constitution, has been developed almost entirely by judicial opinions and the specific meaning varies by issue and has varied greatly over time. In another example, courts in different jurisdictions have developed different interpretations of what is a "tool of the trade" for purposes of debtor property exemptions, based on different interpretations of what tools or instruments are "necessary" for conducting a trade or business. Be alert for recurring words and phrases as you read a line of cases.

Table 2-1. Overview of Research Principles and Techniques,
continued

Tools, Techniques, and Tips	Examples
A. Use the library catalog.	• Use the library's online catalog to find books, periodicals, online databases, and Internet resources. • Use call numbers from the catalog to locate identified items and to discover additional items by shelf scanning and use of shelf lists. • Learn to use subject headings from a found item to locate other items on the same topic.
B. Use finding tools. *1. Indexes*	• Use indexes to locate discussion of a topic within a work. • Use indexes to bodies of literature to locate articles about a topic. LegalTrac is an online index to legal periodical literature. • Try scanning an index quickly to see if you recognize additional relevant terms.
2. Tables of contents	• Use tables of contents to see the organization of a work and to locate relevant discussion.
3. Other finding tools	• Use tables of many kinds to locate legal information. Be sure to see whether a resource contains tables. • Use legal digests to find cases on a very specific topic. • Use citators, such as Shepard's and KeyCite, to identify legal authority citing a known document.
C. Use a known document to find other documents.	• Use catalog subject headings assigned to a relevant book to find other books on the same topic. • Use subject terms assigned to a law journal article in LegalTrac to find other articles on the same topic.
D. Ask a librarian.	• Law librarians are expert legal researchers. They can help you formulate research strategies and use legal resources more effectively.

A challenging aspect of reading legal texts is that seemingly familiar words often have special legal meanings in a particular context. For example, most statutes use defined terms, which have very specific meanings for the purposes of the statutes. You must recognize and understand defined terms when reading a statute. (See Chapter 5, Section II.A.4., on reading statutes.) Remember also that much statutory language has been the subject of interpretation by the courts as they decide cases and that you must read the cases to find the meaning the courts have given the words of a statute.

Terms of art and recurring words and phrases are powerful search terms for locating cases dealing with a particular doctrine. Be sure you understand the significance of these words and phrases and know how to use them appropriately in your research, analysis, and writing.

B. Take Advantage of the Work of Others

Many people have spent a great deal of time mastering an area of the law and publishing in print and online widely available and accessible works on almost any subject. Learn to take advantage of this work by others.

The principle of taking advantage of the work of others has many applications in legal research and practice. In the early stages of a research project, for example, the researcher will often read commentary, such as treatises, in which an expert on a subject has pulled together vast amounts of primary authority and synthesized and summarized it so that the topic can be readily understood. Similarly, the practitioner faced with drafting a procedural document (e.g., a complaint) or a transactional document (e.g., a contract) will generally start with a sample form of a document rather than draft the document from scratch. This use of forms is an ancient practice by which practitioners save time, effort, and money by building on the work of others. Examples of the basic principle of taking advantage of the work of others appear throughout this book.

C. Use the Interconnectivity of American Legal Materials

The body of legal authority in the American legal system is the best organized, most interconnected of any legal system in the world. Many tools have been developed to identify each unique document, ensure that it can be located, and link it to similar documents and to relevant documents in other types of authority. For example, one legal issue may be controlled by a statute, several regulations, and a number of cases. These authorities can be researched using several tools, most of which are cross-referenced or hyperlinked.

Because of this interconnectivity, finding just one relevant authority can lead to a plethora of other sources on point. In fact, if you have one relevant secondary source, statute, regulation, or case, you can follow a trail to essentially all relevant authority. One source leads to another. You can enter the research process almost anywhere and find your way to authority of all types, if you understand the resources and their finding tools. The preceding clause is critical; you must understand the resources you are using, their relations to other resources, and the finding tools that bridge the gaps between different types of authority.

Although it is generally possible to begin the research process at many access points, there is typically a most efficient, logical, and analytically productive path to pursue for most projects. Chapter 1 explains that path. The remaining chapters in this book are devoted to building your knowledge of the types of federal legal authority and the tools that allow you to search within them and to extend your search to relevant documents in the other types of authority.

II. Tools, Techniques, and Tips

A. Use the Library Catalog

A surprisingly underused tool for legal research is the law library's online catalog. The catalog has traditionally contained records describing all the books, journals, magazines, newspapers, and other print items held by the library and used for research. These days, the catalog also typically contains descriptions of and links to the library's online databases and links to many valuable resources on the Internet. Thus, the library catalog is almost certain to provide access to materials useful for any research project.

Once you have located a record of a book, journal, or other resource in the catalog, you can locate the physical item by using the *call number*, which indicates the unique location of that item in the library. An example of a call number is KF5402 .S34 1991.[1] The KF shows that the subject of this book deals with U.S. law. The following number, 5402, indicates the book is within the range of administrative law materials. The .S34 indicates the author's name begins with an S and that the book falls between items with higher and lower numbers following the S. The final number, 1991, indicates the year of publication of the book. This particular call number is assigned to the book *Administrative Law*, written by Bernard Schwartz and published in 1991. By following the sequence of numbers in the KF portion of a library that has this book, you can easily find this unique item on the shelves.

After locating a particular book in the library, scan the other books in the vicinity that concern the same or related subjects. For example, scanning the shelves around the Schwartz book will reveal other books on the subject of administrative law, some of which may prove more useful for your purposes than this book. Note that you can also scan in the online catalog a "shelf list" of books on either side of a book you identified in the catalog by clicking on the hyperlinked call number in the catalog record.

When looking at the catalog record for an item, note the subject headings[2] assigned to the item. *Subject headings* are standardized terms assigned to a work by a cataloger to describe the subjects covered by the item. For example, the Schwartz book has this assigned subject heading: Administrative law — United States. If you click on a hyperlinked subject heading, the catalog will show a list of other books in the library dealing with the same subject. Similarly, by clicking on the author's hyperlinked name, other books written by the same author are identified. Each of the techniques just discussed (shelf scanning, shelf lists, subject heading lists, and author lists) al-

---

1. This example is a call number in the Library of Congress call number system, the system used in the United States by almost all academic libraries, including law school libraries.

2. The Library of Congress recently changed the name from "subject headings" to "descriptors," a more generic term. Most online catalogs, however, still refer to them as "subject headings."

lows you to extend a search from one relevant item to other relevant items in the library.

B. Use Finding Tools

Legal research finding tools are ingenious and powerful. Many finding tools have been developed to locate documents within a particular type of authority, such as statutes. Other tools allow the researcher to use documents found in one type of authority to locate documents on the same subject in other types of authority, for example, citators.[3] A great deal of work has gone into the development of finding tools. Use them whenever possible to save time, effort, and money and to the get the best results possible.

1. Indexes

An index helps you find discussion of a particular subject within a work. An *index* is an alphabetically arranged list of descriptive terms, with page numbers (or sometimes section numbers or paragraph numbers) indicating where in the work the subject is discussed.

Indexes are produced not only for single volumes and series, but also for bodies of literature. LegalTrac, for example, provides citations to the legal commentary published in law reviews, law journals, and other legal periodicals.[4] A well made index contains terms that might not appear in the text of a particular document but which researchers are likely to have in mind when they search or to recognize as relevant. This knowledge added by the indexer allows the researcher to find documents that a keyword search of the same text or texts would not reveal.

---

3. A *citator* lists subsequent sources that have cited a particular authority. By looking up a case in a citator, for example, you can find cases, articles, books, and other sources that later cited that case. Citators are covered in Chapter 10.

4. LegalTrac is the online version of a print index, the *Current Law Index*. It is discussed in Chapter 3, Section III.C.

The power of indexing points out an important secret of re-searching: our ability to recognize relevant terms and concepts is much greater than is our ability to think of all possibly relevant terms from scratch. Learn to take advantage of this power of recognition.[5] When using an index, develop the habit of checking the terms listed under a major term to see which ones might point to useful mater-ial. Follow up on cross-references. When an initial search in the index has not been productive, it sometimes pays to quickly skim the en-tire index to see if any terms jump out at you. Surprisingly often, they will.

2. Tables of Contents

Tables of contents are another type of finding tool. A *table of con-tents* is essentially an outline of the organization of a book or other work. For example, this book's table of contents identifies the chap-ters and the subdivisions of each chapter. If you wanted to determine quickly where statutory research is covered, a glance at the table of contents indicates that Chapter 5 discusses statutory research. Re-viewing the table of contents to a work may reveal material not found either by searching in the index or by conducting a keyword search online.

3. Other Finding Tools

Many other finding tools are used in legal research: A variety of tables are used in many legal publications, such as tables to cross-reference between older law and a more recent version. Legal digests allow the researcher to locate cases dealing with particular subjects.

---

5. Another way the power of recognition can be put to work is by learn-ing to skim long blocks of text for relevant passages. Many treatises and other books have very long discussions of a subject, only certain portions of which are relevant to your needs. Many researchers learn to locate these relevant passages by quickly skimming over many pages of text. The "serendipity" by which experienced researchers come across unexpected insights often results from the skimming of the books in a library's subject area or in similar col-lections online.

Legal citators lead to legal authority that has cited a particular legal document. These and other finding tools are discussed throughout this book.

C. Use a Known Document to Find Other Documents

Much research involves using one known document to find others of the same type. Recall the discussion in Section II.A. of using subject headings in the library catalog to find other items on the same subject. The Library of Congress subject heading system is one example of a widely used kind of finding aid known as *controlled vocabularies*.

Controlled vocabularies are developed to enable precise description and dependable discovery of documents in the databases of many disciplines. Look for a controlled vocabulary when searching in an electronic database or in traditional print guides to subject literature. In this book, numerous examples of this principle are described for effective research in many types of legal authority. For example, Chapter 3 discusses LegalTrac, a database used to find journal articles. LegalTrac assigns "subjects" to the records for articles. Once you have found a relevant article, you can use the subject terms assigned to it to locate other relevant articles. Similarly, Chapter 6 discusses the CRS Legislative Subject Terms used to perform precise research in THOMAS, the website of the Library of Congress.

D. Ask Somebody Who Knows: A Librarian

Professional librarians are experts in legal resources and legal research methods. In an academic library, most or all of the professional librarians have J.D. degrees, as well as professional degrees in librarianship. Law firm librarians have a great deal of experience in legal research and in training others to perform legal research. Whenever you have questions about how to find or use a legal resource, or about the fine points of the legal research process, do not hesitate to ask a librarian. The librarians are there to help you and welcome your questions.

Table 2-2. Questions to Ask Before Using a Resource

General Categories	Specific Questions and Examples
1. Is It Relevant?	• What jurisdiction does a resource cover? • What type of authority does a resource contain? For example, you would use the *Code of Federal Regulations* to find administrative regulations, not the *United States Code*.
2. Is It Authoritative?	• Is a primary authority resource official? Be aware that resources published by a governmental body might not be official; this is especially common with online resources. • If a resource is not official, is it generally recognized as reliable authority? • Is the author of secondary authority, such as a treatise, a recognized authority on the topic? • Is a publisher of a resource recognized for publishing works of reliable authority?
3. Is It Current?	• Has a resource been updated recently? The law changes constantly. Check all resources to be sure they have been kept current. • Use the most current resource available.

E. Ask These Questions Before Using a Resource

Table 2-2 lists crucial questions you should ask before using a legal resource. The questions are explained below.

1. Is It Relevant?

Researchers sometimes spend considerable time and effort searching in a resource that simply cannot provide what they are looking for. The following three tips can help you avoid wasting time and effort in irrelevant resources.

- Before you start to search in a resource, ask yourself what jurisdiction the resource covers. If the relevant law is state law, a search in federal law resources is wasted.
- Ask what type of authority you are seeking. For example, if you need to find federal regulations, be sure to search in a source containing regulations, not statutes.
- If you need journal articles, search in a periodical literature index, such as LegalTrac, rather than in the library catalog

(which will contain references to journals, but not the articles in them).

2. Is It Authoritative?

A challenge for the novice legal researcher is knowing which sources of legal information are authoritative, meaning the sources will provide credible statements about or interpretations of the law. Chapter 1 explained what primary and secondary authorities are. The following discussion explores the criteria for determining how authoritative a source is; the criteria differ for primary and secondary authority.

a. Primary Authority

Primary authority (e.g., statutes, regulations, cases) is most authoritative when it is published in an "official" publication, meaning the relevant governmental body has certified the publication as the definitive statement of the legal texts created by the body. An example of an official publication is *United States Reports*, the official text of U.S. Supreme Court opinions, published by the Government Printing Office. Surprisingly, the fact that a statement of a jurisdiction's law is disseminated by that government does not necessarily mean the statement is official. For example, many governmental bodies publish their statutes and regulations online, but with the explicit warning that the online version is not official and should not be relied upon.

Publications of primary law by private commercial publishers might be recognized as authoritative. In some instances, a government might identify a particular commercial publication, such as a West case reporter, as its official publication. Sometimes, a commercial publication comes to be recognized, in the absence of a truly official version, as the "quasi-official" statement of the law or to be considered as authoritative through long custom and practice. Many West case reporters, such as *West's Federal Reporter* series for federal appellate cases, and some state annotated codes fall within this category.

The novice researcher has several resources available to help identify which primary sources are considered authoritative, and thus properly used and cited. Books such as this one are intended to inform the new researcher as to which resources are generally considered authoritative. Also, the *Bluebook*[6] and the *ALWD Citation Manual*[7] identify the resources that are considered authoritative for U.S. states and the federal government, as well as many foreign countries, including instructions as to which source should be cited when more than one source is available.

b. Secondary Sources

Determining the authoritativeness of the various forms of commentary is more challenging. The authority of each is largely a matter of the reputation that particular publishers, authors, and classes of publications have acquired among experienced researchers. Chapter 3 identifies secondary sources most commonly recognized as authoritative. Bibliographies and research guides often evaluate the authoritativeness of available resources on a subject; many bibliographies and research guides are available online at law school library websites. Experts in an area, such as law professors and experienced attorneys, can identify the most trusted sources in their areas of interest. Law librarians, whose job it is to select the most authoritative resources for their students, are also excellent sources of advice.

3. Is It Current?

The law is constantly changing. Every day new statutes go into effect, new regulations are promulgated, and new cases are published by the courts. For this reason, it is essential to check all primary law sources used to be sure they are as current as possible. For example,

---

6. *The Bluebook: A Uniform System of Citation* (Columbia Law Review Ass'n et al. eds., 19th ed., The Harvard Law Review Ass'n 2010). The *Bluebook* is the legal citation manual compiled by the editors of the Columbia Law Review, the Harvard Law Review, the University of Pennsylvania Law Review, and the Yale Law Journal.

7. ALWD & Darby Dickerson, *ALWD Citation Manual* (4th ed., Aspen Publishers 2010). The *ALWD Citation Manual* is written by the Association of Legal Writing Directors and Darby Dickerson, Dean of Texas Tech University School of Law.

check the date of the pocket parts in an annotated code or the date of the last update for an online database.

Similarly, secondary authority must be checked for currency. Many works in print are supplemented regularly with pocket parts, with supplemental volumes, or by new pages in ring-bound works. Always look to see when a work you are thinking of using was last supplemented. If more than a year has passed (less, for certain subjects) consider finding a more current resource. For most online databases, a "scope note" gives currency and other information about the contents of the database.

III. Choosing Between Online or Print Resources

Many researchers have a strong preference for online or print research. The best researchers, however, recognize that different formats perform better for different types of resources and purposes. An experienced researcher may, for example, perform statutory research in an annotated code in print, and then go online to retrieve cases identified in the annotated code and to update the statutes and cases found. Throughout this process, the researcher might refer to a print treatise as the searches suggest new questions. It is common to see a researcher with a laptop and several books open, turning from one to the other as the research process demands. This part of the chapter discusses factors to consider in making the choice between print and online research. The remainder of the chapter discusses techniques for efficient and cost-effective online searching.

A. Where Is the Document Available?

Virtually all recent primary authority and some older primary authority documents are available online. Many older documents needed by the researcher are, however, available only in print. Essential secondary sources might be available only in print, although they are increasingly available online. Certain finding tools and updating tools are available only online.

B. Is an Online Document Official and Authenticated?

Verifying the official status and unaltered nature of online publications can be problematic. Even some government websites state explicitly that documents available there are not official and not to be relied upon as legal authority. Federal and state governments are developing and starting to apply schemes for authentication of online documents, but implementation is still in the early stages. Researchers are thus often referred to an official print publication for verification.

As noted earlier, official versions are certified by the government as being definitive statements of legal texts. Quasi-official versions lack that formal certification, but they are commonly viewed as authoritative. Many resources are widely used despite being nonofficial (e.g., treatises, many documents on government web pages). When dealing with quasi-official authority or widely used nonofficial authority, the main concern is to ascertain whether the online version faithfully represents the text of the print version.[8] Citation practice generally requires that the print version be checked to confirm accuracy and that citations be to the print version of the authority.

Any document reproduced on nongovernment websites must be viewed with caution because electronic documents are easily altered. A major advantage of using recognized legal information vendors, such as LexisNexis or West, is that they undertake to procure and deliver the official documents and they stake their reputations upon doing this reliably.

C. What Is the Database Scope?

Scope is a key factor determining whether a resource is relevant to the research project. For example, a database of law journal articles

---

8. In the case of statutory codes, the original, official statutes are published by the government and may be checked and cited to confirm that the language printed in a statutory code is a faithful rendition of the language of the original statute or statutes incorporated into a code section. See Chapter 5 for discussion of statutes and statutory codification.

might contain articles only since 1980. The researcher not aware of this limitation might miss important articles.

Many databases include a "scope note," which provides information about the sources of material in the database and the time frame covered. Many scope notes also contain tips for effective searching in the database. Before searching in an online database, determine its scope by locating the link to the scope note. In Lexis and Westlaw, the scope note link is typically a button with an "i." In other databases, the link may simply say "Scope" or a similar word, such as "Contents."

D. How Current Is the Source?

Although online databases are potentially the most current of all resources, you must determine how recently a database has been updated. Many websites have a note at the bottom of the page stating when the page was last updated. Scope notes often give a date of last update or the cutoff dates for documents in a database.

A related question is how soon information is included in a database. For example, some periodicals can be published online only after an embargo period, which is some length of time after the appearance of the print publication. When publication is embargoed, you may need to locate an article in print.

E. What Is the Cost/Time Tradeoff?

Many choices between formats turn on economic decisions. Some online resources are very efficient, but very expensive. Other databases may require more time to search but be less expensive. The choice to use one or the other database may turn on how urgent the request is and the budget available for a project. The materials in an online database are probably also available in print.

Books are free once they have been purchased, but costs are rising, library shelf space is limited, and libraries are cutting print collections. If the print version is close at hand, it may be more economical to use that version than to conduct expensive online searches and printing. If access to the print version would require travel, the on-line choice might be more economical.

F. How Easy Is Searching and Navigating?

Some resources are easier to search online, while others are more readily searched in print. For example, indexes to legal periodical literature are easier and faster to search online, while many experienced researchers find searching statutes and regulations easier and more effective in print.

After you identify relevant documents, some are easier to use online and some are easier in print. Online documents might have links to related parts or to other documents, making navigation quick and easy. On the other hand, some print resources are easier to move back and forth in and to see the relationships between the various parts. Statutes are an example of a resource many researchers find easier to navigate in print.

G. How Easy Is Reading and Skimming?

You may find print is easier to read carefully and to skim for certain purposes. Prolonged, extensive reading is often done more easily in print. For this reason, many people prefer to do preliminary reading in secondary resources in print, even if they used an online search to locate the resource.

Many people find that rapid skimming can be done much more effectively in print. Good researchers are generally experts at skimming large amounts of text in order to identify relevant portions of extensive works.

A related issue is that reading resources in print makes it much easier to keep track of the kind of resources you are using. Documents of different types can appear very similar on a computer screen. The potential for confusion is increased by the ease with which clicking on links can bring the reader to very different types of documents, making it easy to lose the context and the relationship between the documents. Familiarity with the types of legal documents gained from using them in print ultimately allows better control of research in the online environment.

H. Do You Need to Print, E-mail, or Cut and Paste?

A great advantage of researching online is the ease with which text can be extracted, copied, and transmitted. When you need to capture large blocks of text to use later, to quickly transmit to another person or location, or to quickly cut and paste into new documents, online resources are much more useful than their print counterparts.

IV. Online Resources

This part of the chapter explains how to get the most out of online legal research systems. Interestingly, many of the tools developed for print research are now incorporated into online sources due to the power they add to the computerized legal research process.

A. Lexis, Lexis Advance, Westlaw, and WestlawNext

Lexis and Lexis Advance are online research services provided by the publishing company LexisNexis, now owned by Reed Elsevier. Westlaw and WestlawNext are online legal research services provided by West, historically the dominant legal publishing company. West is now owned by another publishing giant, Thomson Reuters.

LexisNexis and West are the predominant vendors of online legal information. Each publishes vast online collections of primary and secondary legal material, as well as extensive news sources, public records information, and practice tools. LexisNexis and West continue to expand the contents of their online legal research services and to develop their search capacities. As a result, online legal research services provided by LexisNexis and West are extremely expensive sources of legal information.

Table 2-3. Commercial Legal Database Providers

Provider	Web Address
Bloomberg Law	www.bloomberg.com/solutions/ business_solutions/law
Casemaker *(free to members of some state bar associations)*	www.casemaker.us
FastCase *(free to members of some state bar associations)*	www.fastcase.com
LexisNexis	www.lexisnexis.com
Loislaw	www.loislaw.com
VersusLaw	www.versuslaw.com
West	www.westlaw.com

B. Other Commercial Databases

Several commercial online legal research services compete with the online services provided by LexisNexis and West. See Table 2-3 for a list of online commercial database providers. The information supplied by these vendors is less extensive and their searching capacities tend to be less refined than those of LexisNexis and West. They are, however, considerably less expensive than the services provided by LexisNexis and West.

LexisNexis and West have responded to this competition by offering inexpensive subscriptions with limited content. These subscriptions typically provide access to federal primary law, the primary law of one state, essential secondary materials for that state, and an online citator.[9] The sole practitioner or small law firm should consider these less expensive alternatives. Keep an eye out for new legal information

---

9. Chapter 10 discusses two citators in detail: Shepard's on Lexis and KeyCite on Westlaw.

providers, as services with innovative search tools attempt to enter the market.

C. Free Online Legal Resources

The websites of governmental bodies, educational institutions, and other organizations provide increasing numbers of free online legal materials. Many researchers reduce their legal research costs by using materials on these sites.

Many resources can be found through the major online directories to free online legal information. Prominent directories are the Library of Congress's Guide to Law Online[10] and Cornell University's Legal Information Institute (L.I.I.).[11] Much of the free online legal information these directories link to is provided at the websites of legislatures, courts, and government agencies.

A private effort to provide legal information online is Google Scholar,[12] which provides access to many law review and law journal articles and to many federal and state judicial decisions through its "Legal opinions and journals" option. An increasingly important source for free access to legal scholarship is the Legal Scholarship Network on Social Science Research Network (S.S.R.N.).[13]

D. Specialized Legal Databases

While Lexis, Lexis Advance, Westlaw, WestlawNext, and other services provide access to vast amounts of legal information, they do not provide everything the legal researcher needs. Other commercial vendors provide subscriptions to specialized legal information. Examples are Bureau of National Affairs (B.N.A.) and Commerce Clearing House (C.C.H.), which provide online databases on such specialized

---

10. The address is www.loc.gov/law/help.

11. The address is www.law.cornell.edu.

12. The address is http://scholar.google.com. Significantly, the site does not currently include statutory law.

13. The address is www.ssrn.com/lsn.

subjects as health law, business and finance, and tax law. Each of these online providers has long been a prominent publisher of legal information. Many of their online resources are adapted from their existing or prior print publications.

Another database that is rapidly increasing in importance is HeinOnline. It provides PDF images of law journal articles and a rapidly expanding collection of other legal authority. HeinOnline is produced by William S. Hein & Co.

Academic and law firm libraries subscribe to specialized legal databases. Be sure to examine your library's web pages to determine which online legal resources are available.

V. Online Searching

Online searching offers many approaches. Some searches simply retrieve a document using a known citation. Other searches proceed topically, with the researcher clicking through layers of an outline to determine which database contains useful documents. Many searches require the use of keywords to identify relevant documents. This part of the chapter reviews both terms and connectors searching and natural language searching, and then provides techniques for powerful and effective online searching.

A. Terms and Connectors Searching

Lexis, Lexis Advance, Westlaw, WestlawNext, and other computerized legal research services provide the capacity to search using "terms and connectors." Such queries consist of search terms and connectors expressing logical relationships between the search terms, the proximity of the terms to each other, or other features of the terms. The system of expressing logical relationships between terms is known as Boolean searching (named for mathematician George Boole).

The symbols used for the connectors differ somewhat between the services. Table 2-4 compares the symbols used by Lexis and Westlaw

Table 2-4. Lexis and Westlaw Connectors and Commands

Goal	Lexis	Westlaw
To find alternative terms anywhere in the document	or	or blank space
To find both terms anywhere in the document	and &	and &
To find both terms within a particular distance from each other	/p = in 1 paragraph /s = in 1 sentence /n = within a certain number of words	/p = in 1 paragraph /s = in 1 sentence /n = within a certain number of words
To find terms used as a phrase	leave a blank space between each word	put the phrase in quotation marks
To control the hierarchy of searching	parentheses	parentheses
To exclude terms	and not	but not, %
To extend the end of a term	!	!
To hold the place of letters in a term	*	*

for common connectors and commands.[14] Many of the commands work the same in both services, but some, such as leaving spaces between words without putting quotation marks around them, work very differently.[15] Other online services use different connectors and commands for Boolean logic searching, although they are beginning to converge on common practices. Those services provide a "Help"

---

14. Some of the Boolean connectors and commands of the beta version of Lexis Advance available in August 2011 differ from those used by Lexis.com.

15. In Westlaw, the terms "judicial" and "notice" with a space between them would be read by the search engine as a command to search for either the term "judicial" or the term "notice." In Lexis, the same query would be read by the search engine as identical to the phrase "judicial notice."

or "Tips" feature that explains their connectors and commands for forming queries in that service.

B. Natural Language Searching

Some online databases, including those provided by LexisNexis and West, provide natural language searching as an alternative to terms and connectors keyword searching. Natural language searching allows the researcher to enter a question, short sentence, or string of search terms as a query. The program converts this unstructured query into a form the search engine can use and returns results ranked by relevance. The exact algorithm behind the natural language searching is different for each database, making comparison between databases difficult.

Although this method may be easier than forming terms and connectors queries, the researcher does not know just what the program is doing or why results are identified as relevant. Experienced researchers often use natural language searching as a backup when terms and connectors searches are not yielding good results or to identify additional documents not captured by terms and connectors searches. Figure 2-1 shows a natural language query in Westlaw. Note that terms and connectors searches can be entered by clicking on the "Terms and Connectors" tab.

C. Getting the Most from Keyword Searching

Although full-text searching in an online database is a popular method of finding documents, the method has inherent problems. Even skilled researchers searching well designed databases typically find only a fraction of the relevant documents in the database. The researcher often cannot think of all terms that might be used to identify relevant concepts. One of the most challenging problems is that text expressing a concept might not contain any words directly representing that concept. Consider how traditional stories, such as folk tales or parables, express abstract concepts without naming them explicitly. A particular problem for the legal researcher is that useful

Figure 2-1. Natural Language Search in Westlaw

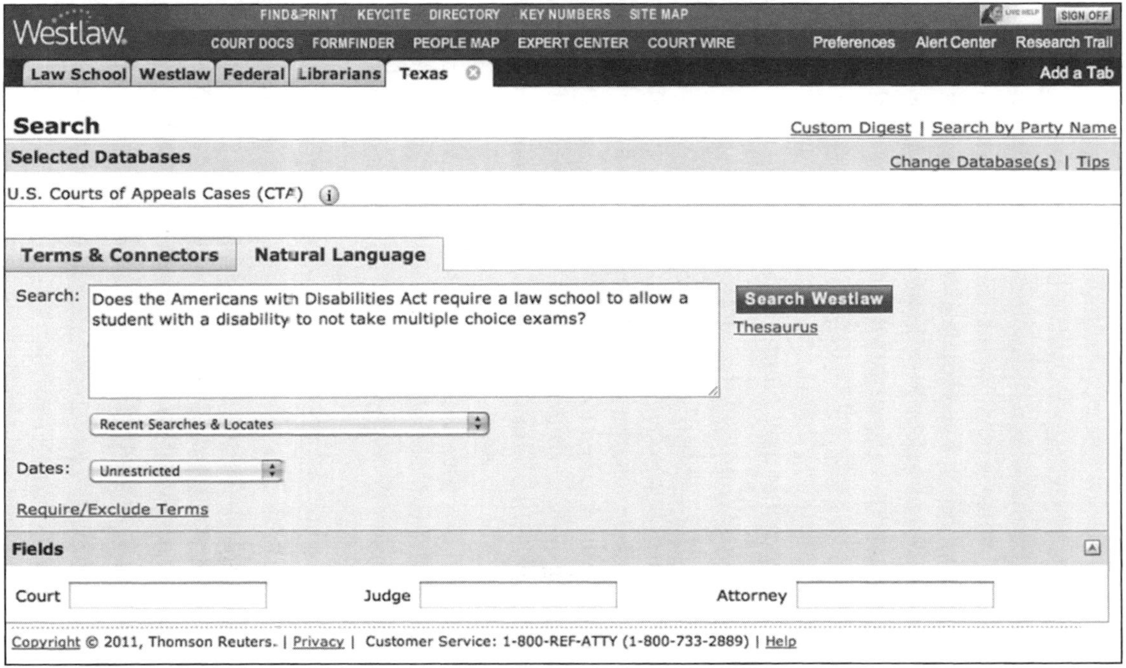

Source: Reprinted with permission of West, a Thomson Reuters business.

analogies might be found in cases with very different facts and using different terms than those the researcher has thought of.

The results of full-text searches are usually a mix of irrelevant documents and some, but not all, of the relevant documents in the database. The goal is to maximize the precision of the search by avoiding as many irrelevant documents as possible, while maximizing the recall of the search by finding as many of the relevant documents in the database as possible. This is a challenging balancing act; two of the techniques expert researchers use to optimize the trade-off between precision and recall include using segments and fields and refining search queries.

1. Using Segments and Fields

Searching for keywords in the complete texts in a database might yield many irrelevant hits, while a search limited to just certain parts of each document might be much more focused. For example, if each article in a database contains abstracts of the full article, the abstracts will probably contain the most relevant terms. If the database allows searching just in the abstracts, relevant articles can be found, while avoiding many articles with those terms appearing in irrelevant contexts in the body of the article. Searches in the title segment may allow similar focus. Lexis uses the term "segments."[16] Westlaw and WestlawNext use the term "fields."[17]

Some fields contain just one kind of information from the documents, such as author, publisher, or subject. For court opinions, fields for judges, attorneys, or docket numbers allow focused searching. Searches can also be limited by date range or by type of publication. Figure 2-2 shows the fields that can be selected for focused searching in the Court of Appeals (CTA) database on Westlaw. The particular fields available vary by database.

---

16. The beta version of Lexis Advance available in August 2011 does not include segments as a search option.

17. Searchable subsets of information in databases are commonly known as "fields." This book will use the term "field" when discussing the concept in general.

Figure 2-2. Fields in Westlaw

Source: Reprinted with permission of West, a Thomson Reuters business.

2. *Refining Queries*

Another way to maximize the recall of a search while focusing with precision is to refine your queries. Carefully consider your search strategy before beginning to enter queries. The initial query should include the terms you believe most likely to appear in the document, with connectors representing the most likely relationships of the terms. Must both terms appear in a relevant document? If so, will they probably appear in the same sentence? In that case, a search structured A /s B might be a good place to start. This search may be too narrow and produce too few or no results. Plan what to do if the search needs to be broadened. Synonyms for terms A and B should be identified and added as alternatives, producing a query such as (A or C) /s (B or D or E). The search could also be broadened by changing the proximity operator, so the terms need only be in the same paragraph or even in the entire document.

Develop a strategy for broadening and narrowing queries before beginning the search. Searching in legal databases can be very expensive and must be performed with maximum efficiency. Law students should use their subsidized access during their years in school to practice the methods that will allow them to be efficient, low-cost searchers in practice. Practitioners should use the training provided by legal database services. All researchers should use the services' toll-free numbers to discuss with representatives how to formulate efficient searches in appropriate databases.

D. Add Power to the Search with Finding Tools

Full-text searching with keywords works very well for some searches and very poorly at other times. For example, an unusual term or phrase, such as "110 tons of tuna," will allow very precise searching. On the other hand, searches consisting of very common terms, such as "fault," "damages," or "plaintiff," will usually yield many irrelevant results. Since legal researchers must be able to locate all relevant documents, not just some, legal database providers have increasingly recognized the need to supply other finding tools. These finding tools were developed to locate information in print resources but have proven equally useful for online searching.

1. Indexes

Good indexes are created by indexing specialists, with subject expertise and knowledge of how people look for information. The indexer considers the concepts and terms researchers will use to find material on a subject. An index created with the insight of a human indexer will often point the researcher to information that would not be found by a simple keyword search of a computer database's master index.

When searching Lexis, Lexis Advance, Westlaw, WestlawNext, or other databases, check whether an index is available. Certain online sources are particularly likely to have an index. For examples, statutes and secondary sources, such as treatises and encyclopedias, often have indexes. The index may be supplied by the vendor as an alternative search mode for a database. Such an index can typically be either skimmed online or searched for words within the index.

2. Tables of Contents

Reviewing a document's table of contents may reveal material not found either by searching in the index or by conducting a keyword search. Tables of contents are now commonly included as an option for searching many online databases. For example, the statutory codes in Lexis and Westlaw often include a table of contents identical to that in the print versions.

3. Lexis's Topic and Headnote System and West's Key Number System

The Topic and Headnote System used on Lexis and the Key Number System used on Westlaw are powerful tools for extending a search from cases found by a keyword search, or from other sources, to find many more cases on the same subject. Effective use of these tools compensates for the often incomplete coverage from searching only with keyword searches. These powerful tools are discussed at much greater length in Chapter 9.

4. Citators: Shepard's and KeyCite

As explained in Chapter 1, Shepard's on Lexis and KeyCite on Westlaw are also powerful tools. Most often, they are used to identify cases that have cited a particular case, allowing a researcher to see whether the particular case is still respected. But these citators also identify references citing statutes, regulations, patents, administrative decisions, and law journals in a number of primary and secondary resources.[18] After finding a relevant case or other document, you can expand the results of the search by using Shepard's or KeyCite to identify other relevant documents. Other legal database services also provide citators, but these citators have not yet reached the degree of development of Shepard's and KeyCite. Citators are very useful in the later stages of research to identify cases or other documents that have been missed by other search techniques. Shepard's and KeyCite are discussed at length in Chapter 10.

E. Cost-Effective Searching

A number of techniques can lower the cost of online searching.

Use free online material. Much primary authority available on Lexis or Westlaw legal research services is also available at government and nonprofit websites. If only the text of a judicial opinion is needed, for example, that opinion might be found at the website of the issuing court.

Read offline when possible. Reading online can be expensive. If you have access to a law library, remember that the reporters, statutes, treatises, and other materials in the library have already been paid for, so using those resources incurs no further costs. Rather than read documents online, consider downloading or printing the list of cites found by the search and going offline to read the documents in the library, at free websites, or printed from the database.

Use the best contract for the purpose. Lexis and Westlaw are available under various contractual terms. Some contracts are more economical for prolonged online reading, while others allow numerous searches at lower cost. A law firm or legal department may have more than one contract. Know the terms of the contracts in your office, and search using the contracts most economical for the particular purpose.

---

18. Be sure to check exactly which resources are included within the citator being used.

Search in the narrowest database containing what you seek. Narrow databases generally cost less to search than do more inclusive databases. For example, if you need cases from a single federal court, search a database containing only that court's opinions. Searching instead in Westlaw's ALLCASES database will cost more per search, as well as return many irrelevant results. On the other hand, be sure a database contains what you are looking for before incurring the cost of a search. Check the scope note before using any unfamiliar database.

Formulate your queries carefully before logging on. A single search on Lexis or Westlaw may cost well over a hundred dollars.[19] Plan how you will broaden or narrow your query if your initial results are too broad or too narrow. Before hitting the "Enter" key, review the query you have written to make sure everything is spelled right, connectors are properly used, and all parentheses are closed.

Use "FOCUS" in Lexis or the "Locate in results" feature in Westlaw. After entering a query and receiving a list of results, you can search the list for the presence of additional terms at no extra cost. Using "FOCUS" or "Locate in results" to find a term in a set of documents is much more cost-effective than conducting a revised search.

Save your searches. All searches should be recorded in a research log, either in print or electronically. Queries and search results can be saved using "History" in Lexis or "Research Trail" on Westlaw. Keeping track of searches run helps prevent time-wasting replication of work already done.

Minimize printing. Print only what you will need. Consider using the books in the library rather than making costly printouts. For large amounts of material, save results to a flash drive or e-mail them to yourself for later review. You can also copy the relevant text and paste it into a word processing document. Be sure you know what will print

---

19. WestlawNext charges for each search and for each document viewed in search results. The charges for searching and document viewing vary by type of contract. The Lexis Advance pricing policy had not been finalized in August 2011.

before clicking on "Print." Are you printing just the cite list or the full text of all documents? If working in an annotated code, are you printing just the text of the statute or all the annotations, too? The difference can be hundreds of pages.

F. Pitfalls of Online Searching and Solutions

Online legal research has brought great speed and flexibility to the research process. Properly used, online research allows doing more, faster. The very nature of online research can, however, lead the inexperienced researcher into serious mistakes.

1. Tunnel Vision and "Law-Bytes"[19]

Experts in legal research instruction have noted that researchers using online resources are prone to focus on an isolated portion of text in a document, without being aware of its relationship to the overall text. It is not uncommon, for example, for novice researchers to cite a case as supporting a certain point based on the court's discussion of the reasoning of other courts' decisions or of hypotheticals. Such citations are generally wrong and may even be totally opposite to the actual holding of the case. A related problem is a tendency of researchers to focus on an isolated block of text as the meaning of the case, rather than perceive the subtleties of the full analysis. These problems stem, at least in part, from reading documents on a computer screen, making it more difficult to keep the larger context in mind.

A solution to these problems is to read the document thoroughly and closely in print, whether printed out from the database or in books. The temptation to cut and paste blocks of text as a substitute for careful consideration and analysis can be combated by developing habits of note-taking and analytical summarization throughout the research process.

---

19. The term "law-byte" was introduced in Molly Warner Lien, *Technocentrism and the Soul of the Common Law Lawyer*, 48 Am. U. L. Rev. 85, 88 (1998).

2. *Inadvertent Plagiarism*

Plagiarism, the unattributed use of the words or concepts of another, is a problem in all kinds of research. In online legal research, it is particularly easy to fall into the trap of unintentional plagiarism when cutting and pasting portions of text from many resources.

The legal researcher must cite all authority relied upon, whether the researcher is developing an objective exposition of the law regarding an issue or marshalling the arguments that support a client's position for a court brief. Citation of authority allows others to find and study the authority relied upon by the researcher. Failing to cite the controlling legal authority that determines the rule or rules of law for an issue weakens an argument and may lead to plagiarism.

Even unintended plagiarism can destroy a career. The solution is to include with all copied text a full citation to the origin of the text. Placing all cut and pasted text, together with full cites, in a research log will help prevent later misuse of the text. Placing the cut and pasted text into the research log also encourages its use in the analytical process. Resist the temptation to cut and paste text from a document directly to a draft of a research paper. If you lose track of what you have borrowed and fail to attribute the source, the penalties may be severe.

3. *Losing Track*

The power of online research is enhanced by the ability to link from cites in a document to the cited documents. Linking allows the instantaneous review of related documents, but it also allows the researcher to leap from document to document, possibly losing track of the path followed and the relationship between the documents. This can result in confusion and much wasted time and expense. The researcher in Lexis or Westlaw can view the History or Research Trail, respectively, as a reminder. Even more effective is keeping track of every step in the research process in the research log, introduced in Chapter 1, with notes on the significance of what is found at each step.

Chapter 3

Secondary Sources

Secondary sources summarize, explain, interpret, or comment on the law. Unlike primary sources, which are the law, secondary sources are *not* the law, regardless of how persuasive they might be. Secondary sources are written by lawyers, law professors, law students, and judges who are not acting in a law-making capacity.

Most researchers are familiar with secondary sources in nonlegal research contexts. Nonlegal secondary sources include dictionaries, encyclopedias, periodicals, and other reference books. These same types of sources are written in the legal context to assist researchers and are the focus of this chapter. In addition, other types of secondary legal sources covered here are *American Law Reports*, loose-leaf services, restatements, continuing legal education (CLE) materials, legal forms, and jury instructions.

I. Why Consult Secondary Sources?

Secondary sources can be helpful to researchers in a number of ways: (1) as background and an overview on an issue or area of law; (2) as finding tools to assist with identifying relevant primary sources; (3) as persuasive authority when no primary authority exists or when the researcher is arguing for a change in the law or a new interpretation of the law; and (4) as a tool to keep a researcher current in a changing area of law.

The first two uses of secondary sources were introduced in Chapter 1. First, when a researcher is unfamiliar with an area of law or with a topic or issue within an area of law, a secondary source can be an effective place to begin research. Secondary sources can identify, explain, and define relevant concepts, and they can alert the researcher to potential issues that should be considered or that may arise. These sources also provide the researcher with additional search terms.

Next, secondary sources may lead the researcher to other relevant sources, both primary and secondary. Some secondary sources, like law review articles and treatises, are heavily footnoted; almost every statement written in an article or treatise is supported by citation to other sources. The researcher can use these footnotes to generate a list of citations to additional sources to review. These footnotes may include citations to cases, statutes, and regulations, among other sources.

The researcher may also learn from secondary sources which authorities govern and which are valued by the courts and scholars working in the particular area of law. For example, a researcher working on a federal jurisdiction question may learn from a law review article that a federal statute is controlling on the issue and may find citations to many federal cases and some well respected treatises. On the other hand, a researcher working on an environmental law issue, such as toxic emissions, may learn that the area of law is controlled by federal regulations, in addition to federal statutes.

Third, secondary sources may serve as persuasive authority for a researcher in three instances. A researcher advocating a change in the law could find support in a well reasoned secondary source like a law review article. Another researcher working in a jurisdiction without relevant, primary authority might cite a treatise as persuasive authority for adopting a particular rule. Alternatively, a researcher may use secondary sources when seeking interpretations of similar laws from other jurisdictions when the governing primary authority has not yet been interpreted to cover the issue presented in the jurisdiction.

Fourth, secondary sources keep researchers current. Secondary sources in this category are like newsletters, providing frequent updates in rapidly changing areas of law. For example, a secondary source published weekly could analyze a recently enacted statute or an important judicial decision that has broad implications.

II. The Persuasive Value of Secondary Sources

Secondary sources vary in their persuasiveness. Some secondary sources are referred to as *secondary authorities* because of their high persuasive value. A source's persuasiveness depends to a great extent on who wrote it, the type of source in which it was published, where it is published, when it was published, and whether it has been cited as authority in the past.

Who. A source is considered more persuasive when it is written by an author who has a reputation as a scholar in the field or on the issue. Further, a source that is written by a judge or a law professor is considered more persuasive than a piece that is written by a law student.

What. Certain types of sources are considered more persuasive than others. For example, law review articles and treatises are more persuasive than dictionaries or encyclopedias. The more specifically the source addresses the researcher's issue and the jurisdiction's law, the more persuasive the source will be. Thus, law review articles and treatises on particular topics are typically considered to be more persuasive than those that provide only general treatment. Further, sources addressing a particular jurisdiction's law are more persuasive than general sources.

Where. Among sources, certain publications are relied upon more than others, often because of a combination of the other factors listed here. For example, *Moore's Federal Practice* and *Wright & Miller's Federal Practice and Procedure*, both legal treatises, are well respected by the federal courts on issues involving federal practice and procedure. These treatises are respected because of their authors' favorable reputations, their consistently high quality, and their focus on particular topics arising in the federal courts. In stark contrast to the persuasiveness of these treatises, a website maintained by an unknown law firm is unlikely to be persuasive analytically even though it might contain helpful research aids.

When. As is true with most sources, persuasiveness is influenced by how current a source is kept. Many secondary sources are kept up to date with pocket parts and supplements (in print) and with additional information (online). Law reviews are not updated in this way; once an article is published, it is not revised at a later date to show changes in the law. However, articles may be checked using citators like Shepard's and KeyCite, which will indicate sources in which the articles have been cited subsequently.

Citation Record. A source's citation record or history may influence its persuasiveness. If courts have looked to a source in the past, the researcher will have evidence that it is respected by the courts. A writer introducing a persuasive authority should consider including a reference to a citation record if one exists. For example, when introducing information that the writer has retrieved from a treatise, the writer can increase the information's persuasive value by pointing out that the treatise has been cited often on the particular point by other courts or, even better, by the relevant jurisdiction's courts.

III. Types of Secondary Sources and the Process for Researching Them

The process for researching secondary sources varies depending on the source. A general outline is provided in Table 3-1.

Table 3-1. Outline for Researching Secondary Sources

1. Search the library's catalog for the location of relevant secondary sources, or search the database list on an online service.

2. Use your search terms in the index or table of contents of a print secondary source, or run a search in an online database.

3. Find the relevant information in the secondary sources in print or online, being sure to check main volumes and pocket parts or supplements in print sources. Reading the commentary will assist your comprehension of the legal issues. Within the commentary, often in footnotes, you will find references to primary authority.

4. Update the secondary source, if possible.

5. Read and update the primary authority.

A. Legal Dictionaries

Legal dictionaries, like other dictionaries, define terms and provide information on the proper pronunciation and usage of words. Legal dictionaries focus on legal words and terms of art; they may also include citations to sources from which definitions were obtained.

Legal dictionaries are available in print and online. They should be consulted by researchers who encounter unfamiliar words in their research, but they should not be considered as sources for conducting original legal research. From time to time, a court will reference *Black's Law Dictionary* or some other legal dictionary, but these sources should never be cited as authoritative.[1]

B. Legal Encyclopedias

1. Overview

Legal encyclopedias provide a general overview of law pertaining to a variety of legal subjects, with references to cases and other practice materials provided in footnotes. The subjects are organized by broad topics (e.g., Contracts) with subsections devoted to more particular issues within the topic (e.g., Counter offers). Because of the general nature of the discussions in most legal encyclopedias, they serve best as sources of background information and as finding tools to identify relevant primary sources. Rarely will it be appropriate to cite a legal encyclopedia discussion, even as persuasive authority on a point of law.

Traditionally, two sets of legal encyclopedias have discussed American law: *American Jurisprudence 2d*, commonly referred to as Am. Jur. 2d, and *Corpus Juris Secundum*, commonly referred to as C.J.S. These encyclopedias provide footnotes to federal and state cases from

---

1. Courts sometimes refer to nonlegal dictionaries to help determine the plain meaning of words. While the courts' opinions are legal authority, the dictionaries themselves are not.

across the United States, but they do not focus on any specific jurisdiction. Rather, they summarize law in the United States and may identify trends in the law and different approaches taken by courts. Both Am. Jur. 2d and C.J.S. provide references to the *American Law Reports* series and to other texts as well as to West topics and key numbers.

In addition to Am. Jur. 2d and C.J.S., some encyclopedias are state specific. For example, *Florida Jurisprudence 2d* summarizes Florida state law, and *Texas Jurisprudence 2d* summarizes Texas law. However, the majority of states do not have their own legal encyclopedias.

Increasingly, online services have begun offering encyclopedias. Their content is sometimes less reliable than that of the traditional encyclopedias; moreover, the online encyclopedias are less likely to offer cross-references to primary authority.

2. Researching in a Legal Encyclopedia

After determining which encyclopedias are available, begin research by selecting a topic in the encyclopedia or turning to the encyclopedia's index with a list of search terms. Most multi-volume sets of encyclopedias are organized alphabetically by topic, with a list of topics printed at the beginning of the set. Additionally, an analysis or outline of what is included within a topic is provided at the start of each topic discussion. Once you have identified potentially relevant topics and sections either by using the index or by using the analysis at the start of a topic, read the identified sections, looking for discussions relevant to the legal issue and for citations to primary sources or other research sources. Check for any supplements or pocket parts to the publication to update the research.

Legal encyclopedias are available online using Lexis and Westlaw. Both services include Am. Jur. 2d and some state encyclopedias. Westlaw also includes C.J.S. On Lexis, use this trail to locate the database identifiers: Search > Legal > Secondary Legal > Jurisprudences, ALR & Encyclopedias. On Westlaw, the database identifiers for legal encyclopedias are listed in the Westlaw directory under "Treatises, CLEs, and Other Practice Materials." You may search on both services using terms and connectors or natural language searches or by browsing the encyclopedia's table of contents.

Finally, encyclopedias provided by free online services typically do not have sophisticated searching available, but they can provide useful information at the early stages of research. For example, the Legal Information Institute (L.I.I.) hosted by Cornell University provides an online encyclopedia/dictionary called Wex.[2] It is a wiki website, meaning that the content is provided by volunteer contributors. Its list of terms is extensive and quite detailed, and it also provides a search box for keyword searching.

C. Legal Periodicals

1. Overview

Most researchers are familiar with researching in periodicals. The researcher uses search terms in an index to locate articles that address the research issue. Research in legal periodicals is similar.

Legal periodicals are usually referred to as *law reviews* or *law journals*; these terms are frequently used interchangeably. The pieces published in law reviews and law journals include articles or essays authored by law professors, lawyers, and judges, as well as comments and casenotes authored by law students. Articles, essays, and comments (sometimes called notes) address a discrete legal issue that the author analyzes in depth. Casenotes report on and sometimes analyze recently decided cases. Articles, comments, notes, and casenotes are typically heavily footnoted, which is especially helpful for locating primary sources and additional secondary sources.

Most law schools publish one or more journals that are edited by student editors selected for journal membership because of their high ranking in their law school classes or their performance in a journal writing competition. Other law journals, both law-school sponsored and not law-school sponsored, are edited by boards made up of lawyers, law professors, and judges.

---

2. The website is http://topics.law.cornell.edu/wex.

Table 3-2. Sample Legal Periodicals

Journal Title	Coverage	Publisher
The Yale Law Journal	General scholarly topics	Students at Yale Law School
Houston Law Review	General scholarly topics	Students at the University of Houston Law Center
Loyola Law Review	General scholarly topics	Students at Loyola University New Orleans College of Law
Rutgers Law Journal	General scholarly topics	Students at Rutgers-Camden Law School
Journal of Environmental Law and Litigation	Specific topics in environmental law	Students at the University of Oregon School of Law
First Amendment Law Review	Specific topics related to the First Amendment	Students at the University of North Carolina School of Law
Legal Communication & Rhetoric: JALWD	Specific topics in the substance and practice of professional legal writing	Law professors in the Association of Legal Writing Directors
Journal of Legal Education	Specific topics related to legal education and legal scholarship	The Association of American Law Schools
ABA Journal	Practice-oriented articles	The American Bar Association

Many law school journals are considered general journals because they publish pieces on a variety of legal topics; some law schools also publish specialty journals that are dedicated to a particular legal subject. Subject-specific law journals are also published by professional organizations of lawyers and law professors. Examples of the various types of journals appear in Table 3-2.

Another type of legal periodical is a *bar journal,* which differs from the law review or law journal primarily in the focus and depth of its pieces. Articles published in bar journals tend to focus on issues of interest to practicing lawyers. Bar journal articles are shorter in length than the pieces in law reviews and law journals, and they are not as heavily footnoted. If a bar journal article addresses the issue you are researching, it can provide a powerful boost to your work, but these articles usually do not cover all aspects of an issue or provide citations to all of the sources that should be researched.

Bar journals are published by bar associations. The American Bar Association publishes the *ABA Journal*, and most state bar associations publish a state bar journal. Bar journals are printed in a magazine format, and they include advertisements, discipline reports, information about bar-sponsored events, and other information that is pertinent to members of the particular association.

2. Researching Legal Periodicals

Legal periodicals are individual publications that may have their own indexes that can be used to conduct research. However, the legal researcher is rarely interested in restricting a search to the articles of one publication. Thus, to locate citations to relevant law journal pieces, use an indexing service that combines references to many law journals. Indexes are available both in print and online. For the reasons stated below, an online index is almost always the best choice.

The indexes available in print are the *Index to Legal Periodicals and Books* (I.L.P.B.) and the *Current Law Index* (C.L.I.). Both the I.L.P.B. and the C.L.I. consist of noncumulative, annual, hardbound volumes, which first appear in softbound pamphlets. The I.L.P.B. for a given year first appears as a series of softbound pamphlets that cover months and then quarters; it eventually appears as an annual hardbound volume. The I.L.P.B., which was originally titled the *Index to Legal Periodicals*, can be searched by looking up either a subject or an author's last name in one combined index. This index is especially helpful for finding older articles because it includes citations to articles published as far back as 1908. The I.L.P.B. table of cases and the table of statutes are also helpful for locating articles discussing particular cases and statutes. Publication of the C.L.I. began in 1980. Researchers may conduct searches in the C.L.I. by looking up a subject, case name, statute, or author/title, each of which is found in its own part of the index.

Entries in both the I.L.P.B. and the C.L.I. include citation information for articles and may include cross-references to other subjects and the names of articles. From these entries, you can make a list of potential articles and locate the journal articles in print or online. For example, if you were referred to "78 Neb. L. Rev. 79" by one of these indexes, you could follow any of the following approaches to locate the text of the article:

- Locate the *Nebraska Law Review* on the shelves of the library, select volume 78, and turn to page 79.
- Determine whether the journal publishes online by conducting a simple search using a search engine such as Google or Yahoo! and retrieve the article from the journal's website.
- Use an online service such as Lexis or Westlaw and retrieve the article by entering the citation in the "Get a Document" or "Find by citation" feature. Be aware that these online services do not include every law journal article. If you are unable to locate an article on one service, try the other service, use another online service with different coverage (such as HeinOnline), look on the journal's website, or retrieve the article in print.

Searching for law journal articles electronically can be more efficient than searching in the noncumulative, print indexes. Several options are available to do this searching online. First, the I.L.P.B. and the C.L.I. both have electronic products to which law libraries may subscribe. The I.L.P.B. is available electronically through a subscription to the online version.[3] Another product, LegalTrac, is a CD-ROM and web-based product that law libraries may purchase to facilitate the use of the C.L.I. Law libraries may devote a computer terminal to LegalTrac or may otherwise make it available on library computers. The benefit of using LegalTrac is that it is cumulative, meaning that you may search in one place for all indexed journal articles rather than having to search in annual volumes of the C.L.I. LegalTrac is updated monthly.

---

3. The address is www.ebscohost.com/wilson.

Another online product that allows the researcher to search the full text of many law journal articles is HeinOnline.[4] To search the HeinOnline database, a researcher must have a subscription, which many law school libraries have. Notably, this database provides links to the articles, which appear in the same format as they do in the printed journals. Some researchers find HeinOnline difficult to use for finding relevant articles; these researchers use the database only to retrieve articles after finding citations through other sources.

A researcher may also search for law journal articles using Lexis and Westlaw, which both have databases devoted to legal periodicals. Choose the proper database (a database could contain all journals provided by the service or a single journal), then type in search terms, which will allow the full-text searching of all articles found in the database. You will retrieve a list of articles that includes the titles of the articles, citation information, and a relevant passage from the article. You can then print the list of citations to locate the articles in the printed journals or a less expensive database. Alternatively, you can click on articles in the list one at a time to review their introductions or the parts of the articles that are most relevant to determine whether the articles are worth printing or downloading for a more careful review. If your search returns too many results, narrow the search by using segments or fields, or by restricting the date. For example, if you are searching for a journal article written by a particular expert in the area of law, you can restrict the scope of your search so as to retrieve only articles written by that author on Lexis by selecting the segment "Author" or on Westlaw by selecting the field "Author."

Finally, Google Scholar[5] allows researchers to identify relevant articles in law journals (as well as judicial opinions). You can search by author, date, and publication. The search engine links to other sources, including HeinOnline and JSTOR,[6] which provide the text of the articles in PDF format.

---

4. The address is www.home.heinonline.org.
5. The address is http://scholar.google.com.
6. The address is www.jstor.org.

D. Legal Treatises and Other Books

1. Overview

a. Treatises

A *treatise* is a scholarly, legal publication written on a particular subject matter. A print treatise may consist of multiple volumes or a single volume. Treatises often provide a comprehensive review and analysis of an area of law, a discussion of issues that frequently arise in an area of law, and a discussion of and citations to primary authorities. The discussions of issues are usually more focused than discussions in general legal encyclopedias, and treatises are more heavily footnoted. Treatises are usually divided into discrete sections that are indexed so that the researcher is able to use parts of the treatise without having to read the entire treatise.

Treatises are regularly updated. Bound treatises are updated through the use of pocket parts, supplements, and new editions. *Looseleaf* treatises are produced in a binder format; they are supplemented by removal of old pages and replacement with new pages, as well as the addition of pages with new material that are often added to the front of the binder on paper that is a different color from the main part of the binder.[7] Treatises have been among the last legal resources to be made widely available online (even on Lexis and Westlaw). When you locate a treatise online, you should find information on how the source is updated.

The value of a good treatise is primarily in the analysis, information, and citations it provides. Further, the reputation of a treatise author and the reputation of the quality of the work will sometimes elevate its value such that courts may turn to it and cite it with approval. Three highly regarded treatises are listed here as examples:

- Federal bankruptcy law: *Norton Bankruptcy Law and Practice* (3d ed., West 2008–2011) provides not only analysis of federal bankruptcy law but also rules applicable in federal bankruptcy courts, relevant forms, and a quick reference guide for the practitioner.

---

7. Looseleaf treatises should not be confused with looseleaf services, which are discussed in Section II.E. of this chapter.

- Federal evidence law: *Wigmore on Evidence* (4th ed., Aspen 2011) has been published for many years and has an excellent reputation.
- Federal Indian law: *Cohen's Handbook of Federal Indian Law: 2005 Edition* (LexisNexis) is a valuable, comprehensive treatise.

b. Monographs

A *monograph* is simply a single book. The usefulness of monographs on legal topics varies widely, depending on how well they are indexed, how often they are updated, how broad or narrow the book's analysis is, and how thoroughly the author has supported statements with citations to primary and other secondary sources. Many monographs are available only in print.

c. Hornbooks, Nutshells, Deskbooks, and Practice Guides

Other recurring types of books on legal topics are hornbooks, *Nutshells*, deskbooks, and practice guides. Hornbooks and *Nutshells* provide a general overview of an area of law. They are marketed to law students as study aides. They are usually not jurisdiction specific, so their value in researching the law of a specific jurisdiction is limited. Hornbooks usually include more citations to primary sources than *Nutshells* do. *Nutshells* are a series of paperback books published by West that serve primarily to bring law students up to speed on an area of law. For the researcher, these books may provide helpful background information or an overview of an area of law before beginning more specific research.

Deskbooks and practice guides are geared to assisting practicing lawyers in a particular area of law. They tend to be more practical, rather than analytical or theoretical like treatises. Also, unlike hornbooks and *Nutshells*, deskbooks and practice guides usually address the law and procedures of specific jurisdictions. They often include (1) explanations of the law and how it has been interpreted, (2) checklists helpful to practitioners, (3) forms, (4) unannotated versions of rules of procedure, evidence, and courts, (5) the text of relevant statutes and regulations, and (6) author commentary on practicing in the jurisdiction or in the particular field of law. Although deskbooks and practice guides all serve similar purposes, their formats vary.

One example of a helpful practitioner deskbook is the West series of state and federal court rules for each state. Each book in the series covers a different state and provides the state and federal rules of court used by the courts located in the state. Another example of a helpful, subject-specific practice guide is the *NEPA Deskbook 3rd Edition* (Environmental Law Institute 2003). It includes the text of the National Environmental Practice Act, the text of relevant statutes, executive orders, regulations, and other documents, forms, and practice advice for lawyers working with environmental law. See Table 3-3 for examples of deskbooks and practice guides on selected issues of federal law.

2. *Researching Treatises and Other Books*

As in researching books in other disciplines, the first step to researching legal treatises and books is identifying the titles in which you will search. Sometimes you will be familiar with the titles covering a particular area of law because of experience in the field or because of other research that has identified the titles. When you are unfamiliar with the treatises or books available on a particular area of law, consult a law librarian, a lawyer with experience in the area of law, or a library catalog to find out which treatises or books are available. Additionally, using an Internet search engine may help you identify relevant titles. Law libraries shelve these publications together by topic, so scan the shelves near relevant books for additional resources. After identifying titles, use search terms in the index or table of contents to the treatise or book to find specific volumes, sections, and pages that seem most relevant to the issue. Then locate those specific portions of the source and review them to determine their value.

Treatises and books are updated in various ways, as noted earlier. Consider whether you are looking at the most recent edition of a treatise or book and whether there are any supplements, pocket parts, or looseleaf inserts to the treatise or book.

An example of researching a specific topic in the treatise *Federal Practice and Procedure* follows. Assume you have a question concern-

Table 3-3. Selected Deskbooks and Practice Guides

Admiralty and Maritime Law:

Charles M. Davis, *Maritime Law Deskbook* (8th ed., Compass Pub. Co. 2010).

Thomas J. Schoenbaum, *Admiralty and Maritime Law* (5th ed., Thomson West 2011).

Geoffrey Gill, *West's Federal Forms: Admiralty* vol. 7-7A (5th ed., Thomson West 2009).

Bankruptcy Law:

Judith K. Fitzgerald, Arthur Gonzalez & Mary F. Walrath, *Bankruptcy, National Edition* (The Rutter Group 2010).

William Hillman & Margaret M. Crouch, *Bankruptcy Deskbook* (4th ed., PLI 2006).

Environmental Law:

Nicholas C. Yost, *NEPA Deskbook* (3d ed., ELI 2003).

Lawrence Lieberman & Rafe Petersen, *Endangered Species Deskbook* (2d ed., ELI 2010).

Federal Procedure:

Florida Rules of Court—State, Federal, & Local (Thomson West 2011) (similar books exist for most states).

William W. Schwarzer, A. Wallace Tashima & James M. Wagstaffe, *Federal Civil Procedure Before Trial, National Edition* (The Rutter Group 2008–2011).

Patent Law:

Ronald B. Hildreth, *Patent Law: A Practitioner's Guide* (3d ed., PLI 1998).

Barry Kramer & Allen D. Brufsky, *Patent Law Practice Forms* (Thomson West 2009–2010).

ing the meaning of the terms *fair play and substantial justice* for determining personal jurisdiction. Begin with the most recent volume of the General Index of *Federal Practice and Procedure*. The index is an easy place to start because the topics are in alphabetical order.

Using the search terms "fair play" and "substantial justice," you quickly find that these terms are discussed in five different sections of the treatise volumes and that all relevant sections are numbered between 1067.1 and 1074. Look at each of these sections to determine their relevance.

The section that is most relevant to your research is Section 1067.2, entitled *Minimum Contacts, Fair Play, and Substantial Justice,* which is shown in Figure 3-1. This section gives explanatory text, footnotes to pertinent cases and other authorities, and cross-references to other relevant sections within the treatise. To complete your research in this publication, check the pocket part of the treatise. The pocket part to this volume at Section 1067.2 provides many additional citations to cases supporting the footnotes of the main text. Sometimes a pocket part will also include supplemental text. You now have some references to the most recent cases on the researched issue as of the publishing date of the pocket part. If there were no reference to Section 1067.2 in the pocket part, you would know that no additional information had been added to the information in the text.

Many treatises and books, such as *Federal Practice and Procedure,* are available online through Lexis and Westlaw. When you scan the directories of these services, identify databases or specific publications in which to run your search. Focus on databases that provide access to secondary sources in general, to subject-specific materials, or to the specific publication(s) in which you wish to search. You can run searches in several databases at one time.

Type in your search terms to receive a list of possible sections that satisfy your query. Your results will include short excerpts from the publications and citation information. Then, click on each section that interests you and assess its value, or print the list of citations to use in the print sources. If you are looking at a source through an online service, be sure to find information about how the source is updated. Sometimes the source will be automatically updated at a regular interval, and sometimes a link to updates will be provided.

Figure 3-1. Excerpt from *Federal Practice and Procedure*

---

§ 1067.1   SUMMONS   Ch. 3
Rule 4

much more encompassing view of the stream of commerce theory that seems to subject a defendant to personal jurisdiction whenever it was forseeable that the product would be marketed in the forum state.[75] A later section explores the current status of the stream of commerce theory.[76]

§ 1067.2 **Minimum Contacts, Fair Play, and Substantial Justice**

This section explores the Supreme Court's treatment of minimum contacts, fair play, and substantial justice as necessary due process requirements of any assertion of personal jurisdiction over a defendant who cannot be served with process within the territory of the forum. The section that follows discusses the apparent limits on the application of this general constitutional principle.[1]

In World-Wide Volkswagen Corporation v. Woodson[2] the Court, in an opinion by Justice White, identified four factors to be considered as elements of "fair play and substantial justice:"(1) the forum state's interest in adjudicating the dispute; (2) the plaintiff's interest in obtaining convenient and effective relief; (3) the interstate judicial system's interest in obtaining the most efficient resolution of controversies; and (4) the shared interest of the several states in furthering fundamental social policies.[3] The Court's discussion of

---

75. Justice Brennan
107 S.Ct. at 1035, 480 U.S. at 117 (Brennan, J., concurring).

76. Later section
See § 1067.4.

§ 1067.2

1. Limits
See § 1067.3.

2. Volkswagen case
1980, 100 S.Ct. 559, 444 U.S. 286, 62 L.Ed.2d 490. This case is discussed in detail in §§ 1067.1 and 1067.4.

3. Four factors
Id. at 564, 444 U.S. at 292.

For a discussion of these factors in the context of general jurisdiction, see § 1067.5.

See also

Ticketmaster—New York, Inc. v. Alioto, C.A.1st, 1994, 26 F.3d 201 (couching

"four factors" inquiry as consideration of five "gestalt factors" encompassing usual four factors, as well as primary concern of defendant's burden of appearing).

Wilson v. Belin, C.A.5th, 1994, 20 F.3d 644, certiorari denied 115 S.Ct. 322, 513 U.S. 930, 130 L.Ed.2d 282.

Ruston Gas Turbines, Inc. v. Donaldson Co., C.A.5th, 1993, 9 F.3d 415 (in assessing assertion of personal jurisdiction, court must examine factors enumerated in Volkswagen opinion).

Hupp v. Siroflex of America, Inc., D.C.Tex.1994, 848 F.Supp. 744.

Frederick v. Hydro-Aluminum S.A., D.C.Mich.1994, 153 F.R.D. 120.

Star Technology, Inc. v. Tultex Corp., D.C.Tex.1993, 844 F.Supp. 295.

U.S. v. Avondale Indus., Inc., D.C.La. 1993, 841 F.Supp. 180.

462

Source: 4 Charles Alan Wright, Arthur R. Miller, *Federal Practice and Procedure* § 1067.2 (West 2002). Reprinted with permission of West, a Thomson Reuters business.

E. *American Law Reports*

1. *Overview*

The *American Law Reports*, known as A.L.R., contains both primary and secondary authority. It is discussed in this chapter on secondary authority because its value is not in its publication of cases, but in its extensive commentary and discussion of the legal issues raised in those cases.

West publishes in A.L.R. certain cases that it deems to address significant legal issues. Each case is published in its entirety, accompanied by an *annotation*[8] that includes a full discussion of a point of law referenced in the case. The annotation provides citations to cases from multiple jurisdictions as well as to other secondary authorities. Headnotes preceding the cases, which are similar to the headnotes in West publications, are tied to A.L.R. digests (these were recently reclassified to correspond to West's digests). The annotation begins with a table of contents, cross-references to other relevant publications, a subject index, and a "Table of Jurisdictions Represented." An introduction identifies the scope of the annotation and provides citations to related A.L.R. annotations. This list of related annotations can prove particularly helpful in leading to annotations that may be even more relevant for the research project.

A relevant annotation can be valuable at the early stages of research because it (1) fully discusses and analyzes an issue; (2) identifies differences among jurisdictions as to their treatment of the issue; and (3) collects relevant cases from all jurisdictions, providing both binding and persuasive primary authority. Each annotation is updated to keep up with changes in the law.

The A.L.R. has been published in eight series. A.L.R., A.L.R.2d, and some early volumes in the A.L.R.3d series include both federal and state law issues. Beginning in 1969, all federal law issues were moved

---

8. The term "annotation" in legal research typically refers to short cross-references between sources. The use of the term for lengthy articles appearing in A.L.R. is unique and sometimes confusing.

to a new series, *American Law Reports, Federal* (A.L.R. Fed.), which is now in its second series.[9] The more modern series, from A.L.R.3d forward, have more features and are similar to each other in format. Each series has multiple volumes organized by volume number.

2. Researching in A.L.R.

Researching to find a relevant A.L.R. annotation can be done both in print and online. In print, if your research deals exclusively with federal law, begin in the ALR Fed Quick Index.[10] Alternatively, the ALR Index to Annotations, which includes references to annotations found in all series from the A.L.R.2d series on, is a more comprehensive index for locating annotations addressing both federal and state law.

Researching in an A.L.R. index is similar to researching in other indexes. Search for key terms, which will lead to citations to annotations related to those terms. Each index entry includes a brief statement identifying the issue addressed in the annotation in addition to its citation. The index also provides cross-references to other terms. Be careful to note the series designation when writing down the annotation citations. Additionally, consult the pocket part to the index to find references to additional annotations.

To search for annotations referencing specific statutes, use the "Table of Laws, Rules, and Regulations" located in the back of the index.

Another method to find relevant annotations is to use the ALR Digest, which includes references to annotations in A.L.R. Fed. and A.L.R. Fed. 2d as well as in A.L.R.3d, A.L.R.4th, A.L.R.5th, and A.L.R.6th. The ALR Digest separates the law into topics and subtopics and gives short summaries of the annotations relating to these topics. Beginning with A.L.R.6th, the digest references have been reclas-

---

9. A.L.R.4th, A.L.R.5th, and A.L.R.6th address only state law issues.

10. To research an issue of state law, begin with search terms in the ALR Quick Index, which covers annotations found in the A.L.R.3d through the A.L.R.6th series. The ALR First Series Quick Index indexes the annotations in the first series. This index should not be consulted unless references in the newer editions of the series do not exist.

sified to correspond to the West Key Number System as have the digest references in the supplements to the other A.L.R. editions. While this digest may be a helpful tool for the researcher who is having trouble finding relevant annotations through an index, an index is generally the better place to begin.

You can also locate citations to annotations online using Lexis and Westlaw. Both of these services provide databases that allow searching the full text of annotations for key terms.

Once you have citations, turn to the corresponding annotations in the volumes or open that portion of the database. Skim the material at the beginning of the annotation, including the introduction, to ensure that the annotation is relevant before reading the entire entry.

The A.L.R. series in print is updated in several ways: (1) by new editions; (2) by pocket parts to supplement the volumes, the indexes, and the digests; and (3) by the "Annotation History Table," which is found in the index. It is important to check pocket parts and the "Annotation History Table" before relying on the annotation printed in the volume because sometimes entire annotations or sections of annotations are superseded by new ones to keep abreast of changes in the law. The pocket part will indicate what changes have been made to an annotation.[11] Online, the A.L.R. material is updated weekly by the addition of relevant cases, and the annotations may be updated using Shepard's and KeyCite.

F. Looseleaf Services

Like the *American Law Reports*, looseleaf services include both primary and secondary authority. They are discussed in this chapter because they compile under one title the statutes and regulations that control a particular area of law, references to cases and administrative opinions, and commentary that takes a practitioner viewpoint. Looseleaf services are popular in areas of law in which regulations

---

11. A.L.R. and A.L.R.2d are updated a bit differently. A.L.R. is updated through the ALR Blue Book of Supplemental Decisions, and A.L.R.2d is updated through the use of Later Case Service volumes.

play a large role; examples include tax law, environmental law, and labor law. Because of their breadth of coverage in one area of law, looseleaf services are sometimes called "mini-libraries." The most well known publishers of looseleaf services are the Bureau of National Affairs (BNA), Commerce Clearing House (CCH), and Research Institute of America (RIA).

In print, looseleaf services are published in three-ring binders; the binder format allows for quick updating as publishers frequently send new pages with instructions for removing outdated pages. To allow this method of updating, information is often indexed and referenced by paragraph number. A "paragraph" might be one actual paragraph or several pages in length; the paragraph reference will remain constant even as pages are inserted and removed. Researching a looseleaf service in print can be complicated, but a "How to Use" section in any looseleaf will provide a useful overview.

Many tools initially available as looseleaf services are not available online. Databases maintained by BNA, CCH, and RIA provide access to resources not always available on Lexis or Westlaw. While some databases track the organization of their print counterparts, others are organized differently. Each service provides a tutorial or guide for how to research the database.

G. Restatements

1. Overview

Restatements summarize or "re-state" American common law on a subject. The American Law Institute (ALI) has published restatements in a variety of fields, including Agency, Conflicts of Law, Contracts, Foreign Relations, Judgments, Law Governing Lawyers, Property, Restitution, Security, Suretyship and Guaranty, Torts, Trusts, and Unfair Competition. Most of these restatements are in their second or third revision, which is designated in the publication's title, such as the *Restatement (Second) of Torts*.

Restatements present common law rules, sometimes including both majority and minority rules and interpretations. Additionally, restatements provide commentary on the rules, illustrations suggesting how the rules should be applied, and citations to and brief summaries of cases in which the restatement section has been interpreted.

Although the common law rules presented in the restatements often look like statutes, they are not statutes. Restatement rules can become primary authority only if a court or a legislature adopts them as such. If the courts of a jurisdiction have adopted a restatement as law, the researcher can use the restatement effectively to locate persuasive authority from other jurisdictions cited in the restatement's discussion.

2. Researching Restatements

You can search for available restatements using a library's catalog by searching for the general subject being researched or for the word "restatement." Once the restatement is located, use search terms in the restatement's index or table of contents to locate relevant sections. Relevant sections of the restatement will include the rule, comments, and illustrations. The corresponding Appendix volumes of the restatement will provide information about citing cases.

Lexis and Westlaw provide restatements in various databases that you can search with appropriate terms. Additionally, you can search for restatement references in other databases, such as databases that include cases or journal articles.

H. Continuing Legal Education Materials

Participating in continuing legal education (CLE) is a requirement for maintaining good standing as a member of most bars in United States jurisdictions.[12] CLE materials consist of the handouts distributed by the CLE instructors, who are generally practitioners, judges, or law professors. The CLE materials usually focus on a particular

---

12. For a summary of CLE requirements by state, visit the map at http://www.americanbar.org/publications_cle/mandatory_cle.html. The following states do not require continuing legal education for their practicing lawyers: Connecticut, Maryland, Massachusetts, Michigan, and South Dakota.

legal subject matter and can be useful to provide introductory material or recent developments on a subject. While CLE materials are probably not the best place to acquire all relevant research or even to begin research, they can be useful research tools because of their practical emphasis. They are rarely cited in judicial opinions or scholarly publications. Moreover, because most CLE materials are not regularly updated, you should update any material gathered from these sources.

The easiest way to locate CLE materials is online. The American Law Institute-American Bar Association (ALI-ABA), the American Bar Association (ABA), and the Practising Law Institute (PLI) publish CLE materials on their websites. CLE materials may also be located on Lexis and Westlaw. On Lexis, search in "Secondary Legal" under "CLE Materials." On Westlaw, search in the database "Treatises, CLEs, and Other Practice Materials." Libraries also catalog and shelve some CLE materials by topic and author.

I. Forms and Jury Instructions

1. Overview

Forms and sample jury instructions are widely available to assist practitioners. The term *forms* is used to refer to sample legal documents, such as contracts, pleadings, wills, and even client letters. The term *jury instructions* refers to the instructions given by a judge to a jury before the jury is sent to deliberate in a case. Sometimes courts will provide attorneys with suggested jury instructions and give the attorneys an opportunity to voice any objections; sometimes courts will ask the attorneys to propose jury instructions.

The most helpful of these types of documents, from a research standpoint, are annotated forms and jury instructions that provide citations to authority to support language found in the documents. The annotated documents lead to primary authorities and other secondary authorities; they provide the information necessary for assessing the relevance of the form or instruction to the client's case. Forms and sample jury instructions also provide valuable information to the practitioner who is new to how things are done in a particular jurisdiction.

Remember when using any of these resources that any document you produce for a client and any instructions you submit to a court must be tailored to your client, your case, and the current, applicable law.

2. *Researching Forms and Jury Instructions*

Forms and jury instructions may be found in several different contexts. First, many free websites provide links to forms and jury instructions. Court websites often include forms for pleadings and other litigation-related documents. Federal appellate courts' websites include links to *model* or *pattern* jury instructions, which are used throughout the federal courts. The United States Fifth Circuit Court of Appeals' library website provides links to all federal court model or pattern jury instructions[13] as does the website of the Federal Evidence Review.[14]

Second, forms and jury instructions may be found in deskbooks and practice guides on particular legal topics, along with significant discussions of the law. See Section III.D.1.c. of this chapter for a discussion of deskbooks and practice guides. To determine which publications are available, check a library catalog under the relevant subject matter as well as under the terms "forms" or "jury instructions."

Several of the publications listed in Table 3-3 include forms relevant to their topics. Some additional examples of form books include *American Jurisprudence Legal Forms* (also available on Westlaw), *West's Legal Forms* (arranged alphabetically by major types of forms), and *Current Legal Forms with Tax Analysis*.

Examples of books focused on jury instructions are *Federal Jury Practice and Instructions* and *Modern Federal Jury Instructions*. Books containing jury instructions are also available organized by civil action, such as *Model Jury Instructions: Employment Litigation*, and *Model Jury Instructions: Securities Litigation*.

---

13. The address is www.lb5.uscourts.gov/juryinstructions.
14. The address is http://federalevidence.com/evidence-resources/federal-jury-instructions.

Third, forms are often found with governing rules of procedure and court rules. For example, the *Appendix to the Federal Rules of Civil Procedure* includes forms for documents that are frequently filed with the federal district courts.

Fourth, forms and jury instructions are available on Lexis and Westlaw, which have databases dedicated to forms and jury instructions.

Chapter 4

Constitutional Law Research

I. Background

The United States Constitution sets out the framework for the federal government, allocates power among the three branches of the federal government, and identifies individual rights regarded as fundamental, such as freedom of speech and free exercise of religion.

The Constitution was written in 1787 and has been in operation since 1789. In 1791, the first ten amendments, known as the Bill of Rights, were added. The Constitution is designed to be difficult to amend and, since 1791, has been amended only 17 times.

The federal Constitution creates and limits national government. The Constitution provides the structure for the federal government by dividing power among three branches: the legislative branch (Article I); the executive branch (Article II); and the judicial branch (Article III). The Constitution provides "checks and balances" to check the power of any one branch of federal government and to balance power among the three different branches. For example, the president may veto a specific legislative act, but Congress can override a presidential veto by two-thirds majorities of both houses. As another example, the Senate must provide advice and consent on key executive and judicial appointments.[1]

The Constitution divides power between the federal and state governments. Federal law takes precedence over state and local laws. Ar-

---

1. United States Senate, *Constitution of the United States*, Introduction, http://www.senate.gov/civics/constitution_item/constitution.htm.

ticle VI of the Constitution, the supremacy clause, provides that "[t]his Constitution, and the Laws of the United States which shall be made in Pursuance thereof; and all Treaties made ... under the Authority of the United States, shall be the supreme Law of the Land." State and local laws may not conflict with federal law or regulate a field occupied by federal law; if they do, the state and local laws are *preempted* by federal law.[2]

Congress itself is supposed to act within the limits of the U.S. Constitution. In *Marbury v. Madison*,[3] the Supreme Court held that it has the power to declare acts of Congress unconstitutional, a concept known as *judicial review*.

The Constitution also limits federal and, after the Fourteenth Amendment in 1868, state government power by protecting the rights of individuals. The Constitution restricts government behavior but does not regulate purely private conduct, a concept known as the *state action doctrine*.[4]

Table 4-1 lists the articles and amendments of the federal Constitution. Articles are cited by article number and section: U.S. Const. art. III, § 1. (This provision appears in Chapter 1, in Figure 1-1.) Amendments are cited by amendment number and section: U.S. Const. amend. XIV, § 2.

II. Locating the Text of the Constitution

The text of the United States Constitution is available in many places. The Constitution is printed in the federal statutory compilations: the *United States Code* (U.S.C.), the *United States Code Anno-*

---

2. However, the federal Constitution sets the floor, not the ceiling, for protection of individual rights: states are permitted to interpret their own constitutions to be more protective of individual rights than is the federal Constitution.

3. 5 U.S. (1 Cranch) 137 (1803).

4. The Thirteenth Amendment, which prohibits slavery and involuntary servitude, is an exception; it regulates private conduct as well as government conduct.

Table 4-1. U.S. Constitution

Article I	Legislative Department
Article II	Executive Power
Article III	Judicial Power
Article IV	Relations between States
Article V	Amendment of Constitution
Article VI	Miscellaneous Provisions
Article VII	Ratification

Amendments

1. Religious and political freedom
2. Right to bear arms
3. Quartering soldiers
4. Unreasonable searches and seizures
5. Criminal actions—Provisions concerning—Due process of law and just compensation clauses
6. Rights of accused
7. Trial by jury in civil cases
8. Bail—punishment
9. Rights retained by people
10. Powers reserved to states or people
11. Suits against states—Restriction of judicial power
12. Election of President and Vice-President
13. Section 1. Slavery prohibited
    Section 2. Power to enforce amendment
14. Section 1. Citizens of the United States
    Section 2. Representatives—Power to reduce apportionment
    Section 3. Disqualification to hold office
    Section 4. Public debt not to be questioned   Debts of the Confederacy and claims not to be paid.
    Section 5. Power to enforce amendment
15. Section 1. Right of citizens to vote—Race or color not to disqualify
    Section 2. Power to enforce amendment
16. Income tax
17. Election of Senators
18. Section 1. National prohibition—Intoxicating liquors

Section 2. Concurrent power to enforce amendment
Section 3. Time limit for adoption
19. Section 1. Woman suffrage
    Section 2. Power to enforce amendment
20. Section 1. Executive and legislative departments—Terms of elective officers
    Section 2. Annual meeting of Congress—Date
    Section 3. Succession to office of President or Vice-President
    Section 4. Death of President or Vice-President—Selection of successor—Choice devolving on either house.
    Section 5. Effective date of amendment
    Section 6. Time for ratification
21. Section 1. Repeal of Eighteenth Amendment
    Section 2. Intoxicating liquors, shipment into dry territory prohibited
    Section 3. Ratification, time limit
22. Section 1. Terms of Office of the President
    Section 2. Ratification
23. Section 1. Representation in the electoral college to the District of Columbia
    Section 2. Enforcement
24. Section 1. Qualification of electors
    Section 2. Enforcement
25. Section 1. Succession to Office of President
    Section 2. Succession to Office of Vice-President
    Section 3. Declaration by President of inability to serve
    Section 4. Declaration by others of President's inability to serve
26. Section 1. Eighteen year old voting rights
    Section 2. Enforcement
27. Compensation of members of Congress

tated (U.S.C.A.), and the *United States Code Service* (U.S.C.S.). Many state code publications include the U.S. Constitution. The text of the Constitution is available for free on the websites of the Government Printing Office,[5] of the U.S. House of Representatives,[6] and of the U.S. Senate, which also provides annotations explaining each provision.[7] The Constitution is available in *Black's Law Dictionary* and in many other resources.

III. Researching Constitutional Issues

Most sources listed above could be used to research constitutional issues. This chapter introduces some efficient and effective ways to research constitutional law. Other chapters of this book provide more detailed explanations of some research techniques covered here.[8]

A. Beginning Research with Secondary Sources

An efficient way to limit legal research time and cost is to begin constitutional research with secondary sources, including treatises and hornbooks, *American Law Reports*, and encyclopedias. As explained in Chapter 3, secondary sources not only give important context and background but also can lead to sources of binding law—constitutional provisions and judicial opinions construing those provisions.[9]

---

5. GPO Access, *Core Documents of U.S. Democracy*, http://www.gpoaccess.gov/coredocs.html.

6. United States House of Representatives, *The United States Constitution*, http://www.house.gov/house/Constitution/Constitution.html.

7. United States Senate, *Constitution of the United States*, http://www.senate.gov/civics/constitution_item/constitution.htm.

8. For more detailed explanations, Chapter 2 discusses searching in online databases; Chapter 3 explains how to use various secondary sources; Chapter 5 covers statutory compilations; Chapter 6 addresses digests; and Chapter 10 delves into citators Shepard's and KeyCite.

9. To locate primary authority by beginning with secondary sources such as treatises, hornbooks, *American Law Reports*, and encyclopedias, follow the steps outlined in Chapter 3. Specifically, search the table of contents or index

Table 4-2. General Constitutional Law Treatises

Author	Title
John E. Nowak & Ronald D. Rotunda	*Treatise on Constitutional Law: Substance and Procedure* (4th ed., Thomson/West 2007) (multi-volume), *available at* Westlaw database CONLAW
Erwin Chemerinsky	*Constitutional Law: Principles and Policies* (3d ed., Aspen 2006)
John E. Nowak & Ronald D. Rotunda	*Principles of Constitutional Law* (4th ed., Thomson/West 2010)
David S. Rudstein, C. Peter Erlinder & David C. Thomas	*Criminal Constitutional Law* (Matthew Bender & Co. 1990 & Supp. 2009), *available at* Lexis database Criminal Constitutional Law

1. Treatises and Hornbooks

A treatise or hornbook can provide an overview of a new area of law, introduce terms of art and the vocabulary of the field, identify current debates, and point to citations to binding current authority. Table 4-2 lists some helpful general treatises on constitutional law.

The Constitution of the United States of America: Analysis and Interpretation is a general treatise by the Congressional Research Service that analyzes U.S. Supreme Court applications of the Constitution. It was published in 2002 and has been supplemented at two-year intervals (2004, 2006, 2008). It is free and available in PDF format on the U.S. Government Printing Office website.[10]

---

for your search terms to find relevant topics; read the secondary source discussion of the topic to become familiar with the new concepts and to choose citations to primary authority; read the constitutional provision and binding judicial opinions construing the provision to confirm their relevance; and update the cases.

10. Cong. Research Serv., Library of Cong., *The Constitution of the United States of America: Analysis and Interpretation* (2004), http://www.gpoaccess.gov/constitution.

Table 4-3. Constitutional Law Treatises on Civil Rights

Author	Title
Sheldon Nahmod	*Civil Rights and Civil Liberties Litigation: The Law of Section 1983* (4th ed., West Group 1997 & Supp. 1998–2011) (multi-volume), *available at* Westlaw database CIVLIBLIT
Martin A. Schwartz	*Section 1983 Litigation: Claims and Defenses* (4th ed., Aspen 1995 & Supp. 2010) (multivolume), *available at* Westlaw database SNETLCD
Ivan E. Bodensteiner & Rosalie Berger Levinson	*State and Local Government Civil Rights Liability* (Thomson Reuters/West 2000 & Supp. 2000–2011) (multi-volume), *available at* Westlaw database STLOCCIVIL
Martin A. Schwartz & Kathryn R. Urbonya	*Section 1983 Litigation* (2d ed., Judicial Ctr. 2008)
Mary Massaron Ross & Edwin P. Voss, Jr., eds.	*Sword & Shield: A Practical Approach to Section 1983 Litigation* (3d ed., ABA Publishing 2006), *available at* Westlaw database ABA-SWORD
Joseph G. Cook & John L. Sobieski, Jr.	*Civil Rights Actions* (Matthew Bender 1983 & Supp. 2010) (multi-volume), *available at* Lexis database Civil Rights Actions

In addition to general treatises on the Constitution, some treatises address specific types of constitutional claims. If the constitutional research concerns a civil claim like freedom of speech,[11] civil rights treatises are efficient tools for becoming familiar with relevant terms and current debates, as well as locating binding authority. Table 4-3 lists some helpful civil rights treatises. If the constitutional research concerns the conduct of police officers, research might begin with treatises focused on police conduct or, even more specifically, on

---

11. The most frequent civil claims are based on the First, Fourth, Eighth, and Fourteenth Amendments.

Table 4-4. Constitutional Law Treatises on Criminal Law

Author	Title
Michael Avery, David Rudovsky & Karen Blum	*Police Misconduct: Law and Litigation* (3d ed., Clark Boardman 2010), *available at* Westlaw database POLICEMISC
Wayne R. LaFave	*Search and Seizure: A Treatise on the Fourth Amendment* (4th ed., Thomson/West 2004 & Supp. 2010) (multi-volume), *available at* Westlaw database SEARCHSZR
John Wesley Hall	*Search and Seizure* (3d ed., Matthew Bender & Co., Inc. 2000 & Supp. 2010), *available at* Lexis database Search and Seizure

search and seizure. Table 4-4 lists helpful treatises focused on those specific topics. If the constitutional research arises in the criminal context and concerns the Fourth, Fifth, Sixth, or Eighth Amendment, you might start with a criminal procedure hornbook, such as Wayne R. LaFave, Jerold A. Israel, Nancy J. King & Orin S. Kerr, *Criminal Procedure* (5th ed., Thomson Reuters 2009), or the same authors' seven-volume treatise, *Criminal Procedure* (3d ed., Thomson Reuters/West 2007, with annual supplements), which is available on Westlaw in the CRIMPROC database.

2. American Law Reports

Annotations in *American Law Reports, Federal* (A.L.R. Fed. and A.L.R. Fed. 2d) provide useful summaries of particular constitutional topics and citations to relevant cases, organized by jurisdiction with new cases added weekly. Some annotations provide the general outline of a theory of constitutional liability and citations to cases applying that theory, such as the state-created danger theory of substantive due process liability.[12] Other annotations are more focused

---

12. *See e.g.* Joseph M. Pellicciotti, Annotation, *"State-Created Danger," or Similar Theory, As Basis for Civil Rights Action Under 42 U.S.C.A. § 1983*, 159 A.L.R. Fed. 37 (2000) (updated weekly).

on a constitutional issue as it is litigated in a specific factual context and can be a rich source of case citations in that specific context. One example is Eighth Amendment claims of deliberate indifference to the medical needs of HIV-positive prison inmates.[13]

To locate relevant A.L.R. annotations: (1) consult an ALR Fed Quick Index, either in the library or on Westlaw or (2) search the "ALR Federal" database on Lexis or Westlaw. In addition, when checking the validity of citations via Shepard's on Lexis or KeyCite on Westlaw, note the citations to relevant articles, including A.L.R. annotations, that appear after the listed primary sources. When searching online databases, you may wish to note the side columns called "Related Content" on Lexis and "Results Plus" on Westlaw, which list relevant secondary sources. While the additional resources suggested in the side columns on Lexis and Westlaw can be helpful if your research is not progressing, be careful not to become sidetracked. When signing off of Westlaw, one last prompt will ask if a particular secondary source might have helped — and often that source is on point.

3. Legal Encyclopedias and Annotated Constitutions

Although encyclopedia entries are less in-depth than the discussions in treatises, hornbooks, or A.L.R., the entries summarize key concepts and provide case citations. A number of legal encyclopedias are available for constitutional law research, several of which were introduced in Chapter 3. Three free, online legal encyclopedias are listed in Table 4-5.[14] Although not specifically labeled an encyclopedia, Justia's annotated discussions of the Constitution provides sim-

---

13. *See e.g.* Robin Cheryl Miller, Annotation, *Federal Constitutional and Statutory Claims by HIV–Positive Inmates as to Medical Treatment or Conditions of Confinement*, 162 A.L.R. Fed. 181 (2000) (updated weekly).

14. Additionally, for a basic introduction to a new area of law, including constitutional law, Wikipedia can be a useful starting place for learning terms of art and perhaps finding citations to relevant authority. Wikipedia should not be relied on as authoritative, as it can contain errors. *See e.g. Bing Shun Li v. Holder*, 400 Fed. Appx. 854, 858 (5th Cir. 2010) (disapproving of "reliance on Wikipedia and ... warn[ing] against any improper reliance on it or similarly unreliable internet sources in the future").

Table 4-5. Free Online Encyclopedias

Name	Address
Legal Information Institute, Wex	http://www.law.cornell.edu/wex
FindLaw	http://www.findlaw.com/casecode/constitution
U.S. Supreme Court Center, Justia	http://supreme.justia.com/constitution

ilar information. Moreover, Justia's table of contents tracks the constitutional provisions and includes hyperlinked explanations of how constitutional provisions have been construed by the Supreme Court (through June 29, 2004), along with hyperlinks to the cited cases.

Beyond the free encyclopedias, the entries in *American Jurisprudence 2d* (Am. Jur. 2d) give general legal overviews, such as explaining the difference between procedural and substantive due process protections[15] or explaining the doctrine of preemption.[16] Am. Jur. 2d and its table of contents are available in libraries and online via Lexis (e.g., under "Secondary Legal," locate "Jurisprudences, ALR & Encyclopedias," select "American Jurisprudence 2d," and then choose "Table of Contents") and Westlaw (e.g., under "Secondary Sources," locate "American Jurisprudence (Am Jur)," and then link to "Table of Contents"). To locate relevant articles, do a word search in the Am. Jur. 2d database or in the table of contents, or instead use the table of contents to move from a general term to a more specific subheading, such as: Constitutional Law > Fundamental Rights and Privileges > Federal Constitutional Guarantees > 14th Amendment and effect thereof > To whom the 14th Amendment applies.[17]

---

15. *See e.g.* 16B Am. Jur. 2d *Constitutional Law* § 953 (2d ed., Thomson/West 2009).

16. *See e.g.* 16A Am. Jur. 2d *Constitutional Law* § 232 (2d ed., Thomson/West 2009).

17. On Westlaw, the layout makes clear that the last is a subheading under "14th Amendment and effect thereof."

Under the last topic heading above, you will find a brief explanation of who is bound by the Fourteenth Amendment, along with case citations and references to other secondary sources, such as A.L.R. Fed., *Am. Jur. Pleading and Practice Forms*, and West key numbers.

The publication *Causes of Action* provides more specific guidance for pleading and proving particular constitutional claims.[18] In addition, it provides citations to cases, secondary sources, West key numbers, law review articles, relevant Westlaw databases, litigation forms, and other potentially useful sources. *Causes of Action* is available in libraries or on Westlaw (e.g., under "Secondary Sources," select "Causes of Action").

Finally, the Congressional Research Service (CRS) prepared an annotated United States Constitution to explain key concepts and provide citations to U.S. Supreme Court decisions.[19] It is available for free online through the Legal Information Institute; online supplements were published until 2000. Like many indexes to secondary sources, the index to the *Annotated Constitution* is a useful introduction to the vocabulary and concepts in the field. For example, a researcher new to Fourth Amendment law might need to locate authority that governs a police search of a client while he was being placed under arrest. Scanning the index to the *Annotated Constitution*, the researcher would glean from the following trail that a relevant term of art might be "search incident to arrest": FOURTH AMENDMENT > SEARCH AND SEIZURE > Search Incident to Arrest. While the *Annotated Constitution* can be a useful introduction to concepts, the citations are limited to Supreme Court cases and have not been updated in over a decade.

4. Blogs and Lexis Preview of Supreme Court Cases

Blogs can be especially useful for identifying current debates in constitutional law and for commentary on recent cases and developments. Blogs devoted to constitutional issues include Constitutional

---

18. *See e.g.* James L. Buchwalter, *Cause of Action for Prison's Failure to Protect Inmate from Assault*, 33 Causes of Action 2d 605 (Thomson Reuters 2007).

19. Cong. Research Serv., Library of Cong., *CRS Annotated Constitution*, http://www.law.cornell.edu/anncon/html/index.html.

Law Prof Blog,[20] First Amendment Law Prof Blog,[21] and the American Constitution Society blog.[22] Other blogs that frequently focus on constitutional issues include The Federalist Society's blog,[23] the American Civil Liberties Union's blog,[24] and the CrimProf blog.[25]

To determine if a constitutional provision currently is pending before the Supreme Court or if a litigant currently is seeking Supreme Court review of that issue, a useful source (in addition to the Westlaw certiorari petition bank explained below) is SCOTUS blog.[26] SCOTUS has commentary on pending petitions and cases before the Supreme Court, including explanations in Plain English.[27] In addition, SCOTUS links to PDFs of petitions seeking and opposing certiorari, briefs on the merits, and amicus briefs, all of which are fruitful sources of potential arguments.

An alternative way to determine if a constitutional provision is pending before the Supreme Court is to search the Lexis Supreme Court materials accessible by following the research trail "Legal," then "Cases—U.S.," and "Supreme Court Cases & Materials," and searching for your constitutional issue in the database "Preview of United States Supreme Court Cases." For example, a search for "Fourth Amendment" would lead you to a brief summary of the facts and

---

20. Steven D. Schwinn & Ruthann Robson, Constitutional Law Prof Blog, http://lawprofessors.typepad.com/conlaw.

21. Josie F. Brown, First Amendment Law Prof Blog, http://lawprofessors.typepad.com/firstamendment.

22. Jeremy Leaming, Nicole Flatow & Alex Wohl, American Constitution Society Blog, http://www.acslaw.org/acsblog.

23. The Federalist Society, FedSoc Blog, http://www.fedsocblog.com.

24. American Civil Liberties Union, Blog of Rights: The Official Blog of the American Civil Liberties Union, http://www.fedsocblog.com (including categories such as Free Speech, Prisoner Rights, Racial Justice, and Voting Rights).

25. Kevin Cole, CrimProf Blog, http://lawprofessors.typepad.com/crimprof_blog.

26. The full name is Supreme Court of the United States Blog, and the address is http://www.scotusblog.com.

27. Lisa McElroy, Archive: *Plain English*, Supreme Court of the United States Blog, http://www.scotusblog.com/category/plain-english.

analysis of the issues in Fourth Amendment cases scheduled to be argued before the Supreme Court.

5. Brief Banks

Once a researcher has a sense of how the research project fits into the big picture of the legal area, a good source of potential legal arguments and current case citations are recent briefs filed in the relevant jurisdiction. Both Lexis and Westlaw have brief banks.

Lexis allows the researcher to search for briefs filed in federal and state courts or in the Supreme Court (without segregating petitions for certiorari). In addition, briefs, motions, and pleadings can be searched by practice area. The "Practice Area Constitutional Law" tool combines briefs on federal and state constitutional law issues.

The Westlaw brief bank has separate databases for briefs and petitions filed to the Supreme Court and to individual circuit courts, all fully text searchable. Briefs and petitions in criminal cases can be searched separately. The database of petitions for certiorari to the Supreme Court is a useful source for identifying constitutional issues that have split the federal circuits, with arguments and citations on both sides. In addition, the Westlaw brief bank organizes Briefs by Topic, including National Civil Rights Briefs.

Briefs filed in the Supreme Court by the Office of the Solicitor General, which represents the United States in the Supreme Court, are available for free on its website. These briefs can be searched by year (1998 forward, with more limited access to 1982–1997) and by broad category (e.g., "Constitutional").[28]

6. The Department of Justice Website

The website of the Civil Rights Division of the United States Department of Justice contains a wide variety of documents useful to constitutional research.[29] For example, documents potentially relevant to Eighth and Fourteenth Amendment research include letters

---

28. United States Department of Justice: Office of the Solicitor General, *Briefs*, http://www.justice.gov/osg/briefs/index.html.
29. United States Department of Justice, http://www.justice.gov/crt.

notifying correctional and mental health institutions of the results of Department of Justice investigations, complaints and briefs filed by the Justice Department in federal court, settlements resolving cases, and annual reports to Congress on Justice Department efforts to enforce the civil rights of institutionalized persons.

7. Other Secondary Sources

Other secondary sources, introduced in Chapter 3, can be useful for constitutional research. These sources include model jury instructions,[30] continuing legal education (CLE) materials,[31] and law review articles. If on point, law review articles can be a rich source of citations to primary authority, as they are generally well researched and footnoted. They can also be a good source for learning about current debates in a field. For a student researcher looking for a constitutional topic for a law review comment or note, a helpful source is the "Emerging Issues Analysis" database on Lexis. This database contains short articles about current debates in specialized areas of law (access "Area of Law—By Topic," select "Constitutional Law & Civil Rights," then select "Emerging Issues").

B. Using Comprehensive Sources of Cases and Case Summaries

1. Free Online Case Databases

In addition to searching for judicial opinions on Lexis and Westlaw, as explained in Chapter 9, you can locate cases construing rele-

---

30. Federal model jury instructions can help researchers to efficiently identify current constitutional issues likely to be considered by a jury. Common examples include claims under the First, Fourth, Fifth, Sixth, Eighth, and Fourteenth Amendments. See Chapter 3, Section III.I. for a discussion of model jury instructions.

31. As an example of a CLE on a constitutional law topic, see Martin A. Schwartz, *Fundamentals of Section 1983 Litigation*, available on Westlaw at 784 PLI/LIT 11 (2008). CLE material is discussed in Chapter 3, Section III.H.

vant constitutional provisions using free online databases. The Lex-isOne database provides free access to federal appellate court deci-sions from the last ten years and U.S. Supreme Court decisions since 1781. The database allows you to limit the search by court, date, judge, parties, and counsel.

The "Advanced Scholar Search" on Google Scholar allows you to limit your search to opinions of particular courts (e.g., "Supreme Court," "All federal appellate courts," or "Eighth Circuit: Appeals and District"), or even more specifically, just Eighth Circuit opinions from Minnesota (by choosing "select specific courts to search"). You can further limit the search results by date.

2. Statutory Codes with Case Annotations

Constitutional law research might effectively begin with the U.S.C.A. or the U.S.C.S. if all three of the following are true: (a) you know which constitutional provision is at issue (e.g., the Fourth Amendment), (b) you know the context or factual scenario in which the client's issue arose, and (c) you know some of the terms of art (e.g., search incident to arrest). The U.S.C.A. and the U.S.C.S. are principally collections of federal statutes, but each includes the an-notated Constitution as a service to readers. Both the U.S.C.A. and the U.S.C.S. are comprehensive sources of abstracts of judicial opin-ions applying particular constitutional provisions and cites to rele-vant secondary sources, such as *American Law Reports*, law review ar-ticles, *American Jurisprudence 2d*, and treatises on federal courts.

Like annotations to statutes, explained in Chapter 5, the annota-tions to the Constitution contain short abstracts of key legal points from federal judicial opinions, preceded by a detailed index of top-ics. Under each topic heading, case abstracts are organized by juris-diction (with the Supreme Court first, followed by federal courts). For example, index headings in the U.S.C.A. under the Fourth Amendment include this progression from general to more specific subheadings, followed by abstracts of key legal points in cases: Fourth Amendment > Seizure of Persons Generally > Conduct constituting a seizure > High speed pursuit of vehicle.

In both the U.S.C.A. and the U.S.C.S., following the most specific heading are the *case abstracts*[32]—summaries of key legal points from individual federal judicial opinions. The case abstracts in the U.S.C.A. also include the relevant West key numbers (e.g., Arrest 68(4)), which are very useful tools for locating additional binding judicial decisions on Westlaw or via *West's Federal Practice Digest* or the *West Supreme Court Digest*. Online searching of the case abstracts in the U.S.C.A. or the digests can be more efficient than using the books because it allows you to combine keywords from the legal issue with connectors specifying the relationship between those terms. For example, to find cases that discuss the specific term "Fourth Amendment" within five words of police and variations of chase or pursuit, you might construct this search: "Fourth Amendment" /5 (police /5 (chas! pursuit)).

The comprehensiveness of the U.S.C.A. and U.S.C.S. annotations to constitutional provisions is both their most and least advantageous feature. In the library, there are in excess of 25 U.S.C.A. volumes and 10 U.S.C.S. volumes devoted to annotations to constitutional provisions. Although the index headings help researchers focus on relevant case abstracts, the volume of index headings can be daunting to someone just beginning to search. Unless you are familiar with the terms of art and can locate a particularly focused index entry, navigating the voluminous index headings to find on-point authorities, even if done online, can be too time consuming to be practical or cost efficient. Similarly, although the U.S.C.A. and the U.S.C.S. contain cites to relevant secondary sources such as annotations in A.L.R. Fed., entries in *American Jurisprudence*, law review articles, and entries in federal courts treatises, the volume of citations to secondary sources

---

32. These case abstracts are sometimes called "squibs," "headnotes," or "case annotations." The term "squib" is an informal term used in legal research, but the other two terms are sometimes misused or used in confusing ways. The case abstracts in West's U.S.C.A. are also the headnotes used in West's digests and on Westlaw; the same is not true of U.S.C.S., as Lexis uses different abstracts. While the term "case annotation" is widely used, it can be confusing because "annotations" are much broader than simply case abstracts.

likely render the U.S.C.A. and the U.S.C.S. too daunting as starting points.

3. Case Annotations in Digests

Beginning research with the Supreme Court digest or *West's Federal Practice Digest 4th* (also on Westlaw) presents similar advantages and disadvantages. Like the table of contents and index to annotations that precede the case summaries in the U.S.C.A. and U.S.C.S., the digests begin with an outline that is a useful tool for learning the relationships between concepts and terms of art. In print, that outline appears under the heading "Analysis" at the beginning of the "Constitutional Law" topic. On Westlaw, the outline appears as an expandable "West Key Number Digest Outline," which is accessible from the Key Numbers link.

4. West Key Number Searches

Another efficient way to begin constitutional research is to search the West Key Number Digest for a relevant key number.[33] From the top horizontal menu on any Westlaw screen, click on "Key Numbers," click on "West Key Number Digest Outline," scroll down to "92 Constitutional Law," and click on the + sign to expand the menu of options. Then select "VII Constitutional Rights in General," and "(B) Particular Constitutional Rights," and finally "k1079 Personal Liberty." If you can locate a particularly on-point West key number, you can use it to efficiently locate relevant court decisions in specific jurisdictions.

Alternatively, to have Westlaw formulate a key number search for you, click on "Key Numbers" at the top of any Westlaw screen, click on "KeySearch," and scroll down to click on "Constitutional Law." From there, select the relevant constitutional topic from the menu (e.g., Fourth Amendment), and then select the relevant subtopics (e.g., Searches and Seizures) until you reach the screen that enables you to choose sources to search. To be efficient and cost effective, select the most narrow set of sources likely to contain the documents you need. For example, if you need court decisions from Ohio, select a limited database such as "Ohio Federal and State" rather than a

---

33. Chapter 9 introduces the West system of topics and key numbers.

Table 4-6. Lexis "Area of Law by Topic"

- Constitutional Law & Civil Rights
  - Search Analysis, Law Reviews & Journals
    - Constitutional Rights of Prisoners [Click "Browse TOC" to continue]
      - Part I Constitutional Rights of Prisoners
        - Chapter 2 Use of Force: Use of Corporal Punishment to Enforce Prison Discipline
          - § 2.8 The Use of Corporal Punishment to Enforce Prison Discipline

broader database, such as "All Federal Cases." (From this last screen, you might also choose to search secondary sources, such as "Encyclopedias and Treatises," or "Journals and Law Reviews.") After you have chosen the sources to search, add any search terms (e.g., police w/25 pursuit), and Westlaw will assemble and run a key number search.

5. Lexis "Area of Law by Topic"

On Lexis, you can locate summaries of constitutional law doctrine with citations to recent cases by accessing the "Area of Law by Topic" library and using the Table of Contents to locate progressively more specific topic headings. For example, to search for authority on physical force used in prisons, you might start with the general topic of "Constitutional Law & Civil Rights" then follow a string of progressively more specific subheadings to arrive at "The Use of Corporal Punishment to Enforce Prison Discipline," as set out in Table 4-6.

The last heading leads to narrative discussion of the use of corporal punishment to enforce prison discipline, with citations to primary and secondary authority. Figure 4-1 shows a Lexis screen with the last, most specific link in the sequence.

A researcher using Lexis who is interested in criminal cases could begin with "Area of Law by Topic" and access the categories listed under "Criminal Constitutional Law."

Figure 4-1. Lexis "Area of Law by Topic"

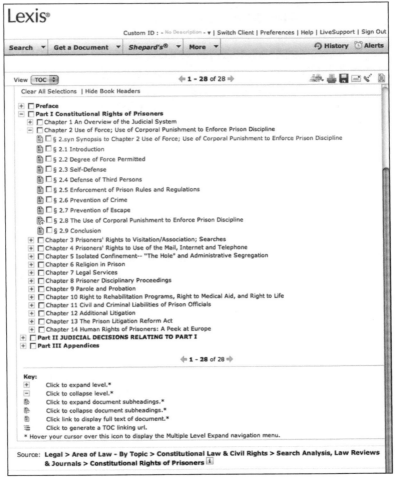

Source: Copyright 2011 LexisNexis, a division of Reed Elsevier Inc. All Rights Reserved. Lexis is a registered trademark of Reed Elsevier Properties Inc. and is used with the permission of LexisNexis.

C. Updating Authority

After locating relevant, binding authority, update those sources via Shepard's on Lexis or Westlaw's KeyCite to confirm their validity and to locate additional, more recent authority. Constitutional provisions can be searched in Shepard's or KeyCite to find cases and other sources that cite the provisions. When Shepardizing or KeyCiting relevant cases, you can limit the report to direct history of the cited case. Alternatively, you can use Shepard's or KeyCite as a research tool to locate citations by more recent opinions. The Shepard's or KeyCite report can be limited in various ways, such as citations by certain jurisdictions, citations by *A.L.R. Federal* or other secondary sources, or citations only to particular headnotes from the original opinion. Updating is covered in detail in Chapter 10.

IV. State Constitutions

Each state has a constitution that functions much like the U.S. Constitution in providing a framework for government and protecting the rights of individuals. Three differences between the federal and state constitutions deserve special note. First, as explained in footnote 2, states are permitted to interpret their own constitutions to be more protective of individual rights than is the federal Constitution. Similarly, state constitutions can provide individuals with rights in addition to those guaranteed by the federal Constitution. A state constitution can, for example, guarantee a system of free public schools, which is not covered by the federal Constitution. Second, while the federal Constitution is restricted to broad principles, state constitutions often cover items that seem more statutory in nature. For example, a state constitution might address the sale of liquor by the glass or ban the use of particular types of nets in fishing. Third, state constitutions are often easier to amend than is the federal Constitution, and many state constitutions have been amended multiple times. Remember, though, that in any conflict between federal and state law, the doctrine of preemption allows the federal law to trump state law.

Chapter 5

Statutory Research

I. Statutes and Codes in American Law

Much law in modern American society is statutory, consisting of the laws enacted by Congress and by state legislatures. Statutes now control many areas once the subject of the common law, and new statutes continue to be passed to address new problems. Although statutory law has replaced the common law for many purposes, the courts have the final authority to decide how a statute is interpreted and whether it complies with constitutional requirements.

Statutory law may be either criminal or civil, but all laws have consequences for noncompliance. Criminal law violations are prosecuted by the government, while noncompliance with civil laws may give rise to enforcement actions, claims for damages, or other claims by individuals, private organizations, or government agencies.

A. Session Laws and Codification

As Congress enacts new laws, these statutes are published first as *slip laws*. Then they are published in volumes compiling the new laws for the legislative session in chronological order of passage; these compilations are *session laws*. Most statutes in the session laws affect the general public, rather than applying only to particular persons.

Federal laws of general application are known as *public laws*. Federal laws that apply only to particular persons are known as *private laws*.[1]

Because a chronological collection of public laws covering many decades would be almost impossible to use for research, the federal government reorganizes the public laws in the statutes into a *code*.[2] Codification involves establishing broad subjects for organizing the law (e.g., Crimes and Criminal Procedure), determining which parts of the statutes are still current, and placing the current statutes into the proper subjects, with further subdivisions within each broad subject (e.g., Arson, Conspiracy, Homicide). As new statutes become law, the code is updated to add new language and to change or remove existing language. Codification allows for effective searching and for maintaining an accessible, current version of the statutory law.

B. Federal Session Laws and Codes

1. Statutes at Large

The United States Congress meets every year, with each year comprising a *session* of a numbered two-year "Congress." For example, the 111th Congress convened in 2009 and 2010, with the session of Congress in 2010 being the 2nd Session of the 111th Congress. One public law enacted during this session was the "National Flood Insurance Program Extension Act of 2010." This law was the one hundred ninety-sixth law enacted during the 111th Congress, so it is Public Law 111-196, which is cited as Pub. L. No. 111-196. For every session, the enacted laws are published in successively numbered volumes of session laws entitled the *United States Statutes at Large* (often called "*Statutes at Large*"). The *Statutes at Large* contains all public

---

1. An example of a federal private law is the *Betsy Dick Residence Protection Act*, Priv. L. No. 109-1, 120 Stat. 3705 (2006), which grants to Betsy Dick the right to remain in her residence in a federal park for the remainder of her life. In state legislation, laws of general applicability are often called *general laws* and private laws are often called *special laws*.

2. All states in the United States also organize their statutes into codes.

and private laws enacted during a session.[3] The *Statutes at Large* citation for Public Law 111-196 is 124 Stat. 1352, which means the law will be printed in volume 124 of the *Statutes at Large* starting at page 1352.[4]

Publication of the *Statutes at Large* began in 1846. At that time, all previous public and private laws and treaties, beginning in 1789, were republished as the first eight volumes of the series. All laws since 1846 have been published in the *Statutes at Large* after the end of a session of Congress. Chronologically published statutes are not practical for effective research, although it is sometimes necessary to check them to confirm the exact wording of a statute.

2. Revised Statutes of the United States

In order to provide an accessible and current version of the statutory law, the U.S. government undertook in the nineteenth century to codify the statutory law originally published in the session laws. The first codification was the *Revised Statutes of the United States*,[5] commonly known as the "Revised Statutes of 1875," authorized by Congress in 1873 and published in 1875. The Revised Statutes of 1875

---

3. Treaties and other international agreements were also included in *Statutes at Large* through 1949.

4. As of late 2011, *Statutes at Large* volume 124 has not yet been published. Because the publication of the *Statutes at Large* is often delayed by several years, like many official publications, the Office of the Federal Register makes the eventual volume and page number available to commercial vendors. This citation was found in West's advance legislative service, known as the *United States Code Congressional and Administrative News* (U.S.C.C.A.N.), for September 2010.

5. Like many law books of the era, the full title as given on the title page is very long and very descriptive: *Revised Statutes of the United States Passed at the First Session of the Forty-Third Congress, 1873–1874; Embracing the Statutes of the United States, General and Permanent in Their Nature, In Force on the First Day of December, One Thousand Eight Hundred and Seventy-Three, As Revised and Consolidated by Commissioners Appointed Under an Act of Congress; With an Appendix Containing "An Act to Correct Errors and Supply Omissions."*

were enacted as a public law, repealing the statutes that had been incorporated into the codification and making the Revised Statutes of 1875 "positive law."[6] In order to correct inaccuracies in the Revised Statutes of 1875, a second edition of the revised statutes appeared in 1878, although this edition was not enacted into positive law. This second edition is commonly known as the "Revised Statutes of 1878."

3. United States Code

In 1926, a new codification was introduced. The *United States Code* codified all portions of the 1875 code (as revised in 1878) still in effect and all subsequent public laws. Since 1934, new editions of the *United States Code* have been published every six years, with annual supplemental volumes in the intervening years. The *United States Code* is the official codification of federal statutes, and commercially produced codes use the same organizational scheme.

The *United States Code* organizes the statutory law into 51 subjects known as *titles*. (See Table 5-1.) The subdivision of titles varies, but the most basic scheme is title, chapter, section, and subsection. Some titles also have subdivisions called *parts*. For example, Title 18 Crimes and Criminal Procedure has multiple parts, including Part I Crimes, Part II Criminal Procedure, and Part III Prison and Prisoners. Part I is divided into 123 chapters, of which Chapter 51 addresses homicide. Section 1111 defines murder. For citation purposes, researchers reference only titles and sections (and any relevant subsections), omitting the part and chapter. To cite Title 18, Section 1111, simply write 18 U.S.C. § 1111.

---

6. *Positive law* is law promulgated and implemented by political entities with power to make binding law. Statutory authority is positive law when it has actually been enacted into law by a legislature. If a codification of existing statutes has been prepared, but the codification has not been enacted into law by the legislature, the original statutes on which the codification is based remain the applicable positive law. In that case, the codification is only *prima facie* evidence of the statutory law.

Table 5-1. Titles of the *United States Code*

1. General Provisions	30. Mineral Lands and Mining
2. The Congress	31. Money and Finance
3. The President	32. National Guard
4. Flag and Seal, Seat of Government, and the States	33. Navigation and Navigable Waters
5. Government Organization and Employees	34. Navy [superseded by enactment of Title 10 as positive law]
6. Domestic Security	
7. Agriculture	35. Patents
8. Aliens and Nationality	36. Patriotic and National Observances Ceremonies, and Organizations
9. Arbitration	
10. Armed Forces	37. Pay and Allowances of the Uniformed Services
11. Bankruptcy	
12. Banks and Banking	38. Veterans' Benefits
13. Census	39. Postal Service
14. Coast Guard	40. Public Buildings, Property, and Works
15. Commerce and Trade	
16. Conservation	41. Public Contracts
17. Copyrights	42. The Public Health and Welfare
18. Crimes and Criminal Procedure	
19. Customs Duties	43. Public Lands
20. Education	44. Public Printing and Documents
21. Food and Drugs	45. Railroads
22. Foreign Relations and Intercourse	46. Shipping
23. Highways	47. Telegraphs, Telephones, and Radiotelegraphs
24. Hospitals and Asylums	
25. Indians	48. Territories and Insular Possessions
26. Internal Revenue	
27. Intoxicating Liquors	49. Transportation
28. Judiciary and Judicial Procedure	50. War and National Defense
	51. National and Commercial Space Programs
29. Labor	

Although the *United States Code* codifies U.S. statutory law, it was not enacted into positive law at its inception. A project to revise each title and enact each revised title into positive law began in 1974 and continues to this day. To date, 24 of the 51 titles have been enacted into positive law.[7] Those titles enacted into positive law are the ultimate authority for the statutory law contained in them. For the titles not yet revised and enacted into positive law, the text of the *United States Code* is only *prima facie* evidence of authority, with the text of statutes in the *Statutes at Large* continuing to be the ultimate source of authority. Tables I, II, and III of each edition of the *United States Code* indicate where sections in the *Statutes at Large*, the Revised Statutes of 1878, or U.S.C. titles that have been completely revised are located in the current U.S.C.

II. Researching Federal Statutes in Print

Although much research is performed in electronic resources, this chapter first discusses researching federal statutes in print, for two reasons. First, the most commonly used electronic resources, those produced by the West and LexisNexis publishing companies, present the most used federal statutory resources in a form virtually identical to the print versions published by West and LexisNexis. Second, most experienced researchers find that statutory research is more efficiently and effectively performed in print.

Because the U.S.C. is published slowly and contains few aids to research, most researchers use the commercially published "annotated" codes by West and LexisNexis. Those annotated codes are the *United States Code Annotated* (U.S.C.A.), published by West, and the *United States Code Service* (U.S.C.S.), published by LexisNexis. These commercially published resources contain many added features that aid in understanding and interpreting the statutes and in locating related

---

7. For a list of the titles that have been enacted into positive law to date, see http://www.gpo.gov/fdsys/browse/collectionUScode.action?collection-Code=USCODE.

authority. Each code section is followed by annotations. *Annotations* are added research references that help researchers understand the language of the statute.

The commercially published annotated codes have the added advantage of being more current than the officially published *United States Code*. Moreover, the commercially published, annotated codes contain not only the codified federal statutes but also the federal Constitution and federal court rules, along with annotations for each. See Chapter 4 for discussion of constitutional research and Chapter 11 for discussion of research of court rules.

A. Researching in the *United States Code Annotated*

The researcher, especially if a beginning lawyer, might be asked to look up a particular statute. That would only require finding the print code volume of the U.S.C.A. by reading the book spines for the code title and range of sections in the volumes, turning to the section, and reading the statutory language (and, of course, checking the pocket parts).

Most projects, however, are more sophisticated and usually require searching in an annotated code for statutory authority on an issue and the cases interpreting it. The steps of this process are outlined in Table 5-2.

1. Search the Index

As discussed in Chapter 1, start by formulating a list of search terms based on the facts and issues in the research problem. Be sure to brainstorm for many search terms, such as by using the journalistic or TARPP approach. As the research process progresses, you will discover new terms of art or words or phrases commonly used to express concepts in the particular subject area.

Search in the index volumes, located near the end of the set, using the search terms developed in the earlier stages of the research process. You will find some of the terms, with compact citations to

Table 5-2. Outline for Research in Print Annotated Code

1. Use search terms to search the index of U.S.C.A. or U.S.C.S. If necessary, search the table of contents.

2. Find the text of statutes and update it using pocket parts and subsequent supplements.

3. Read the statutory text.

4. Find cases interpreting statutes using case abstracts* in annotations and update using pocket parts and subsequent supplements.

5. Examine other annotations for information about statutes and update using pocket parts and subsequent supplements.

---

* An *abstract* is a brief summary of a longer piece of writing. A *case abstract* is a summary of the holding of a case or of some other point of law discussed in the opinion. The case abstracts in West reporters are called *headnotes*.

relevant title and section numbers, such as "11 § 362," indicating the relevant statute is Title 11, Section 362. Under other terms, you might find only a cross-reference to another term in the index. Be sure to follow the cross-references.

The index contains a useful feature for locating precise phrases or combinations of terms. That is the Words and Phrases portion of the index, found alphabetically under "Words." If searches in the rest of the index are not successful, consult the Words and Phrases section.

In addition to the General Index, a specific index exists for each title. If it is likely that relevant sections will be located in a particular title, such as Title 11—Bankruptcy, the index at the end of that title can be used in the same way as described above to locate terms within that title.

2. Find and Update the Statutory Text

Find the sections you identified when searching the index by locating the volumes with title number and range of section numbers on the spine. The sections are arranged by number within each volume.

Be sure to check the pocket part to the volume[8] to see if the statute has been changed by legislation since the cutoff date of the legislation included in the bound volume. While you are doing this, check the cover of the pocket part to see whether the contents include all the laws of the most recent session of Congress. If they do not, or if a session of Congress is in progress, look on the shelves after the bound U.S.C.A. set for paper-bound pamphlets, which update the statutory sections and citing cases beyond the cutoff date of annotated code volumes and pocket parts. This updating service quickly publishes the changes to the code resulting from new acts, putting new sections and changes to sections in their locations within the code, and prints the headnotes[9] of recent cases citing U.S.C. sections. The pamphlets are noncumulative, so five or more supplementary pamphlets may appear on the shelves before the next annual pocket parts are published. The pamphlets also include a table indicating where the sections of new public laws have been placed in the code, a table of U.S.C. sections affected by recent legislation, a Popular Name Table, an index, new court rules, and a special supplement at the conclusion of the congressional session with legislative history documents and presidential signing statements from the session.

3. Read the Statutory Text

After finding and updating the relevant statutes, read them carefully. Statutory language is compact but often complex. Several readings are usually required to get a good understanding. The language

---

8. Sometimes the pocket part material becomes too bulky to fit inside the bound volume. In those instances, a separate pamphlet is printed and shelved immediately after the volume in which the pocket part would have been placed.

9. West editors supply abstracts of the holding and other points of law discussed in each case published in West case reporters. These *headnotes* appear before the text of each opinion. Each headnote is assigned a West topic and key number and included in important finding tools called *digests*. When a headnote discusses a federal statute, the headnote is included in the U.S.C.A. Notes of Decisions for that statute. See Chapters 8 and 9 for detailed discussion of case headnotes and the West Digest System.

of statutes is necessarily general. Consider how the general language may apply to the specific facts of your research problem.

Before reading a section of a statute, scan the definitions section (found in most statutes) so that you will recognize a defined term when you see it. To better understand a section in context, read at least the introductory sections of the statute and also sections on either side of the one your initial search has led to. If the statute has a table of contents, scanning the table of contents might reveal other important sections. For fairly short statutes, it is wise to read all of the sections to get the overall context and be sure of not missing anything relevant to your issue.

When reading a statutory section with a number of elements or factors listed, go immediately to the end of the list and see whether the connector between the last two items is "and" or "or." If the connector is "and," all the elements or factors must be present to satisfy the condition. If the connector is "or," any of the elements or factors will satisfy the condition. Determining this requirement in advance allows you to read the statute with greater comprehension and efficiency.

At the end of every code section is a very brief legislative summary in brackets, citing the original public law and its *Statutes at Large* citation, followed by any subsequent amendments to the language of the statute. The effective dates of the original public law and subsequent amendments are also given. This information is necessary for legislative history research, the subject of Chapter 6. The citations to amending acts are also required if you need to reconstruct the language of a statute as it appeared at some earlier time. For example, if a cause of action arose in 2001 and the section or article was amended by an act in 2003, start with the current statutory language and the text of the 2003 amendment to reconstruct the statute as it read in 2001.

4. Find Cases Interpreting Federal Statutory Law Using the Annotations

Rarely does research end with reading the words of a statute. Much litigation turns on what the words in a statute mean, whether a certain matter is covered by a statute, or whether a statute is unconstitutional or void as against public policy. You must, therefore, examine the cases interpreting the statute. You need to know how the courts have interpreted the statutory language and applied the statute to particular facts in order to understand what the statute means and to predict how a court would decide cases brought under the statute. Following every statutory section in the U.S.C.A. are annotations, which provide a number of research references to help you understand the meaning of the statute.

The annotations contain "Notes of Decisions." These are the headnotes from West reporters for cases that have dealt with the statutory section. See Figure 5-1 for an example of Notes of Decisions for a section of the U.S.C.A. The Notes of Decisions are divided into several classes of issues. Within each class, the headnotes are arranged by court of origin, in chronological order for each court. You can quickly scan the headnotes for the most relevant cases, concentrating on the courts with mandatory authority and usually focusing on the most recent, relevant cases. The headnotes can also provide a quick overview of the historical development of lines of cases. Be sure to check the pocket parts and any subsequent supplementation for headnotes of cases published after the cutoff date of the main volume.

Each headnote contains a citation to the case. You must read the cases. It is not acceptable to cite a case based only on the headnotes, a practice that could lead to serious mistakes and even malpractice.

5. Other Features of the Annotations

The researcher often needs information in addition to case law in order to interpret a statute. The annotations following a code section in the U.S.C.A. often include an "Historical and Statutory Note," which contains historical information about enacting legislation and subsequent amendments. The annotations might also contain "Cross References" to other statutes dealing with similar subjects. Next come "Library References" to West Digest System topics and key numbers relating to the subject of the section. "Library References" also cite C.J.S. encyclopedia sections, A.L.R. annotations, and other readings in secondary sources. There may also be references to *Code of Federal Regulations*

Figure 5-1. Notes of Decisions from the U.S.C.A.

Ch. 2   MINERAL LANDS AND REGULATIONS   **30 § 42**
                                                                   Note 4

Corpus Juris Secundum
    CJS Mines and Minerals § 40, Mill Sites and the Like.
    CJS Mines and Minerals § 48, Extent of Claim.
    CJS Mines and Minerals § 130, Mill Sites and the Like.

Research References

Encyclopedias
    Am. Jur. 2d Mines and Minerals § 57, Mill Sites.

Treatises and Practice Aids
    West's Federal Administrative Practice § 5863, Mill Sites.

WESTLAW ELECTRONIC RESEARCH

    See Westlaw guide following the Explanation pages of this volume.

Notes of Decisions

Generally 1
Abandonment or forfeiture, locator's
    rights 13
Adverse claims, lands subject to appro-
    priation as mill site 6
Construction with other laws 2
Defective patent, title to mill site 11
Definitions 4
Good faith, title to mill site 10
Lands subject to appropriation as mill
    site 5-7
    Generally 5
    Adverse claims 6
    Subsisting claims 7
Locator's rights 12-14
    Generally 12
    Abandonment or forfeiture 13
    Transfer of rights 14
Occupancy outside location 16
Possession of site 15
Purpose 3
Requirements, title to mill site 9
Subsisting claims, lands subject to appro-
    priation as mill site 7
Time for filing application 17
Title to mill site 8-11
    Generally 8
    Defective patent 11
    Good faith 10
    Requirements 9
Transfer of rights, locator's rights 14

---

1. Generally
    This section recognizes the mill site as
a mining possession. Hartman v. Smith,
Mont.1887, 14 P. 648, 7 Mont. 19.

2. Construction with other laws
    A local rule or regulation permitting
the location of mill sites without regard
to the character of the land on which they

are located is in conflict with the provision that mill sites can only be legally
located on nonmineral lands. Cleary v.
Skiffich, Colo.1901, 65 P. 59, 28 Colo.
362, 89 Am.St.Rep. 207.

3. Purpose
    This section is a congressional recogni-
tion that land near, but not contiguous to,
known veins or lodes may be nonmineral,
and if it contains no known valuable mineral deposits it falls into the nonmineral
or agricultural class, however rich in
minerals are the adjoining lands. U.S. v.
Kostelak, D.C.Mont.1913, 207 F. 447.

    The object of this section is to permit
title to land to be acquired for mill sites
located on mineral lands which do not
contain valuable mineral-bearing veins or
deposits, and there is no reason for a
distinction on account of the character of
use, or the ownership or nonownership of
a mine in connection with a mill site.
Cleary v. Skiffich, Colo.1901, 65 P. 59, 28
Colo. 362, 89 Am.St.Rep. 207.

4. Definitions
    The term "mining purposes," as used
in this section, may include any reasonable use for mining purposes which a
quartz lode mining claim may require,
and may consist in the use of a mill site
in connection therewith, and if used in
good faith for any mining purpose in connection with it is sufficient. Silver Peak
Mines v. Valcalda, C.C.Nev.1897, 79 F.
886, affirmed 86 F. 90, 29 C.C.A. 591.
See, also, Valcalda v. Silver Peak Mines,
Nev.1898, 86 F. 90, 93, 29 C.C.A. 591;
Hartman v. Smith, 1887, 14 P. 648, 7
Mont. 19.

379

Source: Reprinted with permission of West, a Thomson Reuters business. An
excerpt of this statute from Westlaw is shown in Chapter 1, Figure 1-2.

(C.F.R.) sections promulgated pursuant to the statute's authority (see Chapter 7 on Administrative Law), citations to law review articles, and other useful information. As with the statutory language and Notes of Decisions, be sure to update material in the other annotations by checking the pocket parts and any subsequent supplementation.

See Figure 5-2 for a page from the U.S.C.A. with the end of a statutory section and the beginning of its annotations.

6. Popular Name Table

Another very useful finding tool is the "Popular Name Table," located at the end of the last index volume of the U.S.C.A. Often, a public law is given a statutory short title, by which the act is meant to be called, in addition to the much longer technical title. Also, many well known acts come to be known by popular names, such as "Blue Sky Law," a name used for the securities laws in many states, or by a descriptive term, such as "Clean Air Act." Since researchers often come to an index with only a short title or popular name for an act, the index lists them in the Popular Name Table. Figure 5-3 shows a page from the Popular Name Table.

7. Other Tables

The U.S.C.A. also has several volumes containing a variety of tables.

Tables 1 and 2 of the U.S.C.A. (called conversion tables) indicate the location in the current U.S.C. of sections originating in the *Statutes at Large,* in sections of the Revised Statutes of 1878, or in sections of a U.S.C. title that has been revised. Although based on Tables I, II, and III of the U.S.C., Tables 1 and 2 in the U.S.C.A. are not as easy to use as the tables in the official U.S.C.

Other tables indicate where executive orders, proclamations, and government reorganization plans are located in the U.S.C.

Figure 5-4 shows an excerpt from a page in the U.S.C.A.'s Table 2. The first column is the public law number for an enacted statute. The second column indicates particular sections or subsections of the public law. The third column is the *Statutes at Large* pinpoint cite for the section or subsection. The fourth column indicates the U.S.C. title and section affected by the section or subsection of the public law. A

Figure 5-2. Annotations for a Statute in the U.S.C.A.

---

30 § 42   MINERAL LANDS AND MINING   Ch. 2

tions in connection with such claim, and is used or occupied by the proprietor for such purposes, such land may be included in an application for a patent for such claim, and may be patented therewith subject to the same requirements as to survey and notice as are applicable to placers.   No location made of such nonmineral land shall exceed five acres and payment for the same shall be made at the rate applicable to placer claims which do not include a vein or lode.

(R.S. § 2337; Mar. 18, 1960, Pub.L. 86–390, 74 Stat. 7.)

HISTORICAL AND STATUTORY NOTES

Revision Notes and Legislative Reports
1960 Acts. House Report No. 1265, see 1960 U.S. Code Cong. and Adm. News, p. 1803.

References in Text
Sections 21, 22 to 24, 26 to 28, 29, 30, 33 to 48, 50 to 52, 71 to 76 of this title and section 661 of Title 43, referred to in subsec. (a), were in the original "this chapter", meaning chapter 6 (sections

2318 to 2352) of title XXXII of the Revised Statutes.

Codifications
R.S. § 2337 derived from Act May 10, 1872, c. 152, § 15, 17 Stat. 96.

Amendments
1960 Amendments. Pub.L. 86–390 designated existing provisions as subsec. (a) and added subsec. (b).

CROSS REFERENCES

Assessment work on contiguous oil lands, see 30 USCA § 102.
Conveyance by mining claim patents issued prior to May 10, 1872, of all rights and privileges conferred by this section, see 30 USCA § 33.
Costs and expenses of surveying mining claims, see 30 USCA § 39.
Evidence of possession and work to establish right to patent, see 30 USCA § 38.
Federal Land Policy and Management Act of 1976 as not affecting this section, see 43 USCA § 1732.
Impairment of rights or interests in mining property, see 30 USCA § 47.
Land use planning, see 43 USCA § 1712.
Lignite, mining, removal, and disposal, see 30 USCA § 541b.
Michigan, Minnesota, and Wisconsin mineral lands, see 30 USCA § 48.
Missouri and Kansas lands, see 30 USCA § 49.
Patents, procurement procedures, etc., see 30 USCA § 29.
Presidential appointment of additional officers to carry out this section, see 30 USCA § 46.
Proof of citizenship, methods of establishing, see 30 USCA § 24.
Resettlement lands transferred to Navajo Indian tribe subject to valid claims located under Mining Law of 1872, see 25 USCA § 640d–10.
Steese National Conservation Area, minerals withdrawn from location, entry, and patent, see 16 USCA § 460mm–1.
Vein or lode within boundaries of placer claim, see 30 USCA § 37.
Verification of affidavits, see 30 USCA § 40.
Withdrawal of lands, see 43 USCA § 1714.

CODE OF FEDERAL REGULATIONS

Mineral patent applications, see 43 CFR § 3861.1 et seq.
Mining claims, nature and classes, see 43 CFR § 3840.1 et seq.

LIBRARY REFERENCES

American Digest System
Mines and Minerals ⊜39, 41.
Key Number System Topic No. 260.

378

Source: Reprinted with permission of West, a Thomson Reuters business.

Figure 5-3. Popular Name Table in the U.S.C.A.

1341   **POPULAR NAME TABLE**

Food Security Commodity Reserve Act of 1996—Continued
Pub.L. 104–127—Continued
> *This Public Law enacted no currently effective sections. For sections affected by this law, see Pub.L. 104–127 in the USCA-TABLES database and the enacting credit set out below.*
Enacting law:
> Pub.L. 104–127, Title II, Subtitle A, § 225(a), Apr. 4, 1996, 110 Stat. 959 (7 § 1736f–1, 1736f–1 note)

Food Security Improvements Act of 1986
Pub.L. 99–260, Mar. 20, 1986, 100 Stat. 45
Short title, see 7 USCA § 1281 note
  Current USCA classifications:

Section of Pub.L. 99–260	USCA Classification
13	7 USCA § 1433c–1

> *This list contains only sections enacted by this Public Law. For all sections affected by this law, see Pub.L. 99–260 in the USCA-TABLES database and the enacting credit set out below.*
Table of Contents for current USCA classifications:
7 USCA § 1433c–1
Enacting law:
> Pub.L. 99–260, Mar. 20, 1986, 100 Stat. 45 (5 § 5312; 7 §§ 259, 608c note, 1281 note, 1431, 1433c–1, 1441–1, 1441–1 note, 1444–1, 1444e, 1445b–3, 1446, 1446 note, 1464, 1466, 1736–1, 1736s, 1736v, 2025 note; 15 § 714b)
Amending laws:
> Pub.L. 108–357, Title VI, § 611(q), Oct. 22, 2004, 118 Stat. 1523 (7 § 1433c–1)

Food Security Wheat Reserve Act of 1980
Pub.L. 96–494, Title III, Dec. 3, 1980, 94 Stat. 2578
  Current USCA classifications:

Section of Pub.L. 96–494	USCA Classification
302	7 USCA § 1736f–1

> *This list contains only sections enacted by this Public Law. For all sections affected by this law, see Pub.L. 96–494 in the USCA-TABLES database and the enacting credit set out below.*
Table of Contents for current USCA classifications:
7 USCA § 1736f–1
Enacting law:
> Pub.L. 96–494, Title III, Dec. 3, 1980, 94 Stat. 2578 (7 § 1736f–1)
Amending laws:
> Pub.L. 99–198, Title X, § 1013, Dec. 23, 1985, 99 Stat. 1456 (7 § 1736f–1)
> Pub.L. 101–624, Title XI, § 1143, Nov. 28, 1990, 104 Stat. 3515 (7 § 1736f–1)
Collateral or Related Acts:
Bill Emerson Humanitarian Trust Act

Source: Reprinted with permission of West, a Thomson Reuters business.

public law section or subsection may add, repeal, or otherwise change a section in the U.S.C. Special notations in the table, not shown here due to space limitations, indicate how a section of the U.S.C. was affected by a section or subsection of a public law. The notations are explained at the beginning of Table 2.

Figure 5-4. U.S.C.A. Conversion Table 2

85–12.....§ 1	71 Stat 9	.26 § 1 nt
§ 2	71 Stat 9	.26 § 11
§ 2	71 Stat 9	.26 § 821....
§ 3(a)(1).............	71 Stat 9	.26 § 4061...
§ 3(a)(2), (3)	71 Stat 9	.26 § 5001...
§ 3(a)(4).............	71 Stat 9	.26 § 5022...
§ 3(a)(5).............	71 Stat 9	.26 § 5041...
§ 3(a)(6).............	71 Stat 9	.26 § 5051...
§ 3(a)(7).............	71 Stat 9	.26 § 5701
§ 3(b)(1)	71 Stat 9	.26 § 5063...
§ 3(b)(2)	71 Stat 10	.26 § 5134...
§ 3(b)(3)	71 Stat 10	.26 § 5707...
§ 3(b)(4)	71 Stat 10	.26 § 5701 nt
§ 3(b)(4)	71 Stat 10	.26 § 6412

Source: Reprinted with permission of West, a Thomson Reuters business.

B. Researching in the *United States Code Service*

The *United States Code Service* (U.S.C.S.), published by LexisNexis, is quite similar to the *United States Code Annotated* and the research process in the U.S.C.S. is essentially the same as that discussed for the U.S.C.A. This section, therefore, begins by briefly noting the similarities but focuses primarily on the significant differences between the two sets.

As stated earlier, both the U.S.C.A. and the U.S.C.S. use the organizational scheme of the U.S.C. and both are heavily annotated with research tools. Importantly, the U.S.C.S. shares with the U.S.C.A. the feature of regular updating. Each volume of the set is updated annually with a pocket part or separate supplemental pamphlet. Further, the Cumulative Later Case and Statutory Service softbound volumes update the set with statutes and cases issued since the cutoff date of the most recent pocket parts.

Turning to differences, the U.S.C.S. contains abstracts of fewer cases than the U.S.C.A. does. While the U.S.C.A. aims for comprehensive coverage of cases, the U.S.C.S. claims to be more selective, resulting in fewer cases for abstracting. Significantly, the case abstracts found in the U.S.C.S. "Interpretive Notes and Decisions" are not the same as the headnotes found in the U.S.C.A. Notes of Decisions, but are written by LexisNexis editors. For this reason, the case abstracts in the U.S.C.S. do not lead the researcher to the topics and key numbers in the West Digest System.

The annotations in the U.S.C.S. also differ from those in the U.S.C.A. in providing more references to administrative law authority. The U.S.C.S. Interpretative Notes and Decisions contain abstracts of not only judicial opinions but also "pertinent" administrative agency decisions; in contrast, the U.S.C.A. Notes of Decisions only contain headnotes of judicial opinions. In addition, the U.S.C.S. "Code of Federal Regulations" annotations tend to contain more cites to *Code of Federal Regulations* (C.F.R.) sections than the U.S.C.A. includes in its "Library References" annotations.

The U.S.C.S. set also contains some resources not found in the U.S.C.A. The International Agreements volume of the U.S.C.S. contains selected U.S. treaties and other international agreements. The two volumes of the Notes to Uncodified Laws & Treaties include research references to aid in researching various uncodified statutes and other authority, including Indian treaties. Another volume contains an index and finding aids to the C.F.R.

The U.S.C.S. also differs from the U.S.C.A. in the placement of court rules. In the U.S.C.S., all court rules volumes are located together after Title 51. The U.S.C.A. places volumes of annotated court rules with related code titles, such as the Federal Rules of Criminal Procedure with Title 18 and the Federal Rules of Evidence with Title 28.

III. Researching Federal Statutes Online

As discussed in Chapter 2, many experienced researchers find researching statutory material in print to be more efficient and effective than researching online. Online resources are generally most useful for locating cites to known code sections. Also, online sources are often more current than even the most recent print resources. A researcher who has located an applicable section of a code by researching in print should check the more current online resources to determine whether changes have occurred since the print resource was published.

A. United States Government Websites

The *United States Code* is available online at government websites and at websites that gather information from the government websites. As one example, the Government Printing Office's online Federal Digital System (FDsys) provides the full text of the current 2006 United States Code and its annual supplements.[10] As another example, the Office of the Law Revision Counsel, under the House of Representatives, provides the 2006 code online, again with updating based on the annual supplements.[11] That site also provides classification tables showing where legislation enacted since the most recent supplement will be placed in the U.S.C. and which sections have been amended by recent legislation, as well as the tables to the U.S.C. The House site is valuable in part because it is easy to determine whether the information is up to date. The office states that "[e]ach section of the U.S. Code database contains a date in the top-right corner indicating that laws enacted as of that date and affecting that section are included in the text of that section."[12]

It is common for federal and state government websites to disclaim official authority of the online versions of laws. The Office of the Law Revision Counsel includes this disclaimer on its website: "While every effort has been made to ensure that the Code database on the web site is accurate, those using it for legal research should verify their results

---

10. The address is http://www.gpo.gov/fdsys/browse/collectionUScode.action?collectionCode=USCODE. FDsys is currently replacing the government website GPO Access, which has long made the *United States Code* available online.

11. See the explanation at http://uscode.house.gov/about/info.shtml for exact information on how each title has been updated at the site.

12. U.S. House of Reps., Office of the Law Rev. Counsel, Currency, and Updating, http://uscode.house.gov/about/currency.shtml.

against the printed version of the United States Code available through the Government Printing Office."[13] A similar notice is posted on FDsys.[14]

A well respected nongovernmental website, the Legal Information Institute (L.I.I.) site at Cornell University,[15] also provides the latest edition of the U.S.C. This site generates its text from information made available from the Office of the Law Revision Counsel, so it is just as up to date. L.I.I. also provides RSS feeds to alert users of recent updates.

Historical versions of the U.S.C. may be necessary when a statute has been amended or repealed since the events at issue took place. For example, when considering the possibility of a suit to recover damages for environmental pollution caused ten years ago, you would need to determine whether at the time of the polluting activities the controlling statute covered the actions causing the pollution. You would need to find and read the text of the controlling statute as it was at that time. The website of the Office of the Law Revision Counsel contains searchable archives of the U.S.C. back to the 1988 version, while FDsys contains searchable archival versions back to 1994.

B. Federal Statutes on Westlaw

Westlaw contains a database of the *United States Code Annotated*, as well as historical versions of the U.S.C.A. from 1990 to present. Westlaw also contains an unannotated U.S.C.A. database. The unannotated code is sometimes convenient, especially when sections with extensive annotations are loading slowly or when you want to print only the statutory text. Most of the time, however, researchers use the annotated version for the features discussed earlier in this chapter.

The U.S.C.A. on Westlaw is very similar to the print version in organization and appearance, although enhanced by hyperlinks for ease

---

13. U.S. House of Reps., http://uscode.house.gov/about/info.shtml.

14. U.S. Gov't Printing Off., F. Digital Sys., About the United States Code, http://www.gpo.gov/help/index.html#about_united_states_code.htm.

15. The address is http://www.law.cornell.edu.

of navigation within the annotations. Westlaw also contains many of the research resources mentioned in the earlier discussion of the annotations, making it easy to navigate to and use those resources during the same online session. The online version has the further advantage of being more current than the print version, both as to the text of the statutes and the case headnotes and other annotations. Be sure to check the date to which the section has been brought current. In Westlaw, click on the link "Currentness" in the first line of the header to a section.

Statutes are generally best searched using the index and the table of contents, as explained in Chapter 2. Westlaw includes links to the index and table of contents of the U.S.C.A. at the search page for the U.S.C.A. database. In the index, use the search terms you developed in the first stage of the research process to identify code sections that may be relevant. Be sure to follow up leads to other terms in the index and watch for relevant terms you might not have thought of. If the index search does not yield a reference to a relevant section, try browsing the expandable table of contents for statutes that may be relevant to your project. The U.S.C.A. database search page also has a link to the Popular Name Table. If you know of a popular name for a key statute on the subject you are researching, look for a link to that statute.

Although the most efficient and effective searching often begins in the index and table of contents, keyword searching in full text is a prominent feature of Westlaw. Keyword searching in statutes is often difficult and may miss the relevant statutes entirely, while returning many irrelevant cites. However, if the statutes you are searching for are likely to include unusual terms specific to the subject you are researching, keyword searching might quickly find the relevant statutes. A tip for reducing the number of irrelevant results returned by keyword searching is to restrict the search to the unannotated code segment (UNANNO) in "Restrict by Search Segment." Restricting the search to just the text of the statutes helps prevent irrelevant results caused by the presence of a search term in an annotation.[16]

---

16. For more guidance on keyword searching, see Chapter 2, Part IV, which provides tips for effective keyword searching, such as limiting searches to particular fields, choice of search terms, and attention to query structure.

Because the U.S.C.A. database is complex, review the scope note before beginning research. This note is accessed by clicking on the button with "i" on it at the U.S.C.A. search page and next to the "U.S.C.A." link in the Directory at "All Databases," then "U.S. Federal Materials," and finally "Federal Statutes."[17] The note provides information about the database contents, effective dates, and tips for searching.

For updating statutory research, legislative service databases are available to track bills under consideration in Congress that might affect the statutory law in the current U.S.C.A. See Chapter 6 for discussion of congressional bill tracking.

C. Federal Statutes on Lexis

The Lexis online service contains annotated and unannotated versions of the current *United States Code Service* and contains historical versions of the U.S.C.S. from 1992 to present. Just as Westlaw is an online version of West's *United States Code Annotated*, the Lexis online annotated code is based on LexisNexis's print publication *United States Code Service*.

The online version of U.S.C.S. is very similar to the print version in organization and appearance, with the advantage of hyperlinks within the annotations to aid navigation. Many of the secondary resources cited in the U.S.C.S. annotations are published by the parent publishing company, so many of the resources cited are readily available during an online session. The online version is more current than the print version of the U.S.C.S. In Lexis, currency is indicated by a note just under the heading of each statutory section.

Unlike Westlaw's U.S.C.A. database, the online U.S.C.S. does not provide an index. However, an expandable table of contents of the U.S.C.S. may be searched by clicking the link "Browse TOC" at the U.S.C.S. search page. The table of contents may reveal sections not found by keyword searching of the source documents. The U.S.C.S.

---

17. If you are using the Law School main page, each database has a link called "SCOPE," which leads to the scope note for the database.

Popular Names Table is available in a separate database, which can be located by searching in "Find a Source" for "USCS Popular Names Table."

The comments about keyword searching in Westlaw also apply to searching the U.S.C.S. database in Lexis.

As with any database, the researcher using the online U.S.C.S. should review the scope note. It is indicated by a button with an "i," which appears at the U.S.C.S. search page and next to each database link at the "Legal" search tab at the main Lexis search page. For updating statutory research, legislative service databases are available to track bills under consideration in Congress that might affect the statutory law in the current U.S.C.S. Chapter 6 discusses congressional bill tracking.

D. Federal Statutes in Other Online Databases

Chapter 2 mentioned less expensive alternatives to Westlaw and Lexis, such as Casemaker, Fastcase, VersusLaw, Loislaw, and Bloomberg Law. Because of the lower cost for obtaining primary law on these databases, many practitioners prefer to use these databases, particularly for obtaining statutes, regulations, and cases.[18] Although each database has its own characteristics, the methods for searching are similar to those discussed for Westlaw and Lexis.

IV. Applying and Interpreting Federal Statutes

As discussed above, statutory research involves finding and reading the text of a statute, finding and analyzing the case law that has applied the statute, formulating the rule of the jurisdiction from this analysis, and applying the rule to the client's facts. Much litigation turns on the meaning to be given to statutory language. The language may be ambiguous on its face, or its application to a particular fact situation might not be evident. The lawyer in the role of advocate

---

18. In 2011, Google Scholar did not include federal or state statutes.

often attempts to inform and persuade the court as to the meaning of the statute as it bears on the client's position.

Courts attempt first to give the statute its plain meaning, but can look to other factors. The courts look to various types of intrinsic and extrinsic evidence in interpreting statutes in order to give effect to the intention of the legislature. *Intrinsic evidence* is evidence drawn from the text of the entire statute and its relation to the larger statutory context. *Extrinsic evidence* is evidence from outside the text that indicates what the legislature may have intended by the language of the statute. Common forms of extrinsic evidence include circumstances surrounding the statute's enactment, the preceding common law, earlier statutes, and administrative construction of the statute. A particularly important extrinsic factor is the legislative history of the statute — the records of the deliberations of the legislature leading to the enactment. Legislative history is discussed in detail in Chapter 6.

Courts will also look to various court-developed maxims, known as *canons of construction*, in attempting to determine the meaning of the language of a statute. These maxims are, however, often contradictory, allowing for choice among the rules and uncertainty as to result. The researcher must look to the case law of the jurisdiction to determine how the courts apply canons of construction. A long-standing authority on statutory construction is *Statutes and Statutory Construction*, commonly known as "Sutherland," after its original author.[19]

Some basic rules of construction of federal statutes are provided in Title 1, Sections 1 through 8 of the *United States Code*.[20] Some states have considerably more detailed statutes concerning the rules of statutory construction for their statutes.

V. Researching the Statutory Law of States

The process of researching statutory law is very similar for the states. Some states have both officially published codes and commer-

---

19. The author of recent editions is Norman J. Singer.
20. 1 U.S.C. § 1–8 (2006).

cial publications. Officially published codes are usually unannotated, but in a few states, such as Montana and Oregon, the state government publishes an annotated code. The commercially published codes most useful for research are annotated codes, with features much like those found in the U.S.C.A. and U.S.C.S.

States differ in how they organize their codes. They might identify all sections only by number (e.g., Wash. Rev. Code. § 2.08.180), or they might divide the codified statutes into a number of subject codes. For example, California's statutes are divided into subject matter codes. An example is the statute of limitations for medical malpractice actions, which is California Civil Procedure Code § 340.5.

Each state also publishes official series of session laws, although the titles given the session laws vary greatly. You must determine which sources are considered official for purposes of citation and to which sources citation is preferred.

State codes are published online by almost all states. Be sure to determine whether these online versions are considered authoritative for purposes of legal research; many states place disclaimers on their online codes, saying they should not be relied upon for legal research purposes. Be sure also to check the currency of the online code.

State codes are available on Lexis, Lexis Advance, Westlaw, and WestlawNext, and the other online databases mentioned in Chapter 2, with each typically available in annotated and unannotated versions.[21] If LexisNexis or West publishes a state's annotated code in print, expect to find that publication on the related online services. The online service that does not have access to an annotated code published by its parent company may have a less thoroughly annotated state code online. If you have access to Lexis, Westlaw, and other online services, compare the code versions available on each service to determine which is more complete. State codes can also be accessed through L.I.I., on the Library of Congress's Guide to Law Online, and at the government websites of the individual states.

---

21. The exception is Google Scholar, which currently does not include statutes.

Chapter 6

Bill Tracking and Legislative History

I. Introduction

Bill tracking allows lawyers to identify pending legislation that might affect their client's interests and follow the bills as they move through the legislative process. In contrast, legislative history[1] research addresses the documents produced during the progress of a bill from introduction to enactment. Courts sometimes consider the legislative history of statutes when interpreting statutory language. Since understanding the federal legislative process is crucial in both tracking bills and performing legislative history research, this chapter begins with an overview of the process by which the Congress enacts new laws.

II. The Federal Legislative Process

The United States Congress consists of the Senate, with 100 members, and the House of Representatives, with 435 members. Congress meets every year, with each year constituting a *session* of a two-year

---

1. The term "legislative history" has several related meanings. This chapter uses "legislative history" to mean the documents produced as a bill progresses through the legislative process to become law. A list of the documents produced by the researcher is called "a legislative history." The phrase "compiled legislative history" is used to describe either a list of documents or a collection of the actual documents gathered by somebody other than the researcher.

Congress. For example, in 2011, Congress was in the 1st Session of the 112th Congress.

Table 6-1 shows the steps of the legislative process from the idea for a bill[2] to its enactment into law and the documents produced at each step of the process. Because the House and Senate have numerous detailed procedural rules too complex to state here, the description is necessarily simplified. A resource explaining the rules at each step in considerable detail is *How Our Laws Are Made*[3] at the THOMAS website.[4]

III. Bill Tracking

A. Bill Tracking in the U.S. Congress

Statutory law is subject to change as new laws replacing, amending, or deleting the existing laws are passed by Congress. Attorneys must know how bills introduced into Congress might affect existing law. Table 6-2 outlines the steps for identifying a pending bill and tracking its progress through the legislature.

1. Researching with a Bill Number

If you already know the bill number, you can determine the bill's status easily and at no cost at the THOMAS website. THOMAS, maintained by the Library of Congress, has many useful links to information about the House and Senate, current legislative information, legislative history databases, guides to performing legislative history research, and information about other branches of government and other resources available from the Library of Congress. Taking

---

2. Legislation may be introduced as either a "bill" or a "joint resolution," although the great majority of legislation is introduced in bill form. Since bills and joint resolutions differ little in practice and may be used interchangeably, the term "bill" will used throughout the discussion in this book.

3. The address is http://thomas.loc.gov/home/lawsmade.toc.html.

4. The address is http://thomas.loc.gov. THOMAS, maintained by the Library of Congress, is discussed in detail throughout this chapter.

Table 6-1. How a Bill Becomes Law

Legislative Action	Documents Produced
An idea for a bill is proposed by an arm of the government, a legislator, a group, or an individual. A legislator agrees to sponsor it. The bill is drafted by a legislator, staff attorneys, or others.	An introduced **bill** may affect a client's interests. If the language of the bill is changed before enactment, the changes may reveal the intent of the legislature.
The bill is introduced in the House or the Senate, numbered, read on the floor of the chamber for the first time, and referred to a committee.	A Senate bill begins with "S." followed by a chronological number; a bill introduced in the House of Representatives beings with "H.R." followed by a chronological number.
The committee holds public hearings and studies the bill. The bill may be amended or another draft substituted for the original in a "markup session." The committee holds a formal hearing and votes, resulting in a favorable report or an unfavorable report.	**Transcripts** of hearings are prepared. **Committee prints**, containing explanations of current law, need for legislation, supporting data and analysis, and the effect of the bill, are prepared by support staff, the Congressional Research Service (C.R.S.), or others. A **committee report** contains the committee's recommendation, explanation, and analysis of the bill language, fiscal effects, and record of the committee vote. The report discusses each section of the bill in paragraph form, making it one of the easier pieces of legislative history to read and understand. See Figure 6-3 for an example of a committee report.
A bill with a favorable report is scheduled for a second reading and debate on the floor of the House or Senate. The bill may be amended by majority vote of representatives or senators.	The *Congressional Record* records the actions on the floor of the House or Senate and the votes. Much of the text in the *Congressional Record* consists of statements by and discussions between representatives and senators, presented in transcript form.*
The bill is read for the third time and debated on the floor. The bill may be amended by vote of representatives or senators. If approved by vote of the representatives or senators, the bill is sent as an engrossed bill to the other chamber.	The **engrossed bill** is the language passed by the first chamber and sent to the second chamber.

---

* See the discussion of the *Congressional Record* at Section IV.B.2.a.v.

Table 6-1. How a Bill Becomes Law, *continued*

Essentially the same process is followed in the other chamber, with some procedural differences. The bill may be amended further by vote. If an amended bill is approved by vote of the other chamber, the bill is sent back to the originating chamber.

Documents produced at each stage are the same as those shown above.

An **amended bill** is sent to the originating chamber.

If the bill was amended in the second chamber and the originating chamber accepts all amendments, the bill is sent as an enrolled bill to the president.

The **enrolled bill** is the version sent to the president.

If amendments in the second chamber are not accepted by the originating chamber, a conference committee is appointed to negotiate matters in disagreement. If the committee agrees on terms, a unified bill includes amendments by the conference committee. The conference committee report is filed and voted on by each chamber.

The **conference committee report** contains the committee's recommendation of the unified bill and discussion of the changes made by the committee.

A **unified bill** shows the markup by the conference committee.

If both chambers adopt the conference committee report, the unified bill is enrolled and sent to the president.

Notice that when the enrolled bill emerges depends on the extent of agreement between the two chambers.

The president has ten days to act on the bill. If the president signs the bill, the bill becomes law. If the president does not sign within ten days, the bill becomes law automatically, except if the bill is not signed by the president before Congress adjourns *sine die*, in which case the bill dies as a "pocket veto."

The president may produce a **signing statement** or **veto statement**.

The *Congressional Record* records the actions on the floor of each chamber and the votes.

If the bill is vetoed by the president, the veto may be overridden by a two-thirds vote of each of the House and Senate. The enacted bill is assigned a session law number, called a public law number. The public law number is a chronological number indicating the Congress in which the law was enacted and the order in which the law was passed.

The enacted public law is published first as a **slip law**, then in the *Statutes at Large*.

The public law is **codified** in the **United States Code** with other statutes on the same topic.

Table 6-2. Outline for Congressional Bill Tracking

1. Go to the THOMAS website.

2. When you know the bill number:

   a. Use "Search Bill Summary & Status."

   b. Select "Bill Number."

   c. Enter the bill number and submit.

3. When you do not know the bill number, use one of the following approaches:

   a. Click on "Search Bill Text for Multiple Congresses." Select the current Congress. Search by one of the following options: word/phrase, subject (index) term, bill/amendment number, stage in congressional process, date of introduction, sponsor/co-sponsor, or committee.

   b. Search using C.R.S. legislative subject terms. If you have already found a relevant bill, you can use subject terms assigned to that bill to find other relevant bills.

   c. Browse lists of bills and amendments sponsored by a representative or senator. Other browse list options are bill number, popular and short title, and Senate and House bills separately. To access the browse options, click on "Browse Bills & Resolutions" at http://thomas.loc.gov/home/LegislativeData.php.

4. Special features: THOMAS allows you to subscribe to RSS feeds of daily actions on the House and Senate floors and the Daily Digest of House and Senate activities.

the time to familiarize yourself with the resources available on THOMAS will make your research more efficient.

To get bill tracking information for a particular bill, look under "Search Bill Summary & Status," select "Bill Number" from the drop-down menu, and enter the bill number. The text of the bill can be selected from a grid containing links to information relating to the bill. Selecting "All Information" opens a page with a full listing of actions since the introduction of the bill, as well as background information about the bill, such as title, sponsor, co-sponsors, related bills, and the last major action on the bill. Other links from the Bill Summary & Status page for a bill provide access to related bills, titles (popular, short, official), a list of co-sponsors, Congressional Budget Office (C.B.O.) estimates, Congressional Research Service (C.R.S.) bill summaries, committees that considered the bill, and related committee documents. The link "All Congressional Actions with Amendments" provides links for particular actions to the *Congressional Record*, records of votes, and reports relating to the bill.

Also available at the THOMAS website are links allowing you to subscribe to RSS updates regarding pending legislation and to share information found with various social network websites.

2. Searching for and Tracking Pending Bills

The researcher often will not have a bill number but will need to search for bills that affect existing law. The most useful resource for this purpose is again the THOMAS website. Several search options are available at the THOMAS site. See Figure 6-1 for the THOMAS website home page.

To search the text of bills, click on "Search Bill Text for Multiple Congresses" and check the box for the current Congress only. To search all the information about a bill, but not the text of bills, use "Search Bill Summary & Status." The advanced search page is searchable by word/phrase, subject (index) term, bill/amendment number, stage in the legislative process, dates of introduction, sponsor/co-sponsor, and committee.

The advanced search page also offers the option of searching by subject terms. Recall the discussion in Chapter 2 of controlled vocabularies and the use of descriptors to extend searching. The descriptors used in THOMAS searches are a controlled vocabulary called "CRS legislative subject terms." An advanced researcher can use subject terms assigned by C.R.S. analysts to find bills dealing with very precisely defined subjects. If you have already identified a relevant bill, the subject terms assigned to that bill are available at the "Bill Summary & Status" page for that bill. The subject terms are hyperlinked so that other bills on the same topic can be identified, an

Figure 6-1. THOMAS Home Page

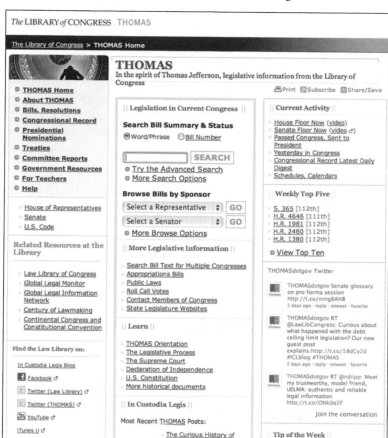

Source: THOMAS, at http://thomas.loc.gov.

example of using descriptors to extend research. THOMAS provides a comprehensive list of subject terms,[5] although trying to search by terms drawn from a subject term list is not consistently productive for those not already expert in their use.

5. The list is available at http://thomas.loc.gov/help/terms-subjects.html.

A third option is to browse lists of bills and amendments sponsored or co-sponsored by each representative or senator, as well as lists by bill number, popular and short titles, and Senate and House bills separately. The numerous options for searching Bill Summary & Status on THOMAS are powerful, but complex. Researchers new to THOMAS should refer to the tip sheet on searching Bill Summary & Status.[6]

Once you have identified bills of interest in the current Congress, you can track them throughout the session. One method is simply to return to THOMAS from time to time and use Bill Summary & Status to check on the current status of the bill, but more sophisticated tracking tools are available at THOMAS. You can subscribe to RSS feeds of daily actions on the House and Senate floors and of the *Congressional Record*'s Daily Digest of House and Senate activities, as well as information about bills presented to the president.

A traditional tool for identifying and tracking new legislation is the *Congressional Index*, a looseleaf service published by Commerce Clearing House (C.C.H.). Its usefulness for current bill tracking has been largely superseded by the powerful online tools provided by THOMAS, but the *Congressional Index* remains useful as a source of histories of actions on past bills, especially those published before the period covered by THOMAS, which starts at the 93rd Congress (1973–1974).

Lexis and Westlaw provide current bill tracking databases and archival bill history databases. The Lexis bill text and bill tracking databases are found using this directory trail: Legal > Federal Legal-U.S. > Find Statutes, Regulations, Administrative Materials & Court Rules > Legislative History Materials.

The Westlaw bill-tracking databases are found by following this directory trail: Directory > U.S. Federal Materials > Bill Tracking. In addition to the basic bill tracking report, found at Bill Tracking Report—Current Congress, a useful database is Congressional Bills Legislative Forecast—Current Congress. The Congressional Bills Legislative Forecast database is based on a service called BILLCAST, which is described by the database scope note as providing a listing

---

6. The information is at http://thomas.loc.gov/bss/bss_help.htm#index.

of public bills currently pending in the House and Senate and statistical odds for a bill's success in committee and on the House or Senate floor. Westlaw contains the BILLCAST archives, but not the reports for the current Congress.

B. Bill Tracking in State Legislatures

Bill tracking has historically been more challenging in state legislatures than in the U.S. Congress. Thorough bill tracking often required the presence of an observer in the capital during the legislative session, although many states eventually implemented "hot lines" that citizens could call to track legislation. In response to the need for current information about legislative developments, commercial publishers created legislative services to help track the progress of bills during a session and update the research in their annotated codes.

In recent years, many states have improved preservation and availability of legislative documents. With the advent of state government websites, legislative materials including legislative activity histories and full-text copies of documents have become widely and currently available online in many states. As a result, bill tracking may often be quite easily performed online.[7] Although the details vary somewhat from state to state, the legislative process in a state will be generally similar to that detailed in Table 6-1 at the beginning of this chapter. Most of the documents produced will also be similar in nature to the documents discussed in this chapter. In some instances, the state bill tracking process may be even easier than the federal bill tracking process, as states continue to upgrade their web service and to explore the newest ways of quickly disseminating news of legislative developments.

One or more law school libraries in a state will almost certainly have published online a research guide to bill tracking for that state. The state library or legislative library will also probably have such a guide on its website. These guides are often excellent. You should look

---

7. For older legislation, it is still often necessary to seek the print files for bills in state libraries or archives, often available only in the state capital.

for and study these online research guides before starting a state bill tracking project.

IV. Federal Legislative History Research

Much litigation turns on the meaning of statutes. When the meaning of words or phrases is not clear, courts often look to related statutes in the jurisdiction. Courts try to find a consistent statutory scheme so that the interpretations of related statutes do not create contradictions within the statutes of the jurisdiction. Courts also look to court opinions that have already interpreted the statute. If these authorities do not resolve the issue, courts may look to other evidence as aids to interpretation. Courts may consider legislative history, the documentary record of the passage of a bill through the legislative process, as evidence of the intent of the legislature.

Judges differ in the extent to which they consider the documents produced during the legislative process as evidence of legislative intent,[8] although the use of legislative history as evidence of legislative intent has become a well established practice.

Federal legislative history research uses many of the same tools already discussed for bill tracking. Rather than following a bill through the current Congress, you will start with information from current statutory resources to discover the bill or bills that became the statute in question. Once you know the bill number and congressional session, the timeline of legislative actions can be determined and available documents obtained and studied.

The availability of federal legislative history resources varies according to when a law was enacted. Legislative history information for federal bills enacted since 1969 is comprehensive and widely avail-

---

8. On the U.S. Supreme Court, for example, Justice Scalia is critical of the use of legislative history, although the Court as a whole continues to refer to legislative history in interpreting federal statutes.

able, while information from earlier years is less comprehensive and is often more difficult to identify and locate.

A. Sources of Federal Legislative History

The documents produced during the legislative process are identified in Table 6-1. Since much of the work done by the legislature is done by committees, many of the documents are produced for or by committees as they consider and recommend bills. This part of the chapter describes the documents you will be seeking and explains their significance. Section IV.B. describes the resources where these documents can be located.

1. Versions of Bills

Each of the versions produced during the progress of a bill from its introduction to its presentation to the president should be studied to determine what changes were made to the bill during its journey. The markup of a bill in committee and the amendments to a bill in committee and on the floor can yield insights to the intent of the legislature. Figure 6-2 shows the caption and part of the text of an introduced bill. Note these features: the bill number, H.R. 4667; the name of the bill sponsor, Congressman Perriello; the caption; and the enacting clause, "*Be it enacted by the Senate and House of Representatives of the United States of America in Congress assembled.*"

2. Committee Hearings

Official committee or subcommittee[9] actions and votes must be open to the public.[10] Committees often solicit testimony for public hearings and may issue subpoenas to compel attendance. Testimony

---

9. The term "committee" is used hereafter in this chapter to refer to either committees or subcommittees.

10. See *How Our Laws are Made, Part VI, supra* n. 3, for a detailed discussion of closed meetings and actions. Hearings and other actions may be closed to the public for certain limited reasons if the committee votes in open meeting with a majority present to close a meeting to the public.

Figure 6-2. Introduced Bill

111TH CONGRESS
2D SESSION

H. R. 4667

To increase, effective as of December 1, 2010, the rates of compensation for veterans with service-connected disabilities and the rates of dependency and indemnity compensation for the survivors of certain disabled veterans, and for other purposes.

IN THE HOUSE OF REPRESENTATIVES

FEBRUARY 23, 2010

Mr. PERRIELLO (for himself, Mr. FILNER, Mr. HALL of New York, Mrs. HALVORSON, Mrs. KIRKPATRICK of Arizona, Mr. DONNELLY of Indiana, Mr. RODRIGUEZ, and Mr. TEAGUE) introduced the following bill; which was referred to the Committee on Veterans' Affairs

---

A BILL

To increase, effective as of December 1, 2010, the rates of compensation for veterans with service-connected disabilities and the rates of dependency and indemnity compensation for the survivors of certain disabled veterans, and for other purposes.

1   *Be it enacted by the Senate and House of Representa-*
2   *tives of the United States of America in Congress assembled,*
3   **SECTION 1. SHORT TITLE.**
4   This Act may be cited as "Veterans' Compensation
5   Cost-of-Living Adjustment Act of 2010".

Source: Federal Digital System, at http://www.gpo.gov/fdsys.

at hearings is recorded and transcripts are produced. Many transcripts are widely distributed. All transcripts are available at the offices of the committee. Videos of many committee hearings are also webcast and archived for later viewing.

While hearings can provide helpful background, take care in using committee hearings as indicators of legislative intent. The witnesses often represent specific interests, and the legislators interviewing them are necessarily motivated by a variety of political considerations.

3. Committee Prints and Bill Analyses

Committees often have studies prepared and published concerning the subjects of bills under consideration. These *committee prints* are primarily intended for use by the committee members and staff, but in recent years they have been made generally available. FDsys[11] archives all committee prints from the 105th Congress (1997–1998) to present. Committee prints are often called the "homework" of the committee. As legislative history documents, they are not as important as committee reports but may cast light on the perspectives and considerations influencing the passage of the bill.

Committees also solicit information and analyses from several outside sources:

- Agencies and government departments that would be affected by a bill are frequently asked to submit comments concerning the bill.
- The Government Accountability Office (G.A.O.)[12] is often asked to submit a report on the value and advisability of the proposed bill.
- The Congressional Research Service (C.R.S.) provides the committee an initial, brief report summarizing the key provi-

---

11. FDsys is currently replacing the Government Printing Office website GPO Access as the main source of government documents online. FDsys is at http://www.gpo.gov/fdsys.

12. The G.A.O. was called the General Accounting Office until 2004, when its name was changed by legislation to Government Accountability Office.

sions of the proposed legislation. Additional C.R.S. analyses of the bill are produced as major actions are taken on the bill throughout the legislative process.

- The Congressional Budget Office (C.B.O.) may be asked to provide estimates of budgetary effects of bills under consideration by the committee, and the C.B.O. is required to produce a statement of budgetary effects and government mandate effects of any bill reported out of committee for consideration by the chamber.

Any of these documents may provide insights into the consideration of a bill by Congress.

4. *Committee Reports*

Congressional committee reports are very influential legislative history documents. United States House and Senate *committee reports* contain detailed discussion of the committee's findings and recommendations, including the projected costs or revenues of the proposed legislation. The report addresses the factual background and policy considerations behind the bill and also contains section-by-section explanations of the committee's interpretation of the bill and its intended purpose in paragraph format. This format makes it quite easy to locate relevant discussion of a section of the bill. A committee report may contain statements by those committee members not in favor of the bill. The report must indicate how the bill will change existing law and provide the text of laws that would be repealed by the bill. A bill that a committee votes to recommend favorably to the chamber is accompanied by a report. The extended analysis may run to several hundred pages.[13] See Figure 6-3 for an example of a committee report. Note particularly the listing of the contents of the report.

---

13. By contrast, committee reports in state legislatures may be quite brief, consisting only of a summary of the vote by the committee, the committee's recommendation, and a markup of the bill text.

Figure 6-3. Committee Report

111TH CONGRESS 2d Session	HOUSE OF REPRESENTATIVES	REPORT 111–452

VETERANS' COMPENSATION COST-OF-LIVING ADJUSTMENT ACT OF 2010

MARCH 22, 2010.—Committed to the Committee of the Whole House on the State of the Union and ordered to be printed

Mr. FILNER, from the Committee on Veterans' Affairs, submitted the following

R E P O R T

[To accompany H.R. 4667]

[Including cost estimate of the Congressional Budget Office]

The Committee on Veterans' Affairs, to whom was referred the bill (H.R. 4667) to increase, effective as of December 1, 2010, the rates of compensation for veterans with service-connected disabilities and the rates of dependency and indemnity compensation for the survivors of certain disabled veterans, and for other purposes, having considered the same, report favorably thereon without amendment and recommend that the bill do pass.

CONTENTS

89–006

Source: Federal Digital System, at http://www.gpo.gov/fdsys.

5. Congressional Floor Debates

A bill recommended by a committee proceeds to the chamber for consideration by the chamber as a whole and a vote. If the bill is discussed or debated on the floor of the chamber, amendments may be proposed, voted upon, and adopted. The arguments presented on the floor for and against the bill and any amendments, as well as the records of votes and often the text of the bill, are published in the *Congressional Record*.[14] Congressional debate is less authoritative than committee reports. The authority level of floor debates is similar to that of committee hearing transcripts because the speakers often represent specific interests and are necessarily motivated by various political considerations. The text of floor debates is most useful when revealing how an author or sponsor of a bill interprets a bill and its intent.

6. Conference Committee Reports

When the two chambers pass different versions of a bill, it is sent to a *conference committee* composed of both representatives and senators. If a conference committee agrees on reconciled language, the unified bill is sent to each chamber with a recommendation for passage and a committee report explaining the changes. Conference committee reports, which include the bill markup and explanation of all changes, are generally considered the most influential of legislative history documents because they explicitly state the intent of those responsible for the statutory language.

---

14. The debates as published in the *Congressional Record* might differ from what was actually said on the floor. Members of Congress may correct the language before publication, and they may insert remarks not delivered on the floor. Before March 1, 1978, the *Congressional Record* does not indicate inserted remarks. From March 1, 1978, through September 7, 1986, a bullet symbol (•) indicates the beginning and ending of inserted remarks. Since September 8, 1986, inserted remarks by representatives are indicated by change of typeface, while inserted remarks by senators continue to be indicated by bullet symbol.

7. Presidential and Executive Agency Documents

The executive branch may submit documents related to a bill at several points in the legislative process. When the president sends proposed legislation to Congress, the proposed legislation is commonly accompanied by a memorandum from the president or an executive agency explaining the reason for the proposed legislation. The affected executive agency may also subsequently provide responsible committees with supporting statements and analysis.

After an enrolled bill is sent to the president, the president may sign the bill or allow the bill to pass into law without signing. Presidents sometimes issue a signing statement, indicating the president's interpretation of the purpose of the bill and intent for executive action to implement the bill. If the president vetoes a bill, a veto message may be issued. The status of presidential signing statements and their use as legislative history is much debated, but signing statements are commonly included among the documents in legislative histories.

8. History of Related Bills

Often the bill that is enacted is one of several on the same matter that were considered in the same congressional session or in earlier sessions. THOMAS, ProQuest Congressional,[15] and other sources of legislative history information often reference these related bills. If these bills received significant consideration, examine their legislative histories in the same manner as you examine the legislative history of the bill finally enacted into law.

B. Preparing a Federal Legislative History

The development of federal legislative histories and acquisition of the documents might be either quite easy or quite onerous. Since 1970, lists of legislative history documents and the documents them-

---

15. This online subscription service is discussed at several points later in the chapter.

selves have been available for all federal public laws. For earlier years, excellent compiled legislative histories are available for selected public laws. A compiled legislative history may be either a collection of the documents developed during the legislative process or simply a list of citations to the documents. If a compiled legislative history is available, your task is much lightened. A compilation of all the documents of a legislative history makes research very convenient. If only a list of documents has been compiled, the cites to the documents can be used to acquire the documents. When no compiled legislative history exists, you must use a variety of resources to identify and acquire relevant documents. Locating and using compiled legislative histories is discussed next.

1. Compiled Legislative Histories

a. Finding Aids for Compiled Legislative Histories

Various individuals and organizations compile legislative histories for particular statutes. A good place to start your search, especially if the statute is of historic importance, is the online catalog of your library; many law libraries hold some compiled legislative histories with all documents produced in the legislative process included. If your library does not hold a compiled legislative history with documents for a particular bill, try searching in other libraries by using the OCLC WorldCat union catalog[16] or by searching in the online catalogs at the library web pages for individual law libraries.

Several well known publications provide listings of legislative histories compiled by others. The *Sources of Compiled Legislative Histories: A Bibliography of Government Documents, Periodical Articles and Books*[17] lists sources of compiled legislative histories of major

---

16. OCLC WorldCat is an online catalog that combines into one "union catalog" the electronic catalog records of thousands of academic and other libraries. OCLC WorldCat not only provides records for all the items held in the participating libraries, but also shows the libraries holding an item. The address is www.worldcat.org.

17. Nancy P. Johnson, *Sources of Compiled Legislative Histories: A Bibliography of Government Documents, Periodical Articles, and Books* (AALL Publication Series, No. 14, 1979) (updated periodically).

federal laws since 1789. This finding aid is available both as a print looseleaf service and online in HeinOnline's Federal Legislative History Library.

Also widely available is *Federal Legislative Histories: An Annotated Bibliography and Index to Officially Published Sources*,[18] which contains citations to 255 legislative histories developed by the staff of congressional committees, by the C.R.S. for congressional committees, or by federal executive agencies during the years 1862 through 1990. The public laws covered by the legislative histories begin with the 4th Congress (1796).

An excellent guide to compiled legislative histories that is available in many law libraries is the *Union List of Legislative Histories*, by the Law Librarians Society of Washington, D.C. area. Currently in its seventh edition, this publication provides compiled legislative histories for several thousand bills, contained in more than 120 libraries in the Washington, D.C. area.

Legislative histories compiled by agencies of the federal government are listed in the Government Printing Office's *Monthly Catalog of United States Government Publications*, which is now available online as the *Catalog of U.S. Government Publications*.[19]

b. Collections of Compiled Legislative History Documents

In addition to compiled legislative history documents found through searching library catalogs, several resources provide access to the legislative histories, with documents, for spans of many years.[20]

i. Congressional Information Service (C.I.S.)

For bills since 1970 that were passed into law or received some action following introduction, the best source of legislative history is

---

18. *Federal Legislative Histories: An Annotated Bibliography and Index to Officially Published Sources* (Bernard D. Reams, Jr., comp. 1994).

19. The address is catalog.gpo.gov.

20. This use of "legislative history" refers to the list of documents. The notation "with documents" indicates that the documents themselves are also available.

the series of legislative histories and related finding aids produced by Congressional Information Service, Inc. (C.I.S.). While the C.I.S. series is comprehensive, it can be challenging to use and the assistance of a law librarian is advised.

This series has several parts, available in different media. For each year, the CIS/Index volume contains indexes to bills, including subject, title, bill number, report number, document number, hearing number, and committee print number indexes, each of which references the C.I.S. abstract numbers for congressional documents. The Abstracts of Congressional Publications annual volume contains abstracts of congressional documents, organized by House, Senate, and joint committee. The Legislative Histories of U.S. Public Laws annual volume (combined with the CIS/Index annual volume for each year before 1984) contains lists of documents comprising the legislative history of a bill, abstracts describing the documents, and identifying numbers used to locate the documents. The series accompanies the C.I.S. Microfiche Library, which contains copies of the documents listed in the legislative history volumes for bills that were passed into law. See Figure 6-4 for a page of a C.I.S. legislative history, including a reference to a C.I.S. fiche number for the referenced document. Note that, in addition to a C.I.S. fiche number, some documents are identified by a "SuDoc" number. This number, which is assigned by the Superintendent of Documents, a department of the Government Printing Office (G.P.O.), allows you to locate the document in federal depository libraries.[21]

The C.I.S. legislative history series are also available through online subscriptions to ProQuest Congressional, a service found in most academic law libraries. The full text of documents is available only from about 1990 to present under many subscriptions.[22] You can use the C.I.S. fiche or G.P.O. fiche to obtain copies of documents from earlier years by using the C.I.S. or SuDoc numbers provided in the legislative histories.

---

21. Many academic law libraries are partial G.P.O. depositories and hold documents identified by SuDoc number in print or fiche.

22. Exact years of full-text availability vary by type of document.

Figure 6-4. C.I.S. Legislative History

August 14, 1989

Public Law

1.1 Public Law 101-82, approved Aug. 14, 1989. (H.R. 2467)

(CIS89:PL101-82   25 p.)

"To provide disaster assistance to agricultural producers, and for other purposes."

Authorizes USDA disaster assistance payments to farmers, orchardists, and commercial forest owners for 1989 crop losses due to damaging weather or related conditions and requires disaster aid recipients to purchase Federal crop insurance for the 1990 crop year.

Amends the Agricultural Act of 1949 and the Agricultural Credit Act of 1978 to authorize emergency assistance for livestock feed, transportation, and water.

Directs the Secretary of Agriculture to make and guarantee disaster loans, including loans for rural businesses; and authorizes refinancing of certain existing loans, including FmHA loans made to Indian tribes.

Amends the Consolidated Farm and Rural Development Act to establish an emergency water assistance program of grants to organizations providing water to rural communities; and amends the Disaster Assistance Act of 1988 to authorize disaster assistance for watershed protection activities.

Amends the Agricultural Adjustment Act of 1938 to revise the shrinkage allowance for peanuts.

Authorizes planting of alternate crops in 1990 under the acreage limitation program.

Amends the Federal Crop Insurance Act to authorize use of new underwriting rules for crop yield coverage.

H.R. 2467 is related to H.R. 2232 and H.R. 1736.

2.2 S. Rpt. 101-93 on S. 1429, "Disaster Assistance Act of 1989," July 27, 1989.

(CIS89:S163-3   40 p.)
(Y1.1/5:101-93.)

Recommends passage of S. 1429, the Disaster Assistance Act of 1989, to amend the Agricultural Act of 1949 and five other acts to extend USDA disaster assistance payments under the Disaster Assistance Act of 1988 to commodity producers who suffered a more than 40% loss in production in 1989 crops due to drought or natural disaster; to provide disaster assistance payments to orchard crop producers who suffered more than 45% tree mortality due to freeze or related conditions in 1989; and to provide credit relief to farmers in disaster areas.

Includes provisions to revise the livestock feed program, provide disaster loans for rural and agriculture-related businesses, and establish an FmHA emergency water assistance program of grants to organizations providing water to rural communities.

Includes additional views (p. 30-32).

S. 1429 is related to H.R. 2467.

P.L. 101-82 Debate

135 Congressional Record
101st Congress, 1st Session - 1989

Source: CIS/Annual 1989: Legislative Histories of Public Laws.

ii. G.A.O. Legislative History Collection

Another very useful set of compiled legislative histories and documents is the G.A.O. Legislative History Collection. It contains the documents for about 20,000 legislative histories compiled by the G.A.O., starting in 1921. Until recently, this set was available only in fiche at a handful of libraries, with coverage from 1915 to 1980. The collection is now available on Westlaw, with expanded coverage from 1915 to 1995. The path to G.A.O. Legislative History Collection in the Westlaw Directory is All Databases > U.S. Federal Materials > Legislative History > US GAO Federal Legislative Histories.

iii. *United States Code Congressional and Administrative News*

A more limited, but widely available, source for quick reference to some documents and abbreviated legislative histories is *United States Code Congressional and Administrative News* (U.S.C.C.A.N.), a West publication published since 1941.[23] U.S.C.C.A.N. is an advance legislative service for federal legislation and related documents. U.S.C.C.A.N. publishes the text of new public laws in monthly pamphlets.[24] At the end of a congressional session, the public laws for the session are published in one or more hardbound volumes and the legislative history information is published in separate hardbound volumes. The legislative history volumes for each session list for each public law enacted during the session the dates when a bill was considered and the volume of the *Congressional Record* in which actions on the floor were recorded. Also listed are the committees that considered the bill and cites to committee reports and conference reports. U.S.C.C.A.N. publishes all or part of the most important committee

---

23. The series title has varied. The current title has been applied to the series since 1952.

24. This quick publication was a valuable service when online government websites did not exist. The *Statutes at Large* volumes are published long after the public laws contained in them are enacted. U.S.C.C.A.N. provides the *Statutes at Large* cite, allowing proper citation.

or conference committee reports, making these critical documents widely available.

iv. Westlaw and Lexis

Westlaw's LH database contains the legislative histories for U.S.C.C.A.N. from 1948 to 1989 and all committee reports published in U.S.C.C.A.N. from 1990 forward, as well as those presidential signing statements reprinted in U.S.C.C.A.N. beginning with 1986. A related database, USCCAN-REP, contains "[a]ll congressional committee reports, including reports on bills that did not become law beginning with 1990."[25] In addition, Westlaw contains compiled legislative histories, with documents, for selected public laws.

Lexis also contains selected legislative histories, with documents, for selected public laws. To determine if Lexis contains a legislative history of an act, start by clicking on "All" on the far left side of the toolbar. Select "Legislation & Politics - U.S. & U.K." From the list that appears, select "U.S. Congress." From the next list, select "Legislative Histories" and see if the legislative history for the act you are researching appears in the list.

2. Compiling Your Own Legislative History

If you cannot locate a compiled legislative history using the resources discussed in the previous section or do not have access to these resources, you may have to compile your own list of documents and locate those documents. Table 6-3 outlines the process.

a. Compiling a List of Documents

Legislative histories providing dates of major actions and cites to documents produced are available from a number of free online and print resources. In general, the online sources provide coverage for relatively recent years, while it is often necessary to use print resources for older bills. Fortunately, many of the print resources are widely

---

25. This information is from the scope note to USCCAN-REP in Westlaw.

Table 6-3. Outline for Compiling Your Own Legislative History

1. Locate the public law number and *Statutes at Large* citation for the statute.

2. Locate the bill number of the bill that was enacted into the public law you are researching. The bill number is the one identifier that will help locate all the relevant documents.

3. Get a list of activities, dates, and documents produced during the progress of the bill from introduction to enactment into public law. The documents include:

   a. Original bill and subsequent versions

   b. Committee hearing transcripts

   c. Committee prints and bill analysis

   d. Committee reports

   e. Records of congressional floor debates

   f. Conference committee report (if the bill went to conference committee)

   g. Presidential and executive agency documents

4. If consideration of related bills in the same or previous Congresses contributed to the legislation you are researching, you may need to perform the previous steps for each related bill.

5. When analyzing the documents you have gathered, keep in mind the relative weights given to the types of documents by the courts.

---

available. Academic law libraries generally contain most or all of the resources mentioned in this section, and non-law academic and public libraries often have some of them.

i.   THOMAS

For information about bills enacted since the 93rd Congress (1973–1974), use the THOMAS website. The "Bill Summary & Status" database contains links to information about bills, including the texts of the bill versions, detailed lists of legislative actions, cites to committee reports and the *Congressional Record*, and texts of C.R.S.

summaries and C.B.O. cost estimates. Coverage varies by type of document. Bill texts are available since the 101st Congress (1989–1990). Committee reports are available since the 104th Congress (1995–1996). The *Congressional Record* is available since the 101st Congress (1989–1990).

ii.   Historical House and Senate Journals

For very old bills, from 1789 to 1875, use the "House Journal" and "Senate Journal" at the American Memory website, maintained by the Library of Congress.[26] The *House Journal* and *Senate Journal* are official publications of the House of Representatives and the Senate, respectively, in which are recorded the daily minutes of the chambers. Full-text searching is available for searching the bills and resolutions of the House after December 1817 and of the Senate after December 1826 by title or bill number.

For earlier years, or as a backup to the full-text search, the site provides a browsing option. To search the House Journal, after choosing a journal for a particular session, use "Navigator" to show a list of contents, scroll down to "Index" and click on the link, and then search the index using the "Find" feature of your browser with the phrase "bills of the house." Use the table "Bills of the House of Representatives" to locate the legislative history using the bill number for your bill. The process of searching the Senate Journals is identical. Sometimes, the process is simplified when a link directly to the bill's history appears in the initial Navigator list.

For the large time span (1876–1972) between the coverage of THOMAS and the historical House and Senate journals, a variety of print sources are widely available at no cost in academic and public libraries.

iii.   U.S.C.C.A.N.

U.S.C.C.A.N., described earlier, is available in almost all academic law libraries and in many general academic and public libraries. In addition to containing the most important committee reports, the

---

26. The address is memory.loc.gov/ammem/amlaw/lwhj.html.

legislative history volumes include lists of actions and cites to documents from 1941 to present.

iv. *Congressional Index*

The *Congressional Index* is a looseleaf service (see Chapter 3 for information about looseleaf services) published by Commerce Clearing House (C.C.H.) since the 75th Congress (1937–1938) as a bill-tracking service. Although the bill-tracking function is less essential now that THOMAS is available, the bound volumes of the final cumulative version for each session contain detailed legislative histories for all bills, along with excellent indexing. Many law libraries hold bound historical volumes of the *Congressional Index*.

v. *Congressional Record*

The daily edition of the *Congressional Record* includes a History of Bills and Resolutions section in the bi-weekly index.[27] The cumulative History of Bills and Resolutions is included in the bound Index volume, which is shelved immediately after the permanent bound volumes of the *Congressional Record* for the session. The History of Bills and Resolutions provides *Congressional Record* cites for actions on bills and cites to some documents. The bound Daily Digest volume, shelved with the Index, contains the History of Bills Enacted into Public Law, which tabulates critical dates, committee assignments, report numbers, and the page of passage in the *Congressional Record*. Since the histories in the Index and the Daily Digest contain somewhat different material, use both to compile a full legislative history for a bill.

vi. House Calendar

The *Calendars of the United States House of Representatives and History of Legislation*, commonly known as the House Calendar, contains

---

27. The *Congressional Record* is published daily during a session of Congress. After a session ends, the materials from the daily edition are republished in a bound permanent volume. See Section IV.B.2.b.iii. for further discussion of this feature of the *Congressional Record*.

a section called the "History of Bills and Resolutions: Numerical Order of Bills Which Have Been Reported or Considered by Either or Both Houses." The legislative histories cumulate during a session for any bill on which some action has been taken in either chamber. The House Calendar at the conclusion of a session will thus contain a complete legislative history for bills introduced and considered during that session.[28]

The Senate also has a calendar, *Senate Calendar of Business*, commonly known as the Senate Calendar. The Senate Calendar is less useful for legislative history research because the House Calendar serves this purpose for both the House of Representatives and the Senate.

vii. *House Journal* and *Senate Journal*

The *House Journal*[29] and *Senate Journal* each contain a History of Bills and Resolutions section. As discussed at length earlier, the Library of Congress's American Memory website makes the journals available for the years from 1789 to 1875.[30] Many law libraries and government document repositories hold the journals for years in which online legislative histories are not available.

viii. *Digest of Public General Bills and Resolutions*

The *Digest of Public General Bills and Resolutions*, published by the C.R.S. from 1936 to 1990, contains digests and legislative histories of enacted public laws. The congressional documents are not included. The collection is available in many libraries.

---

28. The House Calendar since the 104th Congress is online at FDsys. The address is http://www.gpo.gov/fdsys/browse/collection.action?collectionCode =CCAL.

29. The *House Journal* is online at FDsys for the years 1992–1999. The address is http://www.gpo.gov/fdsys/browse/collection.action?collectionCode =HJOURNAL.

30. The address is http://memory.loc.gov/ammem/index.html.

b.   Getting the Documents

Unless you were fortunate enough to locate the compiled documents of a legislative history, you now must obtain the documents listed in a legislative history you have created using the resources just discussed.

i.   Congressional Bills

A number of sources provide the text of bills. For economy of presentation, the most convenient sources are listed for each period. Unless noted otherwise, the sources that provide older bills also provide the text of recent bills.

1989–Present: The free and convenient THOMAS website contains the full text of bills from 1989 to present. FDsys contains bills from the 103rd Congress (1993–1994) to present.

ProQuest Congressional contains bills from the 101st Congress (1989–1990) to present in its legislative history module based on the C.I.S. legislative history series. The Lexis legal research service also contains a database of bills for the same period. Westlaw does not provide a separate bill database.

The G.A.O. Legislative History Collection contains documents, including bill texts, for about 20,000 bills enacted into public law from 1915 to 1980. This series has recently become available online in Westlaw, with extended coverage to 1995, at FED-LH.

1970–Present: The most widely available source of bill texts from 1970 to present is the C.I.S. Microfiche Library, discussed at Section IV.B.1.b.i.

1915–1995: Many bills that were enacted into public laws are included in the G.A.O. Legislative History Collection. Until recently, this set was available only to those with access to the few libraries holding the microfiche set, which covers the period from 1915 to 1980. Westlaw has recently added this collection, with expanded coverage from 1915 to 1995. The database is FED-LH.

Sources for Early and Hard-to-Find Bills: If a bill is not available from the sources listed above, try requesting the text of the bill from a federal depository library.[31] Try also the *Congressional Record*, which sometimes prints the text of bills discussed or amended on the floor of a chamber. Finally, if you have obtained the text of a committee report for a bill, the report might contain the text of the bill, most likely with markups in committee shown.

ii.   Committee Reports and Conference Committee Reports

1990–Present: For free online access, FDsys and THOMAS provide reports since the 104th Congress (1995–1996).

The subscription database ProQuest Congressional provides the full text of most reports since 1990 in its legislative history module based on the C.I.S. legislative history series. If a subscription to ProQuest Congressional includes a subscription to the *Serial Set*, discussed at the end of this section, you have access to a comprehensive historical collection of committee and conference committee reports from 1789 to 1969.

Westlaw contains all congressional reports, including bills not passed into law, since 1990 in the database USCCAN–REP.

1970–Present: The CIS Microfiche Library contains reports from 1970 to present. To locate the report on fiche, use the C.I.S. indexes in print or on ProQuest Congressional to obtain the C.I.S. number.

1941–Present: U.S.C.C.A.N. publishes all or part of selected reports for each bill enacted into public law since 1941. Westlaw includes all U.S.C.C.A.N. published reports from 1990 to present in USCCAN-REP.

1915–1980: The G.A.O. Legislative Histories Collection contains documents, including reports, for about 20,000 bills enacted into public law from 1915 to 1980. This series has recently become available online in Westlaw, with extended coverage to 1995, at FED-LH.

1789–Present: The *Serial Set*, published by the G.P.O., publishes a variety of congressional documents produced since 1789. Notably, committee reports and conference reports are comprehensively published for the entire period. Law libraries usually hold the *Serial Set* in print format, online as a module of ProQuest Congressional, or both.

---

31. A searchable directory of federal depository libraries is at http://catalog. gpo.gov/fdlpdir.

iii. Congressional Debates

The ultimate source for locating all congressional debates is the *Congressional Record* or its predecessors, the *Annals of Congress* (1789–1824), the *Register of Debates* (1824–1837), and the *Congressional Globe* (1833–1873).[32] The *Congressional Record* is widely available in print and on fiche. Online resources primarily cover recent years: FDsys, 1994–present; THOMAS, 1989–present; Westlaw and Lexis, 1985–present; ProQuest Congressional, 1985–present (some subscriptions contain an additional module covering 1873 through 1997).

When using the *Congressional Record*, note that cites may be either to the daily edition, published daily during a session, or to the permanent edition, published later as a bound volume in the permanent Congressional Record series. The daily and permanent editions have different paginations. A cite to the daily edition is identifiable by section letter prefixes: S–Senate; H–House; E–Extension of Remarks; and D–Daily Digest. The permanent edition is repaginated without the section letter prefixes.

iv. Hearings

As with many of the documents discussed in this chapter, the finding aids and accompanying fiche collections produced by C.I.S. are often the most useful sources for legislative history lists and for the text of documents. The C.I.S. legislative history collection provides hearings for all bills on which hearings were held from 1970 to present. ProQuest Congressional provides the digitized hearings from the C.I.S. legislative history set from 1988 to present. Some ProQuest Congressional subscriptions contain C.I.S. hearings indexes and full-text collections of hearings from 1833 to present, as well as some unpublished hearings starting in 1824. If your library does not provide access to these indexes through ProQuest Congressional, check your library's catalog to see if the library holds the following indexes in print and the associated fiche collections: *CIS US Congressional Com-*

---

32. All are available at the Library of Congress web page, http://memory.loc.gov/ammem/amlaw.

mittee Hearings Index (1833–1969); *CIS Index to Unpublished US Senate Committee Hearings* (1823–1976); *CIS Index to Unpublished US House of Representatives Hearings* (1833–1968).

The following online sources provide access to recent hearings transcripts: Westlaw, 2004 to present, and the websites of House of Representatives and Senate committees.

v.   Committee Prints

FDsys provides selected committee prints since the 105th Congress (1997–1998).

ProQuest Congressional contains committee prints, with the years of coverage depending on the modules subscribed to. Depending on subscriptions, coverage may cover the years from 1830 to present. If your library's subscription includes the *Serial Set*, those committee prints that were occasionally printed in the *Serial Set* are available (if not, see if your library holds the *Serial Set* in print).

As with other legislative history documents, the C.I.S. Microfiche Library contains copies of all prints included in the C.I.S. legislative histories since 1970. Another C.I.S. index, the *CIS US Congressional Committee Prints Index*, provides cites to the prints copied in the associated microfiche collection.

V. State Legislative History Research

State courts usually also consider legislative history as evidence of legislative intent when interpreting statutes. Historically, state legislative history has been only irregularly available and difficult to locate. In recent years, some states have improved their preservation of legislative history documents. State government websites have made legislative materials, including legislative histories and full-text copies of documents, widely available online. As a result, legislative history research may be quite easily performed online, at least for relatively recent legislation.[33]

---

33. For older legislation, it is still often necessary to seek the print files for bills in state libraries or archives, often available only in the state capital.

The details of the legislative process vary somewhat from state to state, but both the process and the documents that it produces will generally mirror the description in Table 6-1 at the beginning of this chapter. Sometimes, researching state legislative history might be easier than researching federal legislative history because many or most state documents may be available at one government website.

Legislative history research guides published online by law school libraries in a state or by the state library or legislative library are often excellent places to begin a state legislative history research project.

Chapter 7

Administrative Law Research

I. Federal Administrative Law

The executive branch is one of the three branches of the United States government, along with the legislative and judicial branches. Within the executive branch of government are executive departments, usually headed by a cabinet secretary. In addition to the agencies operating within these departments, there are many independent and quasi-official agencies that are otherwise empowered by the executive, legislative, or judicial branches of government. Together, these administrative bodies are known by many names, such as departments, agencies, administrations, commissions, and boards.[1] These administrative bodies form an integral and important part of the federal government. They each have the detailed expertise required to implement specific legislative, judicial, or executive mandates.

The power granted administrative agencies by the three branches of government mimic the powers of those branches. For example, an agency may be given any or all of the following powers·

- Quasi-legislative power such as drafting regulations[2] in an effort to interpret and implement legislative, judicial, and executive mandates;

---

1. Examples of each include the Department of Transportation, the Environmental Protection Agency, the Social Security Administration, the Federal Communications Commission, and the National Labor Relations Board.
2. Regulations are also called "rules," especially when they are in the process of being proposed or finalized. In addition, some states use the term rules even for their codified administrative regulations.

- Quasi-judicial power, such as decision-making in disputes between citizens and the agency when the agency enforces regulations against citizens;
- Quasi-executive power to issue licenses or orders, investigate whether regulations are being followed, and enforce regulations.

The outcome of the exercise of these powers often produces a form of legal information known as administrative law.[3]

Federal administrative law governs broad and varied areas of law that affect American life generally such as telecommunications, banking, and energy. But administrative law also delves deeply into minutiae of everyday life. For example, federal regulations require that food labeled as "pork with barbecue sauce" must contain at least "50 percent cooked meat of the species specified on the label."[4] These dual characteristics—broad applicability and a concern with minutiae—suggest a sweeping expanse of authority. Actually, administrative law is carefully limited with a detailed system of procedures to facilitate citizen involvement in the adoption of regulations. Each regulation must be supported by authorizing primary law, often specific legislation from Congress. These authority-granting legislative acts are commonly called "enabling acts." When properly authorized, adopted, and implemented, administrative regulations have the full force and effect of law. An administrative regulation is invalid, however, if it exceeds the authority granting the agency the power to create the regulation.

The two basic forms of administrative law of most interest to legal researchers are regulations and agency decisions. This chapter focuses on researching those two forms of administrative law and generically refers to various administrative bodies as agencies. The fundamental process is outlined in Table 7-1.

---

3. The term administrative law can refer either to (1) the law governing agencies or (2) the law produced by agencies. This chapter uses the term with the second meaning.
4. 9 C.F.R. §319.312.

Table 7-1. Outline of Administrative Law Research

1. Learn about the agency through reading secondary sources or reviewing the agency's website.

2. Search for applicable regulations:

    a. Find citations to relevant regulations in secondary sources.

    b. Search annotations to federal statutes to find references to regulations authorized by the statutes.

    c. Browse titles in the *Code of Federal Regulations* (C.F.R.).

    d. Search the index to the C.F.R.

    e. Search the C.F.R. by keyword.

    f. Search the agency's website.

3. Ensure that the regulatory language is current; if not, update it.

4. Locate relevant administrative decisions by the agency.

5. Conduct case research for appeals of agency decisions.

A. Overview

A preliminary approach to a thorough understanding of relevant administrative law may involve learning about the administrative body regulating the area of law being researched. If you do not know which agency governs the area of law at issue, secondary sources typically provide an answer or at least enough information to support an educated guess. Examples of secondary sources potentially providing this information include legal encyclopedias, subject area treatises, *American Law Reports* annotations, and perhaps law review articles.

To help identify which agency might govern a particular area of law, the *United States Government Manual*[5] provides descriptive and logistical information about each agency. The manual is digitally published and updated online as changes occur. Also, "Resources" links

---

5. The manual is available at http://www.usgovernmentmanual.gov.

from the main page provide additional information that might be useful, such as a history of organizational changes or commonly used acronyms. The *Manual* can both assist in identifying which agency is relevant for specific research and provide information about that agency.

Armed with the agency name, you might seek more detailed background information useful in developing an initial understanding of how that area of administrative law is governed. Agencies are now required to provide information online, including the agency's mission, organizational structure, policy statements, and interpretations.[6] Agency websites are excellent resources for that purpose. Using a general search engine such as Google or Yahoo! is a reasonable approach to locating agency websites. A Federal Agency Directory[7] is also maintained by the Louisiana State University Library, linking to many agency websites. USA.gov[8] is also another source for a collection of links to federal agency websites.

B. Administrative Regulations

The relatively broad mandates that Congress or the president (through the executive branch) issues to agencies usually require enormous detail for implementation. Typically, Congress lacks the time or expertise to develop the detailed rules necessary to implement the mandates issued. That duty falls to administrative agencies, which must develop the necessary rules, generally called "regulations" at the federal level once they are finalized and codified. For example, the Nuclear Regulatory Commission has promulgated extensive regulations about the licensing of nuclear facilities in the United States. Figure 7-1 displays an administrative regulation requiring the N.R.C. to notify conservation groups or organizations known to be interested

---

6. *E-Government Act*, Pub. L. No. 107-347, 116 Stat. 2899, 44 U.S.C. § 101; *Electronic Freedom of Information Act Amendments of 1996*, Pub. L. No. 104-231, 110 Stat. 3048.

7. The address is www.lib.lsu.edu/gov/index.html.

8. The address is www.usa.gov/directory/federal/index.shtml.

Figure 7-1. Sample Regulation

> **§ 51.122 List of interested organiza-
> tions and groups.**
>
> The NRC Office of Information Re-
> sources Management will maintain a
> master list of organizations and
> groups, including relevant conserva-
> tion commissions, known to be inter-
> ested in the Commission's licensing
> and regulatory activities. The NRC Of-
> fice of Information Resources Manage-
> ment with the assistance of the appro-
> priate NRC staff director will select
> from this master list those organiza-
> tions and groups that may have an in-
> terest in a specific NRC NEPA action
> and will promptly notify such organi-
> zations and groups of the availability
> of a draft environmental impact state-
> ment or a draft finding of no signifi-
> cant impact.
>
> [49 FR 9381, Mar. 12, 1984, as amended at 52
> FR 31612, Aug. 12, 1987; 54 FR 53316, Dec. 28,
> 1989]

Source: 10 C.F.R. § 51.122 (2011).

in the Commission's licensing and regulatory activities whenever a
draft environmental impact statement from a petitioner is available.[9]

1. General Process of Creating Administrative Regulations

Prior to the 1930s, few uniformly required methods of creating
federal administrative regulations existed. Once regulations were created, the regulations were not required by law to be made available
to the public. Several steps were taken in the 1930s to require the publication and codification of regulations. Congress formalized the

---

9. 10 C.F.R. § 51.122 (2011).

process of creating regulations in 1946 with the adoption of the Administrative Procedures Act.[10]

Briefly summarized, the process of creating federal administrative regulations begins when an agency is authorized to draft and implement regulations in support of a legislative, executive, or judicial mandate. After the agency drafts a regulation, that *proposed rule* must appear in the daily publication, the *Federal Register*.[11] Through this process, the public is invited to comment on the proposed rule by e-mail, letter, or phone call to the agency within a specific period of time, often at least 60 days. Regulations.gov is a federal government website where the public may conveniently find, view, and comment on proposed rules. The agency may hold one or more public hearings at various locations to gather public comments for consideration. The agency then considers the comments received and decides whether any amendments to the proposed rule are warranted. Then a *final rule* is adopted by the agency and must also be published in the *Federal Register*. The agency may include a summary of public comments it received and provide any relevant discussion about how the comments were considered or addressed. At the end of the process, final rules are codified in the *Code of Federal Regulations*, meaning they are arranged by subject.

2. Code of Federal Regulations

All regulations currently in effect are codified in the *Code of Federal Regulations* and arranged by subjects called *titles*. Therefore, the value of the C.F.R. in administrative law is similar to the value of the *United States Code* in statutory law. Fifty titles comprise the C.F.R. Although some of the numbered titles in the C.F.R. and *United States Code* address the same area of law, such as Title 26 addressing tax law, most of the titles between the two codes are not aligned by subject.

---

10. Pub. L. No. 79-404, 5 U.S.C. §500 *et seq.*

11. The *Federal Register* uses continuous pagination throughout a calendar year, meaning that page numbers in the thousands are common.

Each C.F.R. title is divided into *chapters*, which generally contain the regulations of a specific agency. Chapters, however, are often not used in identifying specific regulations. The chapters are further divided into *parts* and *sections*. In the following example, 20 C.F.R. § 416.906, 20 is the title, 416 is the part, and .906 is the section. A lawyer might say "20 C.F.R. section 416 point 906," even though technically 416 is the part. (This regulation appears in Chapter 1, in Figure 1-3.)

Administrative regulations are usually authorized or enabled by congressional legislation. An *authority note* at the beginning of each C.F.R. part cites the statutory authority for the subsequent regulations. A *source note*, found after the authority note, gives the *Federal Register* citation and date where the regulations were officially published. These references have research consequences that will be discussed in Section I.B.5.b. of this chapter.

The C.F.R. is published annually in paperback form by the Government Printing Office (G.P.O.). Rather than publishing the entire 50-title set at one time, however, G.P.O. publishes one quarter of the set every three months so that the entire set is republished over the course of a year. Titles 1–16 are updated and re-published January 1 of each year; Titles 17–27 are updated on April 1; Titles 28–41 are updated as of July 1; and Titles 42–50 are updated every October 1. The paper covers of the individual volumes change color each year, which makes identifying which volumes have been updated much easier. Often, the volumes are months late being updated and distributed, and many volumes trickle from the publisher at different times, even volumes addressing parts of the same title.

In addition to the 50 titles, the last volume of the code is the Index and Finding Aids volume. Like the other volumes, this volume is also updated and republished each year. Although the subject index terms are not very detailed or specific and the indexing points only to parts rather than the more detailed sections, the index might lead to the general area of the code where you could browse the associated headings to find the specific, appropriate sections. Some of the finding aids might be useful, including the "Parallel Table of Authorities and Rules," which lists *United States Code* sections in numerical order authorizing specific administrative regulations. Other authorities authorizing administrative regulations are also listed in the table, including presidential documents such as proclamations, executive orders, and reorganization plans.

The C.F.R. is available from several different sources. In addition to the print version, the Government Printing Office also publishes a C.F.R. annual edition at G.P.O.'s new website, the Federal Digital System (FDsys).[12] This online annual version of the C.F.R. is no more current throughout the year than the print version of the code, except that its availability online bypasses the time-consuming publishing and distribution process that slows the print version.

The G.P.O. also produces the Electronic Code of Federal Regulations (e-CFR),[13] which is an authentic but unofficial editorial compilation of the C.F.R. incorporating the latest regulatory amendments as published in the *Federal Register*. It is typically updated and current within several days of any changes published in the *Federal Register* affecting currently codified regulations. Lexis and Westlaw also provide C.F.R. databases that, like G.P.O.'s e-CFR, are updated within days of changes published in the *Federal Register*. Additionally, Westlaw provides an annotated C.F.R. database called "Regulations Plus,"[14] which includes case annotations like the Notes of Decisions included with the *United States Code Annotated* and a C.F.R. index. Other online services such as Loislaw and HeinOnline also offer subscription access to the C.F.R.

For access to older annual editions of the C.F.R., the FDsys website provides free access to editions since 1996. Lexis and Westlaw provide earlier access back to the 1980s. HeinOnline provides access since the beginning of C.F.R. publication in 1938.

---

12. Over the past year, the G.P.O. has been migrating from the outdated GPO Access website (www.gpoaccess.gov) to the new site, FDsys or Federal Digital System (www.fdsys.gov).

13. e-CFR is a project of G.P.O. and the National Archives and Records Administration's Office of the Federal Register. It may be accessed at http://ecfr.gpoaccess.gov.

14. Westlaw's "Regulations Plus" is not included with the standard academic subscription at the time of this writing.

3. Federal Register

As discussed in the section addressing the process of drafting regulations, the *Federal Register* is a daily, chronological publication including proposed rules, as well as final rules adopted by an agency. It provides official notice as required by the rule-making process and facilitates public participation. The *Register* also publishes notices from federal agencies and some presidential documents such as executive orders. Although the chronological nature is inconvenient and most researchers would access regulations using the C.F.R., the value of the *Federal Register* to legal researchers is the notification role it plays in the rule-making process for regulations currently being considered and its role as a historic window into the rule-making process for regulations currently in effect. Information considered in the rule-making process might assist with interpretation of the final rule in a similar way that legislative history may assist in interpreting statutory law.

Although the *Federal Register* is printed every business day by the Government Printing Office, the best access to the *Federal Register* is provided online by the G.P.O., at the FDsys website,[15] where it is updated every day by 6:00 a.m. It is freely available and both browsable and searchable. Coverage includes volumes back to 1994.

In the summer of 2010, the 75th anniversary of the *Federal Register*, the Office of the Federal Register and the G.P.O. developed a new format of the *Federal Register* as a Web 2.0 version of the traditional *Federal Register* publication.[16] The new experimental website is dubbed "Federal Register 2.0" and is a daily web newspaper-formatted presentation of the information contained in each daily *Federal Register* issue. The website organizes the dense format of the traditional print and online version into news sections:

- Money
- Environment
- World

---

15. The address is www.fdsys.gov.
16. *See* www.federalregister.gov.

- Science & Technology
- Business & Industry
- Health & Public Welfare

While this new product is still being developed, it will clearly play an important role in administrative law research in the near future. The new experimental website version, however, will be unofficial until the Administrative Committee of the Federal Register issues a regulation granting the new site official legal status. Until that time, the traditional *Federal Register* is still being published and is the official version of this information. Be sure to use the official, traditional version of the *Federal Register* until the new product becomes official.

Lexis and Westlaw provide the current *Federal Register* issue. Lexis also provides access to the *Federal Register* back to 1981. Westlaw and HeinOnline both provide access back to 1936 when the *Federal Register* was first published.

4. Researching Federal Administrative Regulations

Due to the complexity of administrative law, the organizational scheme of the code, and indexing issues, it is often easiest to find administrative regulations using a source that does not contain the regulations themselves. The print C.F.R. is notoriously poorly indexed. The single volume index that accompanies the print C.F.R. set lacks sufficient detail. Additionally, the complex, detailed, and precise nature of the terminology and subjects involved makes the selection of search terms difficult, whether searching a print index or selecting search terms to use in a full-text, keyword search. The following are some effective methods of locating relevant regulations.

a. Starting with a C.F.R. Citation from a Secondary Source

Starting research with a secondary source, such as a subject-specific treatise or a law review article addressing the legal topic, is an excellent method of finding citations to relevant administrative regulations. Even if the secondary source fails to provide a citation to administrative regulations, its discussion will likely provide citations to any relevant statutory law. In turn, this might lead to citations to relevant regulations from the annotations in the statutory code. Even if the secondary source might not provide citations to regulations or related statutes, the discussion in the secondary source itself should provide clues about relevant search terms to use in a keyword search should that become necessary.

b. Starting with a C.F.R. Citation from an Enabling Statute

Another excellent starting point in the search for relevant regulations is one of the two annotated versions of the *United States Code,* either the *United States Code Annotated* (U.S.C.A.) or the *United States Code Service* (U.S.C.S.). Since administrative regulations must be authorized by other law, usually statutory law, the enabling act providing that authority, found in one of the annotated codes, would likely cite the related administrative regulations. The U.S.C.S. has traditionally provided more thorough coverage of administrative law in its annotations than has its competitor, the U.S.C.A.

Alternatively, if you already have citations to the enabling statute, you can use the "Parallel Table of Authorities and Rules" in the C.F.R. index to find citations to the regulations authorized by that statute. The enabling statutory citation might also be used in an online search to locate the relevant regulations because of the authority note in each C.F.R. part. This is an excellent approach to the regulations when you already know the enabling statute.

c. Browsing C.F.R. Titles in Print or Online

Browsing the administrative code titles is similar to the title or outline browsing approach to searching statutory codes discussed in Chapter 5. Browsing is most effective when you are familiar with the issue being researched and have used the administrative code to research this issue recently. One danger of this approach is missing relevant material that is hidden in another title whose name might not suggest its relevance to your subject.

You can browse the administrative code titles online. The code is also available from the FDsys website, as well as from Lexis, Westlaw, and other commercial online services.

d. Browsing or Searching the C.F.R. Index

While the annual print index that is included as the last volume of the C.F.R. set is not very effective, other indexing is available. Westlaw provides a useful, browsable index that is hyperlinked to the text of the code.

e. Keyword Searching the C.F.R. in Full Text or by Field

The C.F.R. is available online from many sources as a full-text, keyword searchable database. Differences may exist in the sophistication of the search engine of each source. For example, field searching provides the ability to search just specific parts of each document in a database, allowing you to narrow your results using specific information you might already know. Typically, the free online sources do not provide search tools as sophisticated as premium online services like Lexis and Westlaw.

f. Searching Regulations on Agency Websites

Another alternative is to access relevant administrative regulations on the agency's website. Many agencies have websites with links to their regulations. While these may be searchable and browsable, you should be cautious and make certain you know the source of the regulations at the website. Are the regulations authentic or linked from the official version? What is their source? Are they currently updated? Look for disclaimers on the website about the legal authority of the law posted at the site.

5. Updating Administrative Regulations

Because new regulations are always being promulgated, you must ensure that you are working with the current versions, that no amendments have been made to existing regulations, and that no new regulations have been adopted. Several tools are available for updating regulations.

a. Updating Online

The easiest and least expensive method of updating a federal regulation is to use e-CFR as the starting point. This resource should provide the date through which the most recent changes to regulations were last incorporated into the e-CFR text. Next, use the *Federal Register* issues at FDsys that have been published since the most recent incorporation date from e-CFR. Examine the "C.F.R. Sections Affected" chart in the most recent issue of the *Federal Register* to make sure your section has not been amended.

A similar method should be used if updating the C.F.R. database from Lexis or Westlaw. Very little updating is necessary with the e-CFR, Lexis, or Westlaw databases; one of the benefits of using these services is that they are kept current.

In addition to updating the text of regulations, you should also use citators such as Shepard's on Lexis or KeyCite on Westlaw to find resources citing a specific regulation being researched. Citators list cases and other authorities that have cited a regulation, providing more context for evaluating whether it is still widely followed.

b. Updating in Print

Updating the print version of C.F.R. is more challenging. The challenge includes the annual full-text C.F.R. database at FDsys (not e-CFR), which is no more current than the print version. Regardless of the source, assuming the title is more than one month past publication, there is a two-step process for updating a regulation in print. The updating process is similar to checking pocket parts, except that you will use a separate publication called the *List of C.F.R. Sections Affected* and the back page of the *Federal Register*.

i. *List of C.F.R. Sections Affected* Monthly Pamphlet

For the first step, find the most recent pamphlet (or database on the FDsys website) known as the *List of C.F.R. Sections Affected* (L.S.A.). The L.S.A. is a monthly publication that lists all sections of the C.F.R. that have been affected by recent rule-making activity. Information in the L.S.A. should be current back to the publication date of your paper C.F.R. volume; however, you should cautiously confirm the dates of coverage for the L.S.A. publication or database to ensure coverage. If there is no reference in the L.S.A. to a section containing your regulation, there have been no changes to your regulation between the date the C.F.R. title was last published and the date of the monthly L.S.A. If there has been a change, however, this table will list the *Federal Register* page number for each new agency action that has affected your specific section.

ii.   *Federal Register* "C.F.R. Parts Affected" Table

The second step involves examining a table in the back of the *Federal Register*. The table is called the "C.F.R. Parts Affected for [the current month]." Search the table for reference to the C.F.R. part containing your section. Search this table in each *Federal Register* volume published on the last day of each month since the most recently published, monthly L.S.A. When you reach the current month, search this same table in the most recent *Federal Register* issue for the current month. The chart in the back of the *Federal Register* is always cumulative for the entire month. The paper *Federal Register* will probably be a week or two old due to processing and mailing. If you use the free online issues of *Federal Register* at the FDsys website, which are updated each morning by 6:00 a.m., this process will update your regulation to same-day currency.

C. Administrative Decisions

1. *The Nature of Administrative Decisions*

Federal agencies issue an enormous number of types and levels of administrative decisions primarily addressing conflicts between an agency and a citizen. The basic, initial decision-making process is often informal, perhaps even involving an agency employee and a citizen meeting face to face. The process of reconsidering initial administrative decisions varies widely from one agency to another. Administrative law judges (ALJs) may be involved in reviewing initial or second-level decisions. Typically ALJs issue written opinions, although they are not often widely available. While administrative decisions might not have broad precedential value, the decisions may have some value to researchers focusing on the work of a specific agency.

Beyond the ALJ level, sometimes regional or national councils or boards within an agency will issue final administrative decisions that are published online or in specialized reporters. Once all administrative remedies have been exhausted, dissatisfied parties may have the opportunity to appeal an administrative decision to federal court. Once the issues from a specific administrative decision enter the federal court system, researching the issues becomes case law research, which is addressed in Chapter 9.

2. Researching Administrative Decisions

Federal administrative decisions are extremely variable in nature and widely dispersed. Many agencies' final administrative decisions were traditionally published in individual, official print reporters. For example, *Federal Trade Commission Decisions* was a print reporter for the decisions of the Federal Trade Commission. A number of agency decisions were also published in commercial products by publishers such as Commerce Clearing House (C.C.H.) and Bureau of National Affairs (B.N.A.). These publications are often called topical looseleaf services. While some topical looseleaf services are still produced and widely used, most of the specialized, official, print reporters have ceased publication. For those print reporters still being produced, and the many topical looseleaf services, the decisions are individually indexed by each reporter or looseleaf publication. There is no comprehensive index or digest of all administrative agency decisions. For a selected list of agency print reporters, see Appendix 8 of the *ALWD Citation Manual*, Table T1.2 of the *Bluebook*, or the online "appendix" to the *ALWD Citation Manual*.[17]

---

17. The address is http://www.alwdmanual.com/books/dickerson_alwd/appendices/16ALWD_Appendix_8.pdf.

More recent federal agency decisions are being published directly at individual agency websites. For example, the Federal Trade Commission website now provides current decisions as well as access to commission decisions back to 1949.[18] Agency websites are independent and vary widely in terms of organization and information provided. These websites can easily be found online using a search engine such as Google or Yahoo! Alternatively, you may use a collection of links to "Administrative Decisions and Other Actions" posted by the University of Virginia Library.[19] This site might be particularly useful if you do not initially know which agency might publish the decisions you need or you are uncertain of the level of decision you need from a large agency.

Many agency decisions are also selectively available in databases on Lexis and Westlaw. While not all the agencies' decisions are available from these services, the collections on Lexis and Westlaw will likely include older decisions than agency websites might include, as well as the most recent decisions.

It is also worth noting that the U.S.C.S. includes references to agency decisions from a number of agencies as part of the "Interpretive Notes and Decisions" annotations after each code section. These annotations make the U.S.C.S. a good research tool for identifying administrative agency decisions.

II. Researching United States Attorney General Opinions

The Office of the United States Attorney General was created by the Judiciary Act of 1789. The attorney general is the head of the Department of Justice (created in 1870) and serves as the chief law enforcement officer of the federal government. Among other duties, the attorney general gives advice and issues opinions upon request to the

---

18. The address is http://www.ftc.gov/os/decisions/index.shtm.
19. The address is http://www2.lib.virginia.edu/govtinfo/fed_decisions _agency.html.

president and the heads of the executive departments of the federal government. In 1977, the attorney general delegated to the U.S. Department of Justice Office of Legal Council the duties of providing legal advice to the president and executive branch agencies. These duties include the drafting of the formal Opinions of the Attorney General. As examples, a legal opinion might address the president's authority to use military force in a particular situation[20] or whether the criminal provisions of the Violence Against Women Act apply to otherwise covered conduct when the offender and victim are the same sex.[21] See Figure 7-2.

These opinions are available back to 1992 at the Office of Legal Council website.[22] They are browsable by year. Selected opinions are also variably available on Lexis and Westlaw. If the Department of Justice deemed them appropriate for publication, older opinions may have been published since 1791. Opinions of the Attorney General are not primary law but are persuasive as an educated interpretation of federal law applied to specific facts.

Both annotated statutory codes, the U.S.C.A. and the U.S.C.S., include references to relevant Opinions of the Attorney General as part of the annotations at the end of each code section.

III. Researching Presidential Documents

The President of the United States is the chief executive officer of the government, presiding over the executive branch with some additional powers and duties relating to the other branches as well. In the exercise of that power, presidential actions are documented and collected. Two of the most important forms of presidential documents are executive orders and presidential proclamations.

---

20. Authority to Use Military Force in Libya, 35 Op. Off. Leg. Counsel (Apr. 1, 2011).

21. Whether the Criminal Provisions of the Violence Against Women Act Apply to Otherwise Covered Conduct When the Offender and Victim Are the Same Sex, 34 Op. Off. Leg. Counsel (Apr. 27, 2010).

22. The address is http://www.usdoj.gov/olc/opinions.htm.

Figure 7-2. Justice Department Office of Legal Counsel Opinions as Delegated by the Attorney General

---

WHETHER THE CRIMINAL PROVISIONS OF THE VIOLENCE AGAINST WOMEN ACT APPLY TO OTHERWISE COVERED CONDUCT WHEN THE OFFENDER AND VICTIM ARE THE SAME SEX

The criminal provisions of the Violence Against Women Act apply to otherwise covered conduct when the offender and victim are the same sex.

April 27, 2010

MEMORANDUM OPINION FOR THE ACTING DEPUTY ATTORNEY GENERAL

You have asked us whether the criminal provisions of the Violence Against Women Act ("VAWA") apply to otherwise covered conduct when the offender and victim are the same sex. VAWA includes three criminal provisions: 18 U.S.C. § 2261 (2006), addressing interstate domestic violence; 18 U.S.C. § 2261A (2006), addressing interstate stalking; and 18 U.S.C. § 2262 (2006), addressing the interstate violation of a protection order. Consistent with the views we received, we conclude that each of these provisions applies when the offender and the victim are the same sex.[1]

I.

The first of VAWA's three criminal provisions, section 2261, addresses certain specified types of interstate domestic violence. Subsection (a)(1) makes it a federal crime to travel in interstate or foreign commerce, to enter or leave Indian country, or to travel within the special maritime or territorial jurisdiction of the United States "with the intent to kill, injure, harass, or intimidate a *spouse, intimate partner, or dating partner*" if, in the course of or as a result of such travel, the offender "commits or attempts to commit a crime of violence against that *spouse, intimate partner, or dating partner*." 18 U.S.C. § 2261(a)(1) (emphases added). Subsection

---

Executive orders typically document the exercise of presidential authority in conducting the business of government. For example, President Truman issued Executive Order 9981 to desegregate the United States Military in 1948.[23]

Executive orders are officially published in the *Federal Register*, which is available in print and online as previously discussed. Additionally, executive orders published in the previous year's *Federal Register* are codified the following year in Title 3 of the C.F.R. Therefore, C.F.R. Title 3 retains historical value for presidential documents and is often retained by libraries. HeinOnline provides access to C.F.R.

---

23. Establishing the President's Committee on Equality of Treatment and Opportunity in the Armed Forces, Exec. Or. 9981 (July 26, 1948).

Title 3 for each year since the C.F.R. began publication. The Federal Digital System (FDsys) provides online access to a database of executive orders beginning with orders issued in 1994. Westlaw provides access with coverage beginning in 1936. Coverage on Lexis begins in 1950.

Presidential proclamations are often more commemorative or ceremonial in nature, often aimed at those outside of government. They may, however, document some presidential statement or announcement of importance. For example, Abraham Lincoln issued the Emancipation Proclamation in 1862 (effective in 1863), which included as one objective the emancipation of slaves.[24] Proclamations, like executive orders, are officially published in the *Federal Register* and are also included in C.F.R. Title 3 codification of presidential documents. In addition to many of the locations where executive orders are also found, proclamations may also be found in annual volumes of *Statutes at Large*.

Several important and convenient alternative sources of presidential documents exist. The *Daily Compilation of Presidential Documents* may be the most convenient and comprehensive source. It includes executive orders, proclamations, signing statements, texts of speeches, transcripts of press conferences, nominations, and other documentation. Prior to January 2009, this publication was a weekly rather than daily compilation and the title reflects that difference. Coverage is available at FDsys beginning with 1993 issues. As usual, commercial coverage extends earlier. HeinOnline begins coverage from 1965 when the series began. Westlaw begins coverage with issues from 2000, and Lexis has a slightly different collection of information in a database, Public Papers of the Presidents, with coverage since 1979.

Another important but less official source is the American Presidency Project,[25] an eleven-year-old project based at the University of California, Santa Barbara. The project provides a wealth of older presidential documentation as well as new documentation. The documentation is accompanied by interesting and relevant analysis.

---

24. Declaring the Objectives of the War Including Emancipation of Slaves in Rebellious States on January 1, 1863, Exec. Procl. 93 (Sept. 22, 1862).

25. *See* http://www.presidency.ucsb.edu.

IV. State Administrative Law

Most states have an administrative law system that mirrors the federal administrative law system. An administrative procedures act typically defines the administrative law system in many states, including the process by which regulations are created and how they are published and made accessible to citizens of that state. Many states have codified their administrative regulations and also publish a periodic register (sometimes called a "bulletin") notifying the public of changes to the regulations. This general similarity between the process for creating and publishing federal and state administrative regulations means that skills learned for researching federal administrative regulations are often transferable to researching administrative regulations at the state level. Also, note that many states use the term "rules" rather than "regulations" when identifying administrative law created by their agencies or other administrative bodies.

Each state will likely provide a unique structure for its regulations, but typically they might be organized by titles. The titles may represent specific state agencies. Therefore, it may be useful to begin researching state regulations by noting which state agency likely created relevant regulations. Another useful strategy would be to begin an administrative regulation research project by examining a state annotated code for possible references to the relevant regulations.

State administrative agency decisions are notoriously difficult to find. State agency websites might be a starting point to locate decisions. A state's centralized administrative office of hearings might also publish administrative agency decisions and may be another place to search for decisions.

Chapter 8

Judicial Systems and Judicial Opinions

I. Introduction

Judicial opinions are written to explain the decisions of courts.[1] Not all judicial opinions are published outside of the court record of a case, but those that are published appear in print reporters and electronically on court databases and on services such as Lexis and Westlaw. *Reporters* are books that publish the opinions of certain courts or opinions on a particular topic. As examples, the *United States Reports* is a reporter in which opinions written by the United States Supreme Court are published; the series *Federal Rules Decisions* publishes cases decided by United States district courts that address issues involving the Federal Rules of Civil Procedure and the Federal Rules of Criminal Procedure. The opinions in reporters are usually published in rough chronological order.

The importance of researching judicial opinions is at least threefold. First, prior judicial decisions will often be considered mandatory or binding authority to a court because those decisions are treated as law within the jurisdiction. The legal doctrine of *stare decisis et quieta non movere* (stare decisis) instructs courts to apply the law as it has been set out by a court of a higher rank to the court rendering the decision, and sometimes by a court of the same rank, in subsequent cases. Thus, in researching judicial opinions, the re-

---

1. Both the judicial opinions and the litigation in which they are written are referred to as "cases."

searcher is seeking statements of law. Second, even judicial opinions that are not considered mandatory authority are often quite persuasive and instructive to a court faced with a set of facts or a legal issue similar to one previously decided by another court. And third, judicial opinions provide explanations and interpretations of the law that can help lawyers craft arguments and draw analogies or distinctions to advise clients on future actions and to argue to the court for a certain outcome.

With the easy access almost all lawyers and their staffs have to judicial opinions from courts of many jurisdictions, both in print and online, no lawyer should consider research complete without researching judicial opinions on an issue. This chapter explains judicial systems and judicial opinions; the next chapter addresses how to research judicial opinions.

II. The Federal Judicial System

A. Federal Courts

The federal judicial system includes trial courts (called district courts), intermediate appellate courts (called circuit courts), and the United States Supreme Court. The federal courts are courts of *limited jurisdiction*, which means that they only have the jurisdiction or power to hear certain cases. In general, cases within the federal courts' jurisdiction are cases that arise under federal law or cases between citizens of different states with a sufficient value or amount of money in controversy.

The federal court system also includes specialty courts, which are trial courts whose jurisdiction is restricted by subject matter. As examples, federal bankruptcy courts operate within almost every district to handle bankruptcy matters; the Court of International Trade hears cases involving international trade and customs issues; and the United States Court of Federal Claims hears certain cases brought against the United States. See Figure 8-1 for a diagram of the federal court system.

Figure 8-1. Diagram of the Federal Court System

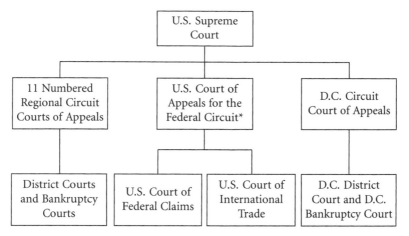

* As explained in the text, the U.S. Court of Appeals for the Federal Circuit also has jurisdiction to hear certain appeals from the U.S. district courts.

The 94 federal district courts serve as the trial courts in the federal system for most cases. Like state trial courts, the federal district courts are the initial forum in which a case filed in the federal system is litigated.[2] Appeals of federal district court decisions are heard by the intermediate appellate court for the particular circuit or region in which the trial court sits. See Table 8-1 for a list of federal appellate courts and the states within their regional jurisdiction. An exception is that the Court of Appeals for the Federal Circuit has jurisdiction to hear appeals from all district courts in cases involving certain issues such as patent law and international trade law, and from all decisions of the Court of International Trade and the Court of Federal Claims.

---

2. As mentioned previously, federal bankruptcy courts operate within almost every district to handle bankruptcy matters, the Court of International Trade hears cases involving international trade and customs issues, and the United States Court of Federal Claims hears certain cases brought against the United States. Tax cases may be brought in the district courts, in the United States Court of Federal Claims, in U.S. bankruptcy courts, or in the United States Tax Court.

Table 8-1. Geographic Jurisdiction of the
United States Courts of Appeals

First Circuit	Maine, Massachusetts, New Hampshire, Puerto Rico, Rhode Island
Second Circuit	Connecticut, New York, Vermont
Third Circuit	Delaware, New Jersey, Pennsylvania, United States Virgin Islands
Fourth Circuit	Maryland, North Carolina, South Carolina, Virginia, West Virginia
Fifth Circuit	Louisiana, Mississippi, Texas
Sixth Circuit	Kentucky, Michigan, Ohio, Tennessee
Seventh Circuit	Illinois, Indiana, Wisconsin
Eighth Circuit	Arkansas, Iowa, Minnesota, Missouri, Nebraska, North Dakota, South Dakota
Ninth Circuit	Alaska, Arizona, California, Guam, Hawaii, Idaho, Montana, Nevada, Northern Mariana Islands, Oregon, Washington
Tenth Circuit	Colorado, Kansas, New Mexico, Oklahoma, Utah, Wyoming
Eleventh Circuit	Alabama, Georgia, Florida
D.C. Circuit	Washington, D.C.

Source: www.uscourts.gov/court_locator.aspx.

When an appeal is filed, a three-judge panel of the circuit court considers the record of the lower court's proceedings and the arguments of the parties. On issues of law, the appellate court may affirm the lower court's decision, modify the decision, remand the case to the trial court for further proceedings, or reverse the lower court's decision to correct the errors that were made. On issues of fact, the appellate court either will affirm the lower court's decision or will reverse the decision and remand the case back to the lower court for a new trial or for further proceedings to correct the errors. The federal appellate court does not have the power to re-examine facts and substitute its own judgment on factual issues.

Once the appellate court renders its decision, litigants wishing to appeal that decision may seek an *en banc* review, which is a review by the entire appellate court,[3] or they may seek review by the United States Supreme Court. The Supreme Court hears only a small fraction of the cases for which review is sought, which means that the appellate court is the court of last resort in most cases.

The Supreme Court is the highest court in the United States. Like the appellate courts, the Supreme Court does not typically sit as a trial court, but it reviews the records from the proceedings of the lower courts. Also like the appellate courts, when reviewing issues of law, the Supreme Court will either affirm the lower courts' decisions or correct any errors that may have been made. Similarly, when reviewing issues of fact, the Supreme Court will either affirm the district court's decision or reverse and remand the case back to the district court for a new trial or for further proceedings to correct the errors found. In addition to hearing appeals from federal courts, the Supreme Court has the discretion to hear appeals from state high courts on issues of federal law.

B. Federal Judges

In the federal court system, district court judges, appellate court judges, and Supreme Court justices are appointed by the president and confirmed by the United States Senate. These judges and justices have a lifetime tenure. Judges of the U.S. Court of Federal Claims are also appointed by the president and confirmed by the Senate. However, they are appointed for fifteen-year terms. Bankruptcy court judges are appointed for fourteen-year terms by the federal appellate court judges. Federal magistrate judges, who assist the district court judges, are appointed by the district court judges to serve eight-year

---

3. The rules of the United States Court of Appeals for the Ninth Circuit allow for *en banc* review by fewer than all of the judges of the Ninth Circuit. 9th Cir. R. 35-3.

terms. Federal magistrate judges handle many pretrial matters in cases filed in the federal district courts, and they may serve as trial judges in civil and non-felony criminal cases with the consent of the parties.

III. Judicial Opinions

A. The Court's Opinion

When courts in the federal system decide cases, they traditionally write opinions that summarize the facts of the cases, summarize the existing law, and explain how they have resolved the cases and why. Courts provide this information, in part, because they know that their opinions serve purposes beyond just explaining to the parties to the dispute how the case has been resolved. A judicial opinion in the United States not only resolves the dispute before the court, but it may also make new law, provide readers with interpretations of the law that will be consulted in future analogous cases, and educate readers on the law.

A typical opinion written by a court in the United States for publication will include some or all of the following, though not necessarily in this order: (1) an introduction to the case in which the court may identify briefly the key facts and issues; (2) a statement of the case in which the court sets out the facts of the case and its procedural history; (3) a statement of the issues the court will address; (4) the applicable law, including enacted law and discussions of previously decided cases; (5) analysis of the case before the court or application of the law to the case before the court; and (6) the disposition of the case, which includes the court's resolution of the case and how that resolution affects any earlier dispositions by lower courts.

The opinion is written by a judge.[4] In a case before a trial court, the one judge who presides will write the opinion, if any. In a case

---

4. The term *judge* is used here to refer to the person who presides over a judicial proceeding. Often, the term *justice* is used to refer to judges who sit on the highest court of a jurisdiction, including the U.S. Supreme Court.

before an appellate court, one of the judges sitting on a panel will be assigned to write the opinion. The opinion expressing the views of a majority of judges sitting on a panel is referred to as a *majority opinion*. A court's majority opinion presents the holding and reasoning of the court and is the only part of a published case that is binding legal authority. A judge who does not join in the majority's opinion might write a concurring opinion or a dissenting opinion; other judges sharing those views can join in the concurring or dissenting opinion. A *concurring opinion* or a concurrence is written by a judge who agrees with the majority of the court's result, but for reasons different from the majority of the court. A *dissenting opinion* is written by a judge who disagrees with the court's result and reasoning. Another possibility is that an appellate court may write a *plurality opinion*, which is an opinion written by the largest number of judges on a court who agree to a result and reasoning, when that number of judges is less than a majority of the court. Finally, a *per curiam opinion* does not have a named author; it is used both for mundane opinions and highly charged opinions.

For example, on a nine-person court like the U.S. Supreme Court, five justices might join in a majority opinion, which is the binding opinion of the court. Three justices hearing the case might join in a concurring opinion in which they state their agreement with the court's ruling, but state their disagreement with the court's reasoning and provide their own analysis. The remaining justice might write a dissenting opinion in which he states his disagreement with the court's ruling and reasoning and provides his preferred result and reasoning. Judges are not required to write concurring or dissenting opinions.

A court's determination of a legal issue that is critical to the court's ultimate decision in a case is the *holding*. Courts often include additional information in their opinions. The term *dicta* refers to statements and discussions included in the court's opinion that are not necessary to support the court's decision. For example, a court may include a discussion of a hypothetical situation and how it might rule on that hypothetical. This discussion may be persuasive authority; it is never considered binding legal authority.

B. Publishers' Research Aids

The opinion issued by a court is called a *slip opinion*. Publishers of reporters often include supplemental material to assist the researcher in reading and understanding opinions and to assist with further research of the issues discussed in opinions. This supplemental material is not authoritative, and it should never be cited.

An example of an opinion of the United States Court of Appeals for the Eleventh Circuit with publisher's research aids is provided in Figure 8-2. (The first two pages of the slip opinion for this case appear in Figure 1-4.) This example is from a West reporter, so West enhancements are shown. The same case on Lexis has different editorial enhancements, though they serve the same purposes. This case may also be obtained from the Eleventh Circuit's website in its original form without publisher's research aids. The original opinion includes the parties' names, the deciding court, the case docket number,[5] the court from which the case was appealed, the representing lawyers' names, the judges' names, the court's opinion, and the court's disposition.

The case in Figure 8-2 is published in West's *Federal Reporter, Third Series*, and includes additional enhancements added by the publisher: a summary of the case (here labeled "Background"), the court's disposition and holding (labeled "Holdings"), and headnotes. These sections are written by the publisher's editorial staff; they do not form part of the court's opinion, and thus they are not authoritative. However, these additions can be helpful to the researcher.

The summary (sometimes called a *synopsis*) is a good place to begin to determine whether to choose the case for further research. The headnotes are also helpful in this task. The *headnotes* are numbered paragraphs in which the publisher has identified key points of law discussed in the opinion. These numbers correspond to bracketed and bolded numbers added by the publisher to the text of the opinion, which identify where the points in the headnotes are discussed by the court. Legal researchers and writers should avoid the

---

5. The *docket number* is the number by which the case is identified by this court.

Figure 8-2. Federal Case with West Topics and Key Numbers

U.S. v. WHITE   **1199**
Cite as 593 F.3d 1199 (11th Cir. 2010)

UNITED STATES of America,
Plaintiff–Appellee,

v.

Ludivic WHITE, Jr., Defendant–
Appellant.

No. 08–16010.

United States Court of Appeals,
Eleventh Circuit.

Jan. 11, 2010.

Background: Defendant was convicted in the United States District Court for the Southern District of Alabama, No. 07-00361-CR-KD, William H. Steele, J., 2008 WL 3211298, of possession of a firearm by a person convicted of a misdemeanor crime of domestic violence. Defendant appealed.

Holdings: The Court of Appeals, Siler, Circuit Judge, sitting by designation, held that:

(1) brief detention of vehicle and patdown search of defendant, an occupant of vehicle, which led to discovery of gun was reasonable under totality of the circumstances, and motion to suppress gun was properly denied;

(2) defendant's prior domestic violence conviction was a predicate offense for purposes of statutory prohibition against possession of firearms by persons convicted of misdemeanor crime of domestic violence; and

(3) Second Amendment was not violated by statutory prohibition against possession of firearms by persons convicted of misdemeanor crime of domestic violence.

Affirmed.

1. Criminal Law ⬅1139, 1158.12

Rulings on motions to suppress evidence constitute mixed questions of law and fact, and on challenges to such rulings Court of Appeals accepts district court's findings of fact, including district court's credibility determinations, unless they are clearly erroneous, but reviews application of law to those facts de novo.

2. Arrest ⬅63.5(4)

Police may stop and briefly detain a person to investigate reasonable suspicion that he is involved in criminal activity, even though probable cause for arrest is lacking. U.S.C.A. Const.Amend. 4.

3. Arrest ⬅63.5(4)

To justify *Terry* stop, officers must have a reasonable, articulable suspicion based on objective facts that the person has engaged in, or is about to engage in criminal activity. U.S.C.A. Const.Amend. 4.

4. Arrest ⬅63.5(8)

In connection with *Terry* stop, officer may conduct pat-down search if he has reason to believe that his own safety or the safety of others is at risk; officer need not be absolutely certain that individual is armed, and issue is whether a reasonably prudent person in the circumstances would be warranted in the belief that his safety or that of others is in danger. U.S.C.A. Const.Amend. 4.

5. Arrest ⬅63.5(4)

"Reasonable suspicion" is determined from the totality of the circumstances, and from the collective knowledge of all the officers involved in the stop. U.S.C.A. Const.Amend. 4.

See publication Words and Phrases for other judicial constructions and definitions.

6. Arrest ⬅63.5(5, 8)

Brief detention of vehicle and its occupants and limited pat-down search which led to discovery of gun on one occupant were reasonable; smell of marijuana alone

---

Source: *Federal Reporter*. Reprinted with permission of West, a Thomson Reuters business.

temptation to cite to or quote the headnotes because they are not part of the court's opinion. Instead, use the headnotes as a guide to the points discussed by the court in the opinion.[6] The headnotes shown in Figure 8-2 also include references to topics and key numbers from the West digest system.

C. Where to Find Judicial Opinions

Judicial opinions are published on court websites, in reporters, and on electronic databases. Regardless of where you find the case, the citation is most often to a print reporter and includes the volume, reporter abbreviation, and first page of the case. The citation for the case in Figure 8-2 is 593 F.3d 1199. Table 8-2 lists the courts within the federal court system, the reporters in which their opinions are reported, the proper citation abbreviations of reporters, and dates of coverage.

U.S. Supreme Court opinions are published in many places, both in print and electronically. In print, these opinions are published in the *United States Reports*; the *Supreme Court Reporter*; the *Supreme Court Reports, Lawyers' Edition*; and *United States Law Week*. The official reporter of these opinions is the *United States Reports*, but its publication is years behind the release dates of the opinions. If a case has not yet appeared in the *United States Reports*, cite to the *Supreme Court Reporter*, if the case appears there.

Electronically, Supreme Court opinions are published on several websites at no charge, including the following:

- The Supreme Court's website, at www.supremecourtus.gov
- FindLaw, at www.findlaw.com/casecode/supreme.html
- Oyez, at www.oyez.org
- Cornell's Legal Information Institute website, at www.law.cornell.edu/supct/index.html
- FedWorld (a program of the Commerce Department), at http://supcourt.ntis.gov.

---

6. Lexis includes as headnotes text that is quoted from the court's opinion. Those quotes, however, are not the opinion of the court and should not be cited. Instead, find the text within the opinion and cite the opinion.

Table 8-2. Reporters for Federal Cases

Court	Reporter	Abbreviation	Coverage
U.S. Supreme Court	*United States Reports* (official reporter)	U.S.	1790 to date
	Supreme Court Reporter	S. Ct.	1790 to date
	United States Supreme Court Reports, Lawyers' Edition	L. Ed. or L. Ed. 2d	1790 to date
	United States Law Week	U.S.L.W.	1982 to date
U.S. Courts of Appeals	*Federal Reporter*	F. or F.2d or F.3d	1880 to date
	*Federal Appendix**	F. App'x	2001 to date
U.S. District Courts	*Federal Supplement*	F. Supp. or F. Supp. 2d	1919 to date
	Federal Rules Decisions (restricted to cases addressing procedural issues)	F.R.D.	1938 to date
U.S. Bankruptcy Courts	*Bankruptcy Reporter*	B.R.	1980 to date
U.S. Court of International Trade	*United States Court of International Trade Reports*	Ct. Int'l Trade	1938 to date
	Federal Supplement	F. Supp. or F. Supp. 2d	1980 to date
U.S. Court of Federal Claims	*Federal Claims Reporter*	Fed. Cl.	1983 to date
	Federal Reporter, Second	F.2d	1960 to 1982

* Cases appearing in *Federal Appendix* are considered "unpublished" and vary in precedential value. Refer to the rules of your circuit before relying on cases published in this reporter.

Supreme Court opinions are included in the Google Scholar database as well as in the less expensive commercial databases discussed in Chapter 2 (see Table 2-3). Opinions are also available on Lexis and Westlaw.

Opinions of the United States Courts of Appeals are published in print in the *Federal Reporter* series, which includes the *Federal Reporter*; *Federal Reporter, Second*; and the *Federal Reporter, Third*. These opinions are also published on the appellate courts' websites, on the FindLaw and Cornell free sites, and on the commercial databases. Some opinions of the courts of appeals are designated by the courts as "not for publication." This designation usually strips the case of some or all of its precedential value, depending on the particular court's rules. The *Federal Appendix* is a reporter in which many of these cases are available. Additionally, some of these "unpublished" cases are available on Lexis and Westlaw.

Some federal district court opinions are published in print in the *Federal Supplement* reporter, which also has a second series, *Federal Supplement, Second*. While many district court opinions are published, they represent a small number of the cases decided by federal district courts. District court opinions addressing issues involving the Federal Rules of Civil Procedure or the Federal Rules of Criminal Procedure may be published in the *Federal Rules Decisions* reporter, instead of the *Federal Supplement*. Electronically, these opinions are published on individual court websites and in both free and commercial services.

Opinions of the U.S. Bankruptcy Courts are published in the *Bankruptcy Reporter* as well as online. Opinions of the U.S. Court of International Trade, which was formerly the U.S. Customs Court, are currently published in the *United States Court of International Trade Reports* and sometimes in the *Federal Supplement* as well. Opinions of the U.S. Court of Federal Claims, formerly the U.S. Claims Court, are currently published in the *Federal Claims Reporter* and sometimes in the *Federal Reporter, Second* for those decisions rendered between 1960 and 1982. Cases from each of these courts are included in Lexis and Westlaw databases and in some less expensive commercial alternatives.

IV. Reading and Analyzing Judicial Opinions

Armed with the knowledge of what components you may find when reading a case, recognize that reading and understanding cases may be very difficult and time-consuming, especially when you are first starting out. Cases, especially older ones, may include "legalese" (e.g., *said, heretofore, aforementioned, hereinafter*) that interrupts a smooth reading and interferes with comprehension. The use of legal terms that are not familiar to you may also slow you down and require you to consult a legal dictionary. Understanding these terms is usually critical to understanding a case, so take the time to gather the necessary information. Courts may refer to parties by name or they may refer to parties by their roles in the case, such as *plaintiff* and *defendant, appellant* and *appellee*, or *petitioner* and *respondent*. Courts may decide cases after a trial on the merits, in which case the courts may reference a jury verdict or a court's *judgment*. However, many times courts dispose of cases before a trial, such as by *summary judgment* or *default judgment*, or based on a post-trial motion, such as a *motion for judgment as a matter of law*. Appellate courts might sit *en banc* or they might hear a case after granting a *writ of mandamus*. Legal dictionaries are available in print and online. Lexis and Westlaw both offer easy-to-use legal dictionaries, allowing you to look up unfamiliar legal terms as you conduct research.

To get the most from your research, you should have a system in place for evaluating and keeping track of cases. This advice applies to all research sources, but it will be discussed here as it applies to cases. After identifying potentially relevant cases as you research, work through these four steps for each case: (1) skim; (2) read; (3) brief; and (4) categorize.

A. Skim

When you first identify a list of potentially relevant cases, skim the syllabus or the synopsis of each case and its headnotes to determine if the case is worth a more careful read. You might also skim the first paragraph of the opinion and the portions of the opinion that correspond to the headnotes relevant to your issue. Consider whether the case has facts that are similar to your facts and whether it addresses legal issues that are similar to the legal issues you are facing. When you are looking at factual similarities, focus on *legally significant facts* (i.e., those facts that were relevant to the court's decision in the case).

In skimming, do not discard cases simply because they do not support your position. A thorough legal evaluation includes a consideration of both favorable and unfavorable decisions, so your analysis should include cases that support your position, if you have a position, as well as cases that do not. Moreover, when arguing to a court, attorneys are bound by ethics rules to present controlling cases on points that are contrary to their positions.

When in doubt about a case's relevance at this stage, either skim through more of the case before making your decision or include the case for a more careful read. Then copy or print those cases that you have identified.[7] Be sure to note on your list of cases the result of your evaluation of each case so that you do not repeat this step unnecessarily.

B. Read

Once you have identified cases by skimming their significant parts, go back to those cases you have chosen for a more careful read. Skim the entire case, but read carefully those parts of the case that are relevant to the issue or issues you are researching. Many researchers highlight or jot down margin notes at this stage, identifying key passages in the case, such as the court's holding, critical facts, or well stated rules.

As you read, make sure you identify and understand the parties and their roles, the legally significant facts, the court's holding and reasoning on the issue or issues in which you are interested, the rules the court is applying to the facts, and any policies or equitable principles that may be driving the court's decision. These are all items you will include in a brief of the case. Additionally, you may begin to categorize cases at this point based on which issue or issues they address. Jot down categories as you read.

---

7. Researchers glean more from the printed page than from scrolling through text on a computer screen because they tend to focus more carefully.

You might determine at this point that a case is not helpful. Record your decision on your list of citations and file the case with other sources that have turned out not to be helpful. Do not discard these sources just yet because as you learn more about the law you might reconsider their value.

C. Brief

Briefing is a way to take notes on a case. Typically, briefs include information organized by categories, which may vary by researcher and by type of project. Students briefing cases for a particular class may use categories recommended by a professor or stressed by a professor through class questioning. For example, briefs for a civil procedure class will typically include a procedural history section documenting the path the case has taken to get to the deciding court, and they will focus on the procedural issues discussed by the court. These briefs will be used to assist the student in discussing the case in class and in preparing for exams. On the other hand, researchers in law practice writing briefs addressing client matters should focus only on the issues pertinent to their research, even if the cases include other issues. Researchers might also limit the information they include to what they will need to analyze the issue and write their analysis.

Some researchers skip the briefing step; they highlight and write more detailed notes on their case copies during the reading step. If you choose this approach, make sure that you fully understand the information that you are highlighting or marking in cases. Briefing requires you to interact more with the information than does simply reading, helping to ensure a better understanding. For example, it is fairly simple to drag a highlighter across words representing the court's holding without carefully reading those words; briefing will prompt you to read the words more carefully to make sense of them before paraphrasing them in a brief. You may quote certain parts of the court's opinion, such as rules or tests applied by the court, but paraphrasing other parts of the opinion usually improves understanding.

For whatever purpose the brief is being written, the following categories will help to organize notes on a case.

Heading. Include the name of the case, the court, the exact date the case was decided, and the citation for the case (volume, reporter abbreviation, and first page). Be sure to include all information necessary for properly citing the case so that you will not have to backtrack to gather information. You may also include a unique word or phrase about the case to identify it to you, such as *child labor case* or *dog bite case.* Once you begin to categorize cases based on the points you want to make or the issues they address, you might also include the category here as well.

Issue or Issues. Identify the question or questions addressed by the court that are pertinent to your research.

Facts. Include legally significant facts and necessary background facts. If emotional facts appear to have played a role in the court's decision, include those as well.

Holding and Reasoning. Identify the court's response to the issue or question presented by the case and the reasons for that response. The reasoning provides the analysis behind the court's holding. Thus, the holding might be, "Yes, the contract was binding," and the reasoning will include the *why* behind that holding.

Rules. Identify the rules, principles, and policies the court applied to the facts to reach its holding. This section may overlap with the reasoning, but unlike the reasoning it will be set forth in more general terms, not tied to the facts of the particular case. It may include a statute, it may include a principle from a prior case, and it may include a public policy or an equitable principle.

Other. Use this section for notes about how this case will work for or against you and why it is significant. For example, identify how this case fits with your other cases, statutes, or regulations. It might modify, change, or further interpret the law. Identify points on which this case is particularly helpful or harmful to the legal issue in your case. The court may have stated the law particularly well or explained the meaning of a term. The case may be a good one to compare to your case on a point or you might need to distinguish the case from yours.

D. Categorize

Although this step is listed fourth, you should always work with an eye toward imposing order on your research and on the final product of the research, whether it is a memorandum, a court brief, a client letter, an oral report, or some other result. Categories for sorting cases might be based on such things as (1) the elements of a tort or a particular cause of action, (2) the requirements for a valid contract, (3) a majority and a minority view in an area of law, or (4) one jurisdiction's law versus another's. Some cases might fall into more than one category. You may decide to outline the project by category and list the cases that are helpful next to each category in the outline. You might decide to physically stack cases by category. You could use a numbering system or a color-coding system to categorize with a number or color associated with specific categories.

All of these suggestions represent ways to keep track of what you have found. When you know what you have and how it fits with the law and with your other sources, you will have a better sense of what you may still need to research and when you have finished researching.

V. State Judicial Systems and Judicial Opinions

In the United States, most state judicial systems are primarily made up of three tiers of courts: (1) trial courts; (2) intermediate appellate courts; and (3) a court of last resort, often called the "supreme" court. State court systems may also include some *inferior courts* or *specialty courts*, which are trial courts whose jurisdiction is restricted by maximum amount of recovery or by subject matter. Examples include municipal courts and probate courts. States with smaller populations may not have an intermediate appellate court.

Opinions of state appellate courts are published in state or regional reporters. Seven regional reporters collectively cover state appellate court opinions in every state: the *Pacific Reporter* (abbreviated P., P.2d, P.3d), the *South Western Reporter* (S.W., S.W.2d, S.W.3d), the *Atlantic*

Reporter (A., A.2d), the *Southern Reporter* (So., So. 2d, So. 3d), the *North Western Reporter* (N.W., N.W.2d), the *North Eastern Reporter* (N.E., N.E.2d), and the *South Eastern Reporter* (S.E., S.E.2d).[8] Most state trial court opinions are not widely published or disseminated because they tend not to create law.

---

8. Note that the regional reporters do not cover the same geographic area as the federal circuits. For example, the *Southern Reporter* publishes cases from Alabama, Florida, Louisiana, and Mississippi, but the states that comprise the Eleventh Circuit are Alabama, Florida, and Georgia. The states in each regional reporter are shown on a West website at http://lawschool.west law.com/federalcourt/nationalreporterpage.asp. The federal circuits are available at a link from the United States Courts website, at http://www.uscourts. gov/Court_Locator.aspx.

Chapter 9

Case Law Research

While the fundamental research process presented in Chapter 1 includes case law research as the fourth step, a researcher is likely to encounter references to judicial opinions throughout the research process. Thus, the researcher often begins case law research with citations in hand. Sometimes secondary sources refer to cases. In other situations, the researcher might know a relevant statute and need to find relevant cases. In still other circumstances, however, the researcher might begin to search for judicial opinions with few leads.

This chapter first addresses situations in which the researcher knows a citation to a relevant statute or case. Then it discusses digests and related tools and strategies for efficiently and effectively locating relevant judicial opinions in print and online.

I. Beginning with a Citation to a Relevant Statute

When you know that enacted law—a particular statute, constitutional provision, or court rule—governs a legal issue, you can easily locate the annotated version of the enacted law, either in print or online. Recall that most researchers use the annotated codes for federal statutes: the U.S.C.A., published by West, and the U.S.C.S., published by LexisNexis. The section of the annotations labeled as Notes of Decisions in the U.S.C.A., and called Interpretive Notes and Decisions in the U.S.C.S., includes brief summaries of the legal issues discussed in cases in which the enacted law has been cited. Each summary pro-

vides a citation to a case.[1] If working in the print version of the enacted law, be sure to check any pocket parts or supplements for the
most recent annotations. Collect the citations to the cases that seem
most relevant. Then locate the cases by using the appropriate volumes
of the reporters, clicking on hyperlinks to the cases, or searching for
the cases online by citation. In addition to retrieving cases electronically by citation using commercial services, you can locate most cases
on free websites. Some of those websites, however, might not use
common case citation forms. For instance, some court websites require searching by date or by docket number.

After identifying relevant cases, use those cases to find additional
cases by one of the methods discussed in the next part.

II. Beginning with a Citation to a Relevant Case

Some research begins with a citation to a relevant case. A supervisor might give you a citation to a relevant case and ask you to fully
research the issue beyond the one case, you might discover the case
in a secondary source or when using annotations to enacted law, or
an adversary might cite the case in a brief. Using the citation, locate
the relevant case in print or online and read it carefully. If it proves
significant, search for additional, relevant cases by (1) retrieving the
cases cited by the court in the relevant case that address the issue; (2)
updating the relevant case using a citator service; and (3) using the
headnotes in the case to identify additional cases through subject
groupings on Lexis or Westlaw, or in West digests. The first of these
methods needs little explanation. When working online, you can
quickly link to each case and skim it. Further, the Table of Authorities (TOA) function of both Shepard's on Lexis and KeyCite on West-

---

1. The headnotes provided in Notes of Decisions in West's U.S.C.A. are
the same headnotes that appear in cases published in West's reporters and
on Westlaw. However, the case abstracts in the U.S.C.S., published by Lexis-
Nexis, are developed specifically for the U.S.C.S. and are not the same as the
headnotes appearing in cases on Lexis.

law provides a convenient list of the cases cited in a particular case. The second and third methods are discussed below.

A. Using a Citator to Find Additional Cases

As introduced in Chapter 1 and explained in depth in Chapter 10, citators allow researchers both to determine whether a particular case is still respected, current law and to expand the research universe. A citator service like Shepard's or KeyCite provides the prior and subsequent history of the case you know is relevant; provides a list of citations to cases, secondary sources, and court documents in which that case has been mentioned; and indicates how these new sources have treated that case.

Those cases listed as "citing references" or "citing decisions" mention specifically the case you know is relevant. This list is a potential source of additional, relevant cases for your research. You may click on the citing cases one at a time to review them, or you may print the citation list and locate the cases in print reporters. Which one of these options you choose may depend on the terms of your contract with the service. If you have free access to a service, accessing the cases online is probably the most efficient use of your time. Moreover, even if you are being charged to use the service, you may save time and money by quickly skimming the cases on the list online to determine which ones are worth a more careful read and which ones are not helpful. Then, you may either print just those cases or read them in reporters.

B. Using Headnotes from a Case to Find Additional Cases

Another way to use a relevant case to find additional cases is to use the headnotes from your relevant case on Lexis or Westlaw or in a print West digest. Headnotes are short paragraphs at the beginning of a case in which the publisher has identified key points of law discussed in the opinion. Editorial staff at LexisNexis and West create these paragraphs; some are taken directly from the text of the case, while others are written by the editorial staff. Both Lexis and Westlaw organize headnotes in subject groupings that you can review in order to find additional cases on point. After finding a case that is relevant to your legal issue, you may use the pertinent headnotes in that case to identify additional cases in which that same point of law has been discussed.

Sometimes the initial case is from the jurisdiction whose law you are researching. At other times, the initial case is from another jurisdiction or the court in that case is applying the law of a different jurisdiction. You may still use the headnotes to locate cases on the same legal point from your jurisdiction because of the interconnectivity of materials within the Lexis and Westlaw research systems.

The Lexis headnotes are linked to the feature "Search by Topic or Headnote," while the Westlaw headnotes are part of the "Key Number System," which is also available in print in West digests. All are discussed below. The West system is introduced first because it is used in West's print reporters, which new researchers often encounter early in their careers.

III. Using the West Digest System to Begin or Continue Research

Using a digest is one of the most efficient ways to locate citations to cases on the issues you are researching. In print, West publishes many digests as multi-volume sets of books. Online, the West Digest System is a powerful research tool that links to cases throughout Westlaw. Both in print and online, the West digest organizes headnotes (summaries of legal issues from cases)[2] by subject and provides citations to the cases. Think of the digest as an especially thorough index to the cases. While reporters publish cases chronologically, digests are organized by topic.

---

2. The headnotes developed for cases in West reporters are also used in West digests, West annotated codes, and the West publication *Words and Phrases*. Some researchers refer to these headnotes as "annotations," though technically that term applies more broadly to include other references in annotated codes.

West publishes many different reporters that together contain judicial opinions from all federal courts and all state appellate courts, and it publishes print digests to provide access to these opinions. (West digests are listed in Table 9-1 later in this chapter.) The same digest information is available on Westlaw.[3] Once aware of the various features of the digest, you will be able to choose the best entry point into the digest system to collect citations to relevant cases. For example, the previous section discussed the best entry point into the digest when you already have a relevant case and are looking for additional cases.

A. Organization by Topics and Key Numbers

West digests are organized initially by *topics*. Currently, there are more than 400 topics into which the legal points made in cases are organized. These topics fit under one of seven main divisions of law identified by West as Persons, Property, Contracts, Torts, Crimes, Remedies, and Government. An alphabetical, numbered list of topics is included in the front of each volume of each West digest and at the Westlaw link "Key Number Digest Outline." The numbers assigned to each topic are not particularly useful to the researcher in the print digest, but the numbers may be used in searches on Westlaw. Topics are broken down into subtopics, which are identified by numbers called *key numbers* because of the figure of a key that precedes them.

The research tool is a topic and key number combination. In print, an example is "Elections 311.1" where the key number "311.1" represents the subtopic "Campaign literature, publicity, or advertising." On Westlaw, the topic "Elections" is represented by the number "144," so the topic and key number combination is "144K311.1." This topic and key number combination is assigned to several headnotes in the landmark case *Citizens United v. Federal Elections Commission* from 2010.[4] In every U.S. jurisdiction, headnotes that discuss the same issues of

---

3. The discussion following focuses on the features of West digests. Digests published by other publishers will have some of these same features.
4. The case citation is 130 S. Ct. 876 (2010).

election campaign literature, publicity, or advertising will be assigned this topic and key number. Thus, once you have a relevant topic and key number, you can find relevant cases in any American jurisdiction.

B. Researching West Digests

1. Researching a West Digest in Print

Volumes of the digest are arranged alphabetically by topic, with the first and last topics included in a particular volume listed on the spine of the volume. Some topics, such as "Criminal Law," span the text of many volumes of the digest. Other topics, such as "Dead Bodies," span only a handful of pages within one volume of the digest.

a. Beginning with a Relevant West Topic

If you already know a relevant West topic for your legal issue, you may go straight to that topic in the digest. At the beginning of each topic, a statement of the "Subjects Included" under the topic and the "Subjects Excluded" is provided, as are cross-references to other related topics. Next, a topical "Analysis" precedes the headnotes. The Analysis is organized like a table of contents, identifying the subtopics and their respective key numbers. The Analysis is essential for researching a topic such as Criminal Law that spans multiple volumes of the digest.

Following this prefatory material are the headnotes, which are arranged within the key number subtopics by court and date. The headnotes include a court abbreviation, the year in which the case was decided, a summary of the legal issue from the case, the case name, and the case citation. The headnotes are the same ones that precede the courts' opinions in West publications of cases, as explained in Section II.B. Thus, the West topic and key number associated with a headnote in a case provide an address where the researcher might find additional cases on that legal issue in the West digest.

As noted earlier, the West system uses the same topics and key numbers across all U.S. jurisdictions. The topics and key numbers are the same in any West reporter or digest. That means you can use the topic and key number from a case in one state to research the same point of law in another state or in the federal court system. For example, assume you are researching federal kidnapping law and learn of a case decided by a Florida state court applying the same point of law. The relevant topic and key number from the Florida case will yield similar results in *West's Federal Practice Digest 4th* as well. West uses the same topics and key numbers in all of its reporters and digests, which makes research information gained from one jurisdiction transferable to other jurisdictions' digests.

See Figure 9-1 for examples of entries from *West's Federal Practice Digest 4th* and the *Florida Digest* under the same topic and key num-

Figure 9-1. Digest Excerpts

Excerpt from *West's Federal Practice Digest 4th*	Excerpt from the *Florida Digest*
1 — Nature and elements of offenses.	1 — Nature and elements of offenses.
U.S.N.J. 1999. Kidnapping is a unitary crime, which, once begun, does not end until the victim is free. 18 U.S.C. (1994 Ed.Supp.III) § 1201. U.S. v. Rodriguez-Moreno, 119 S.Ct. 1239, 526 U.S. 275, 143 L.Ed.2d 388.	**U.S.Fla. 1964.** The Federal Kidnapping Act is not limited to kidnappings for pecuniary gain or for an otherwise illegal purpose. 18 U.S.C.A. § 1201. U.S. v. Healy, 84 S.Ct. 553, 376 U.S. 75, 11 L.Ed.2d 527.
C.A.D.C. 1997. Federal offense of kidnapping did not conclude once victim was abducted and transported across state lines, but rather continued while victim remained held for ransom. 18 U.S.C.A. § 1201(a) U.S. v. Seals, 130 F.3d 451, 327 U.S. App. D.C. 222, rehearing denied, certiorari denied D.C. 222, rehearing denied, certiorari denied 118 S.Ct. 2323, 524 U.S. 928, 141 L.Ed.2d 697, certiorari denied Sweatt v. U.S., 119 S.Ct. 111, 525 U.S. 844, 142 L.Ed.2d. 89.	**C.A.Fla. 1978.** Action of husband in driving his estranged wife across state lines against her will, handcuffed part of the way and at point of a gun part of the way, did not fall outside federal kidnapping statute on ground that statute does not cover kidnapping of a spouse, especially since divorce proceedings had been instituted. 18 U.S.C.A. § 1201(a). U.S. v. Vickers, 578 F.2d 1057, rehearing denied 584 F.2d 389.

Sources: *West's Federal Practice Digest 4th* and *Florida Digest*. Reprinted with permission of West, a Thomson Reuters business.

ber: "Kidnapping 1." Note that the same point of law is being discussed in the different digests.

The headnotes are not the law and should never be cited as authority. Use the headnotes first to identify potentially relevant cases for your review and then to determine which portion of each case is most likely to be on point. If a case proves to be relevant, cite directly to the court's opinion.

West's print digests are updated through the use of pocket parts and supplements and through the inclusion of a list of topics and key numbers in the front of each advance sheet of the West reporters. Thus, each of these sources should be consulted to ensure a thorough digest search.

For example, to research bribery in a case involving allegations that someone bribed a judge, you might begin by looking at the West Outline of the Law, which is found in the front of any West digest volume. Under the heading "Crimes," you would find that "Bribery" is a digest topic. You could then select the digest volume that includes the topic "Bribery" and scan the topic analysis for subtopics and key numbers that appear to be relevant. Next, you would turn to those subtopics and key numbers in both the main volume of the digest and any pocket parts or supplements and read the headnotes to locate citations to potentially relevant cases. After making a list of case citations, locate those cases either in print reporters or online, and read the cases to determine their relevancy. If cases are relevant to your analysis, update them to make sure that they are valid statements of the law.

b. Using the Descriptive-Word Index

Sometimes you will not be familiar with an area of law and will not be able to choose a topic in which to begin research. Sometimes the research issue will seem to fall within several digest topics. Other times the topic will have so many subtopics that you will want more specific direction.

In any of these circumstances, the Descriptive-Word Index is the best entry point into the digest. It is an index that spans several volumes near the end of the digest set. After generating search terms, look for those terms in the Descriptive-Word Index to identify potentially relevant topics and key numbers. The Descriptive-Word Index does not provide case citations. Rather, it directs the researcher to topics and key numbers within the digest. The index is updated with pocket parts and supplements.

For example, to research case law on freedom of the press, you might turn to the Descriptive-Word Index of *West's Federal Practice Digest 4th* rather than turning to a digest topic. Using the Descriptive-Word Index and looking up the term "speech" in the main volume, you will find the following entry: "See heading Speech, freedom of" and "See also heading Press, Freedom of. Generally." Checking the pocket part to that same volume and looking up the term "speech," you will not only be cross-referenced to freedom of the press but also find an entire listing of subheadings and references to topics and key numbers relevant to free speech. You can use other search terms within this entry to focus in more particularly on the issue. (See Figure 9-2 for an excerpt from the Descriptive-Word Index of this section.) Make a list

Figure 9-2. Excerpt from the Descriptive-Word Index

References are to Digest Topics and Key Numbers	SPEECH, FREEDOM OF—Cont'd ACCESS to courts—Cont'd
SPEECH, FREEDOM OF See also heading **PRESS**, FREEDOM of. Generally, **Const Law, 90**	Prisoners, **Const Law 90.1(1.3)**
ABORTION protests, **Const Law 90.1(1)**	ACTIONS to vindicate free speech rights. See heading **CIVIL RIGHTS, ACTIONS**
ABSOLUTE nature of speech in general, **Const law 90(3)**	ADOPT-A-HIGHWAY program, **Const Law 90.1(4)**
ABSTENTION by federal courts, **Fed Cts 53**	ADULT bookstores, **Const Law 90.4(1)**

ACCESS to courts,
  Generally, **Const Law 90.1(3)**
  Press, **Const Law 90.1(3)**
	ADVERTISEMENT,
	  Generally, **Const Law 90.3**
	  Attorneys, **Const Law 90.1(1.5)**
	  Libel and slander, **Const Law 90.1(5)**

Sources: *Federal Practice Digest 4th.* Reprinted with permission of West, a Thomson Reuters business.

of the topics and key numbers that seem most relevant and select those corresponding volumes of the digest to locate case headnotes.

As in using any type of index, if your initial search terms are unsuccessful, brainstorm even further to develop additional terms.

c. Using Words and Phrases

When researchers are looking for the basic definition of a legal term, they typically consult a legal dictionary. Legal dictionaries, like other types of dictionaries, provide general definitions of words and terms. However, when researchers need to identify the definition of a particular legal term according to the courts of a particular jurisdiction or the courts within a particular court system, the Words and Phrases section of the digest is the place to start.

Words and Phrases is a feature of the digest with an alphabetical listing of legal terms. You can browse the list to locate judicial definitions of terms, which are accompanied by the court, date, case name, and case citation of the case in which the term was defined. Also included is the relevant headnote that corresponds to the court's discussion of the term, a listing of relevant topics and key numbers, and identification of any relevant enacted law referenced by the court. See Figure 9-3 for an example of an entry from Words and Phrases.

Figure 9-3. Excerpt from Words and Phrases

SPEECH
U.S.Ark. 1991. Cable television operator is engaged in "speech" under First Amendment, and is, in much of its operation, part of the "press" since it provides to its subscribers news, information, and entertainment. U.S.C.A. Const. Amend. 1.—Leathers v. Medlock, 111 S.Ct. 1438, 499 U.S. 439, 113 L.Ed.2d 494, on remand Medlock v. Pledger, 808 S.W.2d 785, 305 Ark. 610, opinion supplemented 809 S.W.2d 822, 306 Ark. 178, on remand 842 S.W.2d 428, 311 Ark. 175, certiorari denied 113 S.Ct. 2929, 508 U.S. 960, 124 L.Ed.2d 680.— Const Law 90.1 (9).

Source: *West's Federal Practice Digest 4th.* Reprinted with permission of West, a Thomson Reuters business.

The cases identified using Words and Phrases may also be identified through a search using the Descriptive-Word Index. However, Words and Phrases specifically focuses the researcher only on those cases in which the particular term has been interpreted and defined, while the Descriptive-Word Index will include a broader set of cases.

d. Using the Table of Cases

The Table of Cases is a helpful tool to locate a case when you have learned the name of one or both of the parties to a case, but do not have a citation to the case. It is another entry point into the digest because each case entry includes a list of topics and key numbers for the legal issues raised in the case.

The Table of Cases volumes are located near the end of the digest set. The Table of Cases is arranged alphabetically, with primary plaintiff's and primary defendant's names appearing together in one table. In addition to the parties' names and the relevant topics and key numbers, each entry includes an abbreviation for the deciding court and a citation to the case.

2. Researching West's Digest System Online

Westlaw provides the West Digest System online. When viewing a relevant case on Westlaw, clicking on the topic and key number link for a particularly useful headnote will connect you to a list of other cases with the same topic and key number. When you do not have a relevant case at this stage of your research, follow one of the approaches below.

From the main screen of Westlaw, select the "Key Numbers" link. From this screen, select your jurisdiction and enter search terms to search the digest for relevant topics and key numbers, similar to searching the Descriptive-Word Index in print. This search will identify a list of topics and key numbers under which your search terms are found. From this list, choose the entries that seem most relevant, then click "Search." You will retrieve a listing of headnotes, just as you would get if you were looking in the print version of the digest under those topics and key numbers. Note that online the topic is represented as a number, rather than a word or phrase (e.g., the topic "Products Liability" is assigned 313A), so a topic and key number tool online consists of two numbers separated by a "k" (e.g., 313Ak147 represents the topic "Products Liability" and the key number "Proximate Cause"). Each headnote is assigned a topic and key number, as in print, and will include the point of law discussed, the case citation, and a link to the case.

Alternatively, from the Key Numbers screen, click on "West Key Number Digest Outline" to view a listing of all West digest topics and key numbers. Once you reach this screen, you may either enter the topic number and key number separated by a "k" or you may check the boxes preceding those topics and key numbers in which you wish to search. Then, type in your search terms and run your search. Your search will yield a list of headnotes similar to the description above.

Another possibility is to select "KeySearch" at the Key Numbers screen, which will identify 30 broad topics and many subtopics to which you can direct your search. Once you choose your topics and subtopics, you will be prompted to choose a jurisdiction and enter search terms. You will retrieve a list of cases with citation information and links to the cases, as well as the part of the case in which your search terms are found.

IV. Using the Lexis Topic and Headnote System to Begin or Continue Research

Lexis has developed its own system of topics and headnotes, which allows you to focus research on particular topics and restrict research to relevant headnotes. Note that these topics and headnotes do not correspond directly to the topics and headnotes in West publications or to the case abstracts that LexisNexis publishes in the U.S.C.S.

To begin research, use the feature "Search by Topic or Headnote." You will then have the option of selecting "Find Legal Topic" or "Explore Legal Topics." The first option prompts you to enter a description of your legal issue, after which the system will select topics that might be relevant to your issue. Review the options and select the most relevant, after which you will be given a search screen. The second option allows you to browse topics on your own and select those topics that are most relevant. Once you have chosen topics, you will be given a search screen.

At the search screen, you may select the sources to search and the jurisdiction and run a terms and connectors or natural language search. You also have another option. You may choose a jurisdiction and run a search to retrieve all headnotes classified to the topic or cases that discuss the topic. With both of these options, you may restrict your search by date.

To continue research on Lexis when you have a relevant case, skim the Lexis headnotes at the beginning of the case. When you find a relevant headnote, click "More Like This Headnote."

V. Digest Coverage

An important part of digest research is deciding which sources to search. In online digest searches, you will be prompted to select a jurisdiction. For example, when using KeySearch, you could search a subject for all federal cases, just cases within one circuit, or cases in an individual state. A variety of alternatives are available.

Similarly, when using a print digest, you must consider digest coverage when choosing in which digest to research so that your research will yield relevant cases. The coverage of a digest is usually based on geography, court or court system, or subject matter. See Table 9-1 for a listing of West digests and their coverage.

Most print digests are updated by pocket parts. In addition, some digests, like *West's Federal Practice Digest* series, are also updated by the publication of new editions in the series. Each edition covers a set period of years. The newest edition is updated by pocket parts.

A. Digests for Court Systems or Particular Courts

Some digests include references only to cases decided by the courts within a particular court system. On issues of federal law, begin with

Table 9-1. West Digests

Type of Digest	West Digests and Coverage
State court cases	Each state publishes its own digest with the exceptions of Delaware, Nevada, North Dakota, South Dakota, Utah, Virginia, and West Virginia. North and South Dakota cases are included in the *Dakota Digest*, and Virginia and West Virginia cases are included in the *Virginia and West Virginia Digest*. For research of Delaware, Nevada, and Utah cases, see the regional digests.
Regional state cases	*Atlantic Digest* (states included: Connecticut, Delaware, District of Columbia, Maine, Maryland, New Hampshire, New Jersey, Pennsylvania, Rhode Island, and Vermont)
	North Western Digest (states included: Iowa, Michigan, Minnesota, Nebraska, North Dakota, South Dakota, and Wisconsin)
	Pacific Digest (states included: Alaska, Arizona, California, Colorado, Hawaii, Idaho, Kansas, Montana, Nevada, New Mexico, Oklahoma, Oregon, Utah, Washington, and Wyoming)
	South Eastern Digest (states included: Georgia, North Carolina, South Carolina, Virginia, and West Virginia)
Federal cases (from lower federal courts and the U.S. Supreme Court)	*West's Federal Digests* (cases prior to 1939)
	West's Modern Federal Practice Digest (1939–1961)
	West's Federal Practice Digest 2d (1961–1975)
	West's Federal Practice Digest 3d (1975–1987)
	West's Federal Practice Digest 4th (1984–present)
U.S. Supreme Court cases	*United States Supreme Court Digest* (1754–present)
Cases from these specific federal courts	*West's Military Justice Digest*
	West's Bankruptcy Digest
	West's Federal Claims Digest
	West's Veterans' Appeals Digest
Federal and state cases (known as the American Digest System)	*Century Digests* (1658–1896)
	First-Eleventh Decennial Digest (1897–2004)
	General Digests 11th (2004–present)
Subject-specific cases	*West's Education Law Digest*
	West's Federal Sentencing Guidelines Digest
	West's Texas Family Law Digest

a digest that specifically includes citations to cases from the federal court system, the *West's Federal Practice Digest* series. Once you identify topics and key numbers, you can focus on cases decided by the courts within your circuit. This series includes five sets of digests covering cases decided over different periods of time. *West's Federal Practice Digest 4th* covers cases decided by federal courts from 1984 to the present. On most issues, researchers use this most current digest to research federal court issues because its coverage spans the last thirty-plus years.[5]

An example of a digest that includes headnotes to cases decided by a particular court is the *United States Supreme Court Digest*. This digest includes headnotes to cases decided by the U.S. Supreme Court. This type of digest is helpful in those circumstances when the researcher's focus is limited to the rulings of a particular court, which will probably not be often for most researchers. Most researchers interested in finding citations to Supreme Court cases will also be interested in cases decided by other federal courts, and *West's Federal Practice Digest 4th* includes citations to all of these cases.

B. Subject Matter Digests

Digests are also published that include references to cases decided on particular topics. Examples of these digests include *West's Bankruptcy Digest* and *West's Military Justice Digest*. Additionally, other specialized reporters such as *American Maritime Cases* and *Environment Reporter Cases* publish indexes or digests periodically or as an index to the volume in which the cases are reported. The latter two digests are not West publications.

---

5. *West's Federal Practice Digest 3d* covers cases decided by federal courts from 1975 through 1987. *West's Federal Practice Digest 2d* covers cases decided by federal courts from 1961 through 1975. The *Modern Federal Practice Digest* covers cases decided by federal courts from 1940 through 1960. The *Federal Digest* covers cases decided by federal courts through 1939. You will probably turn to these earlier editions of the digest only when you are conducting historical research or when you are focusing on an issue that has not been litigated often.

These subject matter digests are especially helpful for researching in a discrete area of law in which the number of cases decided is limited. When courts face issues that are not frequently litigated, they are usually interested not only in cases that are mandatory authority, but also in persuasive cases that provide guidance on the law and how to apply it. These digests are also helpful for researching trends across jurisdictions on particular legal issues.

C. Geographically Based Digests

Some digests include references to cases decided by the courts within a particular state or region. These digests are best for researching most state law issues. Choose the digest that will include citations to cases decided by courts interpreting the law applicable to the research issue. These cases will most directly assist you in identifying the law and understanding how it has been interpreted within the relevant jurisdiction.

State-specific digests generally include headnotes to all cases reported by federal and state courts sitting within the state, as well as to U.S. Courts of Appeals and U.S. Supreme Court opinions in cases first brought in that state. A state digest is available for each state except Delaware, Nevada, and Utah. In contrast, a digest with regional coverage includes annotations to all state court cases—but not federal cases—reported by courts in the specific region. Current regional digests are available for cases reported in the *Atlantic Reporter*, the *North Western Reporter*, the *Pacific Reporter*, and the *South Eastern Reporter*.

D. All-Inclusive Digests

The American Digest System is West's comprehensive digesting of all cases decided in the United States that are reported in the West National Reporter System. Included within this system are the *Century Digest*, which includes cases decided between 1658 and 1896, and the *Decennial Digests*, which include cases from the subsequent ten-year periods of time.[6] The *Decennial Digests* use the same topics and key numbers as the other West digests, and cases are arranged within key numbers by jurisdiction and date. Because volumes cover specific time periods, researchers must consult multiple volumes of the digest. Between publications, the *General Digest* is published to update the *Decennial Digest*.

Because of their comprehensive coverage of jurisdictions and the way they are updated, these digests are not the best place to start most research projects. These digests would be helpful for surveying American law for a limited time period, trying to identify trends in American law over a limited time period, and researching an issue where the case law is thin. Additionally, these digests may be used to locate persuasive authority from multiple jurisdictions on an issue that has not been litigated in the relevant jurisdiction. Otherwise, you should choose to research in a more limited-coverage digest.

VI. Researching Cases Online

Cases are available online on both commercial and free sites. This part explains researching cases online on Lexis and Westlaw. It also includes a section on Google Scholar.

A. General Case Research

1. Lexis and Westlaw

Similar to selecting an index or digest in which to conduct research, you currently need to select a database in which to conduct case research on Lexis or Westlaw. (Lexis Advance and WestlawNext do not require selection of a database to begin searching.) Lexis and

---

6. From 1976 through 1996, the *Decennial Digests* were published in two parts, one for each five-year period of the decade. The *Eleventh Decennial Digest* was published in three parts, one for 1996–2001, one for 2001–2004, and one for 2004–2007.

Westlaw sometimes combine federal and state cases from geographic areas into one database.

Once you select a database, you will input a query based on your search terms that will identify relevant cases. Your query might use terms and connectors or natural language, as explained in Chapter 2. Both services allow you to search all parts of the case, including material added by publishers and concurring and dissenting opinions, or to restrict your search only to certain parts of the case, called fields or segments.

The search result will be a list of cases retrieved with the relevant text showing the search terms. You can choose to see the full text of the cases online or see a list of the cases with citations. You will also have easy access to Shepardizing or KeyCiting cases retrieved, and the cases retrieved will include links to most of the sources cited within those cases.

2. Google Scholar

Google Scholar is a relatively new search engine in the legal research arena. Just since late 2009 have researchers been able to access reported cases from United States courts using this search engine. Its database includes reported opinions from federal courts from 1924 forward and reported opinions from state appellate courts from 1950 forward. Using the "Advanced Scholar Search" feature, you can enter search terms for full-text searching of judicial opinions. You can research all reported cases in the database or restrict the search to cases from federal courts, state courts, or a particular state or states' courts.

The search produces a list of cases with brief views of the terms found in the cases that can be accessed by clicking on the case name. After choosing a case, you can read, save, and print the case. You also have an option to click on a "How cited" tab, which reveals a list of cases in the database that have cited to the chosen case. (This feature is similar to Shepard's and KeyCite, though it contains fewer citing sources.) The cases listed in How cited may be accessed by clicking on their names in the list.

Novice researchers should not rely exclusively on this search engine just yet if they have access to print research tools or to commercial services because (1) its coverage is limited by date, (2) it is not yet considered a proven and reliable research resource in legal circles, and (3) it lacks some of the helpful research tools other publishers provide, such as headnotes and updating using the reputable services, Shepard's and KeyCite. On the other hand, Google Scholar is an alternative to commercial services in that it allows researchers to quickly and inexpensively locate cases on legal issues.

B. Online Topic Searching

1. Westlaw Search by Topical Practice Area

In addition to the West digest features available on Westlaw discussed in Section III.B.2. of this chapter, Westlaw allows you to restrict your search by broad topic area. These searches are run in databases that are essentially topical libraries aggregated by Westlaw. To search for cases in a database that focuses on a broad topic area, click on "Topical Practice Areas" from the Westlaw main page or directory. Identify the appropriate topic area for your search, and then select a database that includes cases from the jurisdiction whose law you are searching. Note that the Topical Practice Areas feature allows you to search legal sources other than cases, as well.

2. Lexis Search by Area of Law

Lexis allows you to search a source that collects documents relevant to a broad topic area or to search by more specific topics and headnotes, similar to the Westlaw system just described. To search for cases in a source that focuses on a broad topic area, click on "Area of Law — By Topic" on the main screen of the Lexis research system. Identify the appropriate topic for your search, and then select a source that includes cases from the relevant jurisdiction.

For example, to find pleadings on subprime lending, you could begin with the topic "Bankruptcy." Under "Emerging Issues," click "Subprime Lending." Then select "Federal and State Subprime Lending Pleadings Combined." From the search screen, enter either a terms and connectors or a natural language search. As on Westlaw, this type of topical search can also be run to locate documents in addition to cases.

C. Searching with Fields and Segments

As explained in Chapter 2, searching specific parts of a document may produce more focused results. Field searching on Westlaw allows you to tailor your search using some of the features of the West digest system. The fields are the parts of the case in which you want the research system to search. After choosing to search on Westlaw in a particular database, you have the option of using either terms and connectors or natural language. You then have the option of restricting the dates of cases in your results. Following the date restrictors, you will see the field search option, which has a pull-down menu. To restrict your search to some of the features of the cases, choose from among the following fields: words and phrases, topics, headnotes, or digest. You may also select the shortcut to find a case by party name if you have that information available about a particular case or you may search the "title" field for a party's name.

Just as Westlaw provides field searching, Lexis allows you to customize searches using segments. Segments are parts of the case or its editorial enhancements—including names of parties, counsel, judges, headnotes, syllabus—in which the system searches. When you choose a database and run a terms and connectors search or a natural language search, the segment possibilities appear in a pull-down menu. You also have the option of restricting the dates of cases the search retrieves.

Chapter 10

Citators

I. Introduction

A *citator* is a research tool that lists subsequent citations to a particular authority. For example, looking up the case *Citizens United v. Federal Election Commission*[1] in a citator, a researcher would find a long list of the cases, administrative decisions, secondary sources, court documents, and other materials that have cited that case since it was decided in 2010. Citator lists serve two fundamental functions in the legal research process: (1) they allow the researcher to ensure that legal authorities like cases, statutes, and regulations are still valid and (2) they expand the research universe. This chapter explains how to use citators for both functions. Together these functions are called "updating." Some attorneys call the process "Shepardizing" because the print series *Shepard's Citations* were the first citators.[2]

Turning to the first function, citators allow a researcher to determine whether an authority is still valid. For a case, a citator will show whether later cases reversed, overruled, questioned, or distinguished the case. For a statute, a citator will show whether a case has held the statute unconstitutional or whether subsequent legislation has repealed or amended the statute. In each instance, the researcher is determining whether an authority is still "good law." Validation is almost always a time-consuming activity, primarily because of the number of sources

---

1. 130 S. Ct. 876 (2010).
2. *Shepard's Citations* are still available in print, but they are outdated almost before they are published and each year fewer libraries maintain current print volumes. To use a print citator, seek the assistance of a reference librarian or follow the guidance at the front of each volume.

that must be read and analyzed. But thorough legal research requires validation of each authority that will be used in a legal argument.

As for the second function, citators are invaluable research tools because they expand the research universe. After identifying a case as relevant to your research, you can use a citator to find cases, secondary sources, and other documents that have cited that case. Those cases, secondary sources, and other documents may be relevant to your research because they cited a case that you already know is relevant. Similarly, once you know a statute is important to your research, you can use a citator to list the cases that have applied or interpreted that statute; some of those cases are likely to be relevant to your research as well.

Online citators are now used almost exclusively. This chapter will focus on the most developed and user-friendly citators: "Shepard's" on Lexis and "KeyCite" on Westlaw. Other online citators exist, including "V.Cite" on VersusLaw, "How cited" on Google Scholar, "CASEcheck" on Casemaker, "Authority Check" on Fastcase, "BCite" on Bloomberg Law, and "GlobalCite" on Loislaw.

II. Citator Basics

Understanding the process of using a citator requires familiarity with two basic terms: the cited source and the citing sources. The authority you are validating or using as a springboard to further research, in the following example the *Citizens United* case, is the *cited source*. The cases, secondary sources, and other documents listed in a citator that refer to that authority are *citing sources*, although they are sometimes referred to as *citing references* or *citing decisions*. Although the terminology is very similar, for each citator search there is only one cited source while there may be many citing sources.

Using citators to compile a list of citations is quite easy. For some services, you can link to a citator list while viewing a document. Some services allow you to type a citation in a box and run a citator search. Table 10-1 provides an outline for using a citator.

One complexity to Shepard's on Lexis and KeyCite on Westlaw is that they offer two lists of citing sources: a shorter list is available just

Table 10-1. Outline for Using a Citator

1. Access the desired citator list.
2. Analyze the analytical symbols provided by the citator.
3. Consider limiting the list of citing references by jurisdiction, headnote, date, or other function.
4. Prioritize and read the citing sources.
   a. To validate, analyze the impact, if any, these sources have on the cited source.
   b. To expand research, decide whether the citing sources provide clearer explanations of the law, analyze facts that are closer to your client's, or otherwise impact your issue in significant ways.

for validating the cited source and a more complete list expands research by referring to many subsequent authorities. The researcher must understand the differences between the two lists and know when to use each. Another reason using citators on Lexis and Westlaw is complex is that those services use a variety of symbols and notations to indicate the relationship between the cited source and the citing references, so understanding the search results can be difficult and tedious.

The coverage of sources in Shepard's and KeyCite is extensive but not identical. Both Shepard's and KeyCite include as cited sources federal cases, federal statutes, federal administrative regulations, and patents. Increasingly, Shepard's and KeyCite include state primary law and secondary sources.

III. Shepard's on Lexis

A. Access the Citator List

You may access Shepard's from two points on Lexis. When viewing a relevant document, you can access the citator simply by clicking on the "Shepardize" link. Otherwise, click on the "Shepard's" tab and type the citation into the box. (If you need help with the format used by Shepard's, click on the "Citation Formats" link.) To determine which

Table 10-2. Selected Symbols for Shepard's

Shepard's Symbol	Meaning for Cases	Meaning for Statutes
Red stop sign	Negative treatment; the case may no longer be good law	Negative treatment; the statute may no longer be good law
Red exclamation point	—	Negative case treatment
Orange "Q"	Validity questioned by citing references	Validity questioned by citing references
Yellow triangle	Possible negative treatment	Possible negative treatment
Green diamond	Positive treatment	Positive treatment
Blue "A"	Citing sources are available with analysis indicated	Citing sources are available with analysis indicated
Blue "I"	Citing sources are available	Citing sources are available

list of citing sources you retrieve, select one of the radio buttons. "Shepard's for Validation" will provide a limited list of citing sources, intended to show only whether your case is still good law. To obtain a full list of citing sources, click on "Shepard's for Research." One benefit of Shepard's is that the full list of citing sources is set as the default, both from the "Shepardize" link and from the "Shepard's" tab.

B. Analyze the Citator Symbols

The top of the results page has a symbol that indicates Shepard's opinion of the effect subsequent authorities have had on the validity of your cited source. While researchers should never rely on the symbols without reading the citing sources for themselves, the symbols do provide a quick reference. To learn what a particular symbol means, rest your cursor over the symbol. For a full list of symbols and their meanings, scroll down to the legend provided at the bottom of any Shepard's result screen. A partial list of symbols is provided in Table 10-2.

The Shepard's screen on Lexis begins with a summary of results. Clicking on an underlined term will allow you to skip through the search results to each citing source that treats your case in that way.[3] To go to the cases that distinguish your authority, for example, click on "Distinguished" in the summary box. Figure 10-1 shows the first screen of the *Citizens United* case, using Shepard's for Research. Citing sources are arranged first by jurisdiction (federal cases by circuit and then state cases); within each jurisdiction, cases are listed in reverse chronological order. Secondary sources appear after cases.

Lexis precedes each citing source with bold terms that explain how that source treated the cited authority, as shown in Figure 10-2. Examples include "Followed by," "Explained by," and "Cited by." Clicking the hyperlinked name of the citing source will take you to that source, as will clicking one of the pinpoint pages listed below the case name.

Each citing source is shown with its own Shepard's symbol at the end of the source's citation in the Shepard's results list. (If you do not see these symbols, click on "Display Options" and select "Citing Ref. Signals.") Clicking on the Shepard's symbol at the end of the source's citation will take you to the Shepard's list for that case. Remember not to confuse these symbols with the symbol for the case you are validating. In Figure 10-2, the citing decision *Republican National Committee v. FEC* treats *Citizens United* in four different ways including distinguishing it. As a separate matter, *Republican National Committee v. FEC* has received no negative treatment from its own citing sources, as shown by the blue "A" at the end of the citation. It would be a mistake to interpret the blue "A" next to *Republican National Committee v. FEC* as commenting on the relationship between it and *Citizens United*.

C. Limit the Search Results

Sometimes Shepard's will list more citing sources than you can possibly read. In other instances, Shepard's will list more citing sources than are relevant to your work, perhaps because they are cases

---

3. Some browsers do not support this function. An alternative is to use the "find" function on your computer.

Figure 10-1. Shepard's for Research

View: KWIC | Full	⇓ 1 - 50 of 807 Total Cites ⇑	
Display Options ▶	Save As *Shepard's* Alert@ | Unrestricted | All Neg | All Pos |	
	FOCUS™- Restrict By	
	Shepard's® △ **Citizens United v. FEC,** 130 S. Ct. 876 (TOA)	

Signal: △ Caution: Possible negative treatment
Trail: **Unrestricted**

Citizens United v. FEC, 130 S. Ct. 876, 175 L. Ed. 2d 753, 2010 U.S. LEXIS 766, 22 Fla. L. Weekly Fed. S 73, 187 L.R.R.M. (BNA) 2961, 159 Lab. Cas. (CCH) P10166 (U.S. 2010)

SHEPARD'S SUMMARY ⊟ HIDE

Unrestricted *Shepard's* Summary

No subsequent appellate history. Prior history available.
Citing References:

△ Cautionary Analyses:	**Distinguished (15)**
Positive Analyses:	Followed (41), Concurring Opinion (18)
Neutral Analyses:	Dissenting Op. (19), Explained (20)
Other Sources:	Law Reviews (390), Statutes (6), Treatises (19), Annotations (1), Other Citations (4), Court Documents (204)
LexisNexis Headnotes:	HN1 (6), HN2 (16), HN3 (15), HN4 (11), HN5 (18), HN6 (1), HN7 (3), HN8 (17), HN9 (43), HN10 (27), HN11 (6), HN12 (1), HN13 (1), HN14 (2), HN16 (16), HN17 (27), HN18 (3), HN19 (4), HN21 (1), HN23 (62), HN24 (16), HN25

Figure 10-2. Citing Decisions on Shepard's

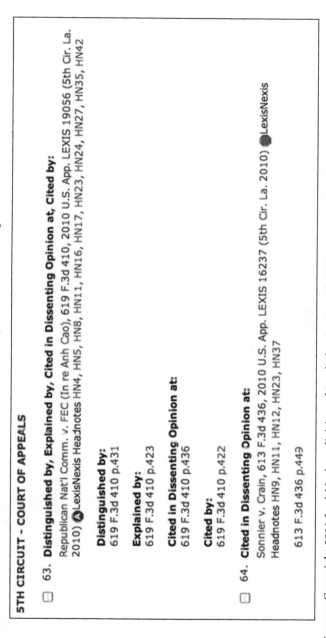

5TH CIRCUIT – COURT OF APPEALS

☐ 63. **Distinguished by, Explained by, Cited in Dissenting Opinion at, Cited by:**

Republican Nat'l Comm. v. FEC (In re Anh Cao), 619 F.3d 410, 2010 U.S. App. LEXIS 19056 (5th Cir. La. 2010) Ⓐ LexisNexis Headnotes HN4, HN5, HN8, HN11, HN16, HN17, HN23, HN24, HN27, HN35, HN42

    Distinguished by:
    619 F.3d 410 p.431

    Explained by:
    619 F.3d 410 p.423

    Cited in Dissenting Opinion at:
    619 F.3d 410 p.436

    Cited by:
    619 F.3d 410 p.422

☐ 64. **Cited in Dissenting Opinion at:**

Sonnier v. Crain, 613 F.3d 436, 2010 U.S. App. LEXIS 16237 (5th Cir. La. 2010) ● LexisNexis Headnotes HN9, HN11, HN12, HN23, HN37

    613 F.3d 436 p.449

Figure 10-3. Shepard's Restrictions

FOCUS™ - Restrict By: △ **130 S. Ct. 876**   Help

[Apply] [Cancel]

Clear Form

No subsequent appellate history. Prior history available.

Type: Analysis, Focus, Jurisdictions, Headnotes, Date

Restrict By: **** No Jurisdiction, Analyses or Headnote restrictions are currently set ****

Analysis available in FULL: Select All   Clear All

Negative:
☐ Distinguished (15)

Positive:
☐ Followed (41)

Other: Select All   Clear All
☐ Concurring   ☐ Dissenting Op.   ☐ Explained (20)
   Opinion (18)   (19)

FOCUS Terms:
Return a list of citations to cases that contain your terms.

FOCUS HINT: The FOCUS search will only identify citing references that have corresponding documents available in the LexisNexis® service. The FOCUS feature is not available if your current results contain more than 2000 documents.

Jurisdictions available in FULL: Select All   Clear All

Federal: Select All   Clear All
☐ U.S. Supreme Court (7)   ☐ 4th Circuit (21)   ☐ 8th Circuit (12)   ☐ D.C. Circuit (8)
☐ 1st Circuit (8)   ☐ 5th Circuit (11)   ☐ 9th Circuit (20)   ☐ Admin. & Agency Dec. (1)
☐ 2nd Circuit (12)   ☐ 6th Circuit (9)   ☐ 10th Circuit (8)   ☐ Ct. App. Vet. Claims (1)
☐ 3rd Circuit (5)   ☐ 7th Circuit (7)   ☐ 11th Circuit (5)

State: Select All   Clear All

decided outside your jurisdiction or because they discuss points of law that are not at issue in your work. Use "FOCUS—Restrict By" to filter your citator results by treatment analysis (negative, positive, or other), jurisdiction, headnotes, dates, and terms. Figure 10-3 shows some of the restriction options available for *Citizens United*.

D. Read and Analyze the Citing Sources

The most important part of using a citator is reading the citing sources. Clicking on the pinpoint link for a citing source will take you to the point in that source's text where your case is cited, making it easy to determine whether the source is relevant to your research. In validation, you must read the citing sources carefully enough to decide the impact they have on your case. In expanding your research, reading the citing sources will tell you whether they add to your understanding and analysis of the issue.

IV. KeyCite on Westlaw

A. Access the Citator List

KeyCite can be accessed in four different ways: through a "KeyCite" link at the top of a search screen; by typing a citation into the KeyCite box in the left frame; and from any source that displays a KeyCite symbol, either by clicking on the symbol in the right frame or by selecting "Full History" or "Citing References" in the left frame. This section begins with the KeyCite link because it provides essential information, including an overview of analysis symbols used for updating, a list of publications that can be updated using KeyCite, and tips on a number of KeyCite topics.

The KeyCite link connects to a page that is divided into left and right frames. The right frame explains the symbols used to show the relationship between the citing references and the cited source (i.e., the authority being updated). In the left frame is a box for typing in the citation. If you do not know the citation format or whether a particular publication is included in KeyCite, click on the "Publications List" link in the left frame.

After you enter the citation and click "Go," a list of "Full History" sources will appear in the right frame. (This list is similar to "Shepard's for Validation." Take care in using KeyCite, as this default is not the full list of citing references.) The first sources listed show the litigation process involving your case, i.e., the "Direct History" of the case.[4] This list of sources will show, for example, whether the case was affirmed on appeal or whether it reversed and remanded a lower court decision. Next in Full History, KeyCite lists "Negative Citing References." These are sources that KeyCite has identified as providing important negative treatment of your case. If you have limited time to update the case, you should at least skim the sources appearing under Full History. To open a separate window showing the actual text of a citing source, click on the number immediately preceding that source's entry in the history list. Similarly, to pull up the KeyCite report for a citing source, click on the treatment symbol (e.g., a yellow flag) preceding that source's entry in the list.

To obtain a more comprehensive list of citing sources — the list that is used for expanding research — look in the left frame of the KeyCite screen and click on "Citing References." (This list is shown in Figure 10-4; it is analogous to "Shepard's for Research.") The sources are arranged by type and depth of treatment. The Citing References page first lists those citing sources that have treated your case negatively. These negative sources are listed by treatment (e.g., "Declined to Extend by" and "Distinguished by") in reverse chronological order. The non-negative citing sources come next, organized according to Depth of Treatment stars, then jurisdiction, and then date of decision. A source that quotes your case will be noted with quotation marks.

---

4. "Direct History (Graphical Display)" provides that information in flowchart format.

Figure 10-4. Citing References on KeyCite

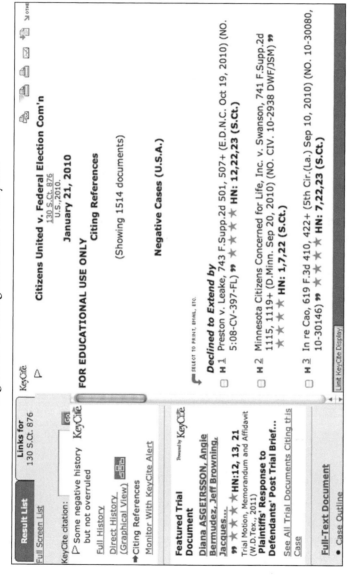

Source: Westlaw. Reprinted with permission of West, a Thomson Reuters business.

B. Analyze the Citator Symbols

KeyCite assigns a symbol to each authority that can be updated. The symbol for the cited source is given both in the left frame and at the top-left of the right frame. This symbol is intended as a quick reference to help you determine whether the cited source is still good law. A summary of these symbols is provided in Table 10-3. Remember that the symbols are only preliminary indicators and do not relieve you of the burden of reading significant citing references and determining for yourself the continued validity of your cited source.

Additional symbols precede each citing source. These symbols show the KeyCite assessment of the strength of each citing source, as opposed to that of the cited case. If a citing source has a negative symbol, its impact on your case may be minimal; because other sources disagree with that source, its overall authoritative value is decreased. Again, do not confuse the KeyCite symbol showing how a citing source has been treated by later authorities with the terms showing how a citing source has treated the authority you are checking.

C. Limit the Search Results

If your case has been cited numerous times, use "Limit KeyCite Display" to focus the results. For *Citizens United*, you can limit KeyCite by type of document (cases, secondary sources, administrative materials, and court documents), jurisdiction, relevant headnotes, and date. You can also restrict the search to documents containing keywords by using the "Locate" feature.

D. Read and Analyze the Citing Sources

The most important part of updating is reading the history cases and citing references. While KeyCite alerts researchers to possible problems through colored flags and treatment stars, only you can decide the impact of an authority on the case you want to use in your analysis. Reading these authorities is easy online. Clicking on an authority in the KeyCite list will take you to the point in the corresponding document

Table 10-3. Selected Symbols for KeyCite

KeyCite Symbol	Meaning for Cases	Meaning for Statutes
Red flag	Negative treatment; the case is no longer good law for at least one legal point	Negative treatment; the statute has been amended, repealed, superseded, or held unconstitutional (in whole or in part)
Yellow flag	Some negative history, but the case has not been reversed or overruled	Proposed legislation might affect the statute; the statute has been limited on constitutional or preemption grounds; a prior version of the statute received negative treatment in a case
Blue "H"	The case has some history	—
Green "C"	Citing sources are available (case has no direct history or negative citing sources)	Citing sources are available (statute has no history)
Stars	The number of stars shows how extensively a citing source discusses the case (four stars indicates an extensive discussion while one star suggests a mention in a citation)	—
Quotation marks	The citing source quotes the case	—

where your case is cited. You can quickly skim that portion of the document and decide whether the authority is relevant to your research.

As you read the citing sources, decide whether they address the legal issue in your client's problem. If a source analyzes only points of your case that are not relevant to your client's situation, disregard that source. If a source is on point, analyze its impact on your case:

Does this new source change the rule announced in your case, either by reversing or overruling it? Or does it follow your case by simply restating the rule and applying it to a similar fact pattern? Does the new source distinguish or criticize your case? If so, why and how? Be very wary of unfavorable criticism of your authorities—opposing counsel will be certain to point it out.

V. Updating Details

In working with either Shepard's or KeyCite, keep in mind the following details.

A. Colored Symbols

The colored symbols provided by Shepard's and KeyCite are simply quick references. A careful reading of the citing sources is required to determine whether the symbols are accurate and relevant to your research problem. A red stop sign on Shepard's or a red flag on KeyCite might mean that a lower court in another jurisdiction disagreed with the analysis of the case you are updating. That citing source has no impact on the weight of your case. As another example, a red symbol might mean that the case has been overruled for one issue but remains valid for all other issues discussed.

Moreover, neither citator's view of an authority is definitive, and in some instances they disagree. In other words, Shepard's might determine a case is no longer good law and assign a red symbol, while KeyCite determines that a case has merely been distinguished and assign a yellow symbol. You must read the citing sources and determine their impact for yourself.

The placement of symbols is important. A symbol *next to* a citing source (after the source on Shepard's and before the source on KeyCite) refers to that source, not to the cited source. Thus, in the Shepard's example for *Citizens United* in Figure 10-2, the stop sign next to the *Sonnier* case means that *Sonnier* has received negative treatment. It does not mean that *Sonnier* treats *Citizens United* negatively.

B. Headnotes

When Shepard's or KeyCite lists relevant headnotes, those head-notes are from your cited case. In the Shepard's example in Figure 10-2, the headnote references following *Sonnier* (e.g., "HN9" and "HN11") are to headnotes of *Citizens United*. Clicking on a particular headnote reference will take you to the place in the citing source that discusses the point of law in that headnote of *Citizens United*.

Never assume that the headnotes in Shepard's and KeyCite are the same. The two services are competitors; while their headnotes are often similar, they are typically not identical.

C. Prioritizing Citing Sources

If time allows, read *every* citing source to determine its impact on the case you are updating. When pressed for time, prioritize the citing sources you will read according to the following criteria:

- Focus on any negative treatment. Look for any case that reverses, overrules, criticizes, or distinguishes your case.
- Read cases from your jurisdiction before reading cases decided elsewhere, which are only persuasive authority.
- Read cases from the highest appellate court, then the intermediate appellate courts, and finally the trial courts (if trial court cases are published) in your jurisdiction.
- Start with more recent cases rather than older cases.
- Choose cases cited for the headnotes that are on point for your research.

D. Table of Authorities

Both Shepard's and KeyCite provide a link to a case's "Table of Authorities," sometimes indicated by "TOA." This function lists the cases cited by the case being updated; in other words, it looks back from the date of the cited case, while the other citator lists look forward.

The Table of Authorities is valuable for two reasons. First, it provides a list of cases that you may need to read. If the case you are updating relied on these cases, they may be relevant to your research in their own right. A very recent case might not have many citing sources, but its opinion might refer to the most important cases in the area of law you are researching. Second, the Table of Authorities indicates whether the cases in that list are still respected. If they are not, the case you are updating may be on shaky ground because authority it relied on is no longer valid.

VI. When to Use Citators

Citators are valuable research tools at several points in the research process. Whenever you first encounter a case, statute, or other source with a citator symbol, quickly check the colored symbol to see whether the source been treated negatively. If so, explore that treatment before beginning to place much reliance on the analysis in that case, statute, or other source.

Later, when you have determined that a case or statute is relevant to your research, carefully review its list of citing sources to find other authorities that discuss the same points of law. Reading the citing sources produced by a citator search may lead to cases in which the court's reasoning is explained more fully or to cases with facts more similar to your client's. As you discover more cases that are on point for your issue, look for trends in frequency and treatment of case citations. In general, cases that have been cited frequently and followed extensively should form the basis of your analysis. You can exclude from your analysis a case that has been ignored by later cases unless the facts are very similar to your client's or the reasoning is especially relevant. You will have to counter any cases that criticize or distinguish a case or statute you rely on in your analysis.

You should continue updating cases and other authorities until the moment your final document is submitted or your argument is presented to a court. Shepard's and KeyCite are continually publishing updated information; the case you Shepardized or KeyCited two weeks ago could have been overruled yesterday.

VII. Citators and Legal Ethics

While using citators as a research tool is optional, using them to validate authorities is an ethical obligation. Courts expect lawyers to use citators to ensure that their arguments are supported by current, respected authorities.[5] Failing to cite current law or disclose adverse authority may result in sanctions, malpractice suits, public embarrassment, and a damaged professional reputation. In one instance, a judge ordered a major law firm to copy for each of its partners and associates an opinion chastising the firm for failing to cite a case adverse to the client's argument.[6] In another case, an attorney was suspended from practice for dishonesty to his client, misuse of client funds, and failure to file the client's claim within the limitations period. In reviewing the facts of the case, the court noted that the attorney "had not Shepardized the cases he relied on regarding the statute of limitations."[7]

---

5. One court noted that "failure to 'Shepardize' a key case [is] not excusable." *See McCarthy v. Oregon Freeze Dry, Inc.*, 976 P.2d 566, 567 (Or. App. 1999).

6. *Golden Eagle Distribg. Corp. v. Burroughs Corp.*, 103 F.R.D. 124, 129 (N.D. Cal. 1984) ("For counsel to have been unaware of those cases means that they did not Shepardize their principal authority....").

7. *In re Tway*, 919 P.2d 323, 325 (Idaho 1996).

Chapter 11

Court Rules and Rules of Professional Responsibility

I. Introduction

In addition to knowing the applicable substantive law, a lawyer must know what court rules of practice, procedure, and evidence apply to proceedings in a particular court. Often, more than one set of rules will apply. Further, lawyers and judges must abide by the rules of professional responsibility that govern their conduct. Specific information on the various court rules and rules of professional responsibility is given in this chapter.

II. Court Rules

The term *court rules* is used to refer to two types of rules: (1) rules of procedure and evidence applicable in a particular jurisdiction, and (2) rules established by a particular court or courts that supplement federal or state rules of procedure, sometimes known as *local rules*. Both types of rules play an important role in litigation in these courts. They instruct parties on all facets of litigation, from filing pleadings and motions, to conducting formal discovery, to handling litigation before, during, and after trial. Failure to abide by these rules can significantly change the outcome of litigation. In addition, some judges publish preferred procedures for their own courtrooms, often available on the court's website.

A. Rules of Procedure and Evidence

1. Background

Rules of civil, criminal, and appellate procedure must be followed to litigate in trial and appellate courts. These rules have the force of law. They exist at both the federal and state level; in fact, many state rules are based on and are similar to the federal rules.

In the federal system, a federal statute gives the Supreme Court "the power to prescribe general rules of practice and procedure and rules of evidence for cases in the United States district courts (including proceedings before magistrate judges thereof) and courts of appeals."[1] The rules promulgated pursuant to this power include the following:

   (a) the Federal Rules of Civil Procedure, including the Supplemental Rules for Certain Admiralty and Maritime Claims,
   (b) the Federal Rules of Criminal Procedure,
   (c) the Federal Rules of Appellate Procedure, and
   (d) the Federal Rules of Evidence.

The Federal Rules of Civil Procedure govern cases brought in federal court arising out of disputes between individuals or entities in which a party, the plaintiff, is seeking damages or some other civil remedy from another party, the defendant. The rules of civil procedure cover topics such as the types of pleadings that may be filed, the style of those pleadings, when and how parties must be served with process, what parties may be joined, how discovery is to be conducted, what motions may be filed, and how juries must be selected.

Courts apply rules of criminal procedure to cases based on criminal law. Criminal cases are brought by the government, the prosecution, which is seeking a judgment against an individual or entity, the defendant, punishing the defendant under criminal law. The Federal Rules of Criminal Procedure identify such topics as the types of documents that must be filed to initiate prosecution, the steps that must be taken to move a case along, and procedures for entering a plea and for sentencing.

---

1. 28 U.S.C. § 2072 (2006). This statute is part of the Rules Enabling Act, codified at 28 U.S.C. §§ 2071–77 (2006).

Rules of appellate procedure govern both civil and criminal actions before appellate courts. They dictate the procedures for filing a notice of appeal or a writ seeking permission to file an appeal as well as what must be filed with the court and when. In the federal system, these rules are known as the Federal Rules of Appellate Procedure.

The Federal Rules of Evidence govern the introduction and admissibility of evidence into civil and criminal proceedings in federal courts. State court rules of evidence govern in state courts; many states have based their rules of evidence on the federal rules.

Additionally, the Supreme Court has the power to prescribe rules governing practice and procedure in bankruptcy cases.[2] These rules are known as the Federal Rules of Bankruptcy Procedure.

The federal rules mentioned above are promulgated in a unique way, different from the way federal statutes are enacted. Through the Rules Enabling Act,[3] Congress authorized the judiciary to prescribe rules of practice, procedure, and evidence to govern in the federal courts. Pursuant to this authority, the Supreme Court created the Committee on Rules of Practice and Procedure, which in turn appoints subcommittees to review these rules, entertain comments on the rules and on rule changes, and recommend changes to the Supreme Court. If the Court approves proposed rules, they are sent to Congress. They become effective if Congress does not act to reject or modify them within a certain period of time. Once the rules become effective, they have the force of law and courts enforce them in the same way they enforce statutory law.

2. Researching Federal Rules of Procedure and Evidence

The federal rules of procedure and evidence are published with the federal statutes in the U.S.C., the U.S.C.A., and the U.S.C.S.[4] The Federal Rules of Civil Procedure, the Federal Rules of Appellate Proce-

---

2. 28 U.S.C. § 2075 (2006).
3. 28 U.S.C. §§ 2071–77 (2006).
4. Because the U.S.C. tends to be published more slowly than the other publications, it is not the best source in which to research current rules. Thus, you should use the U.S.C.A. and the U.S.C.S.

dure, and the Federal Rules of Evidence are published as an appendix to Title 28 of the United States Code in the U.S.C. and the U.S.C.A.; the Federal Rules of Criminal Procedure are published as an appendix to Title 18, and the Federal Rules of Bankruptcy Procedure are published as an appendix to Title 11. The U.S.C.S. publishes separate volumes devoted to rules that are found after the titles of the United States Code, except that the Federal Rules of Evidence are published as an appendix to Title 28. You may research these rules using search terms in the General Index to these publications of the United States Code or using search terms in the separate indexes that follow each set of rules.

These rules are also readily available online from free and commercial web services. For example, court websites provide links to the rules applicable in the specific courts. The United States House of Representatives Office of the Law Revision Counsel provides free online access to the United States Code.[5] The site allows researchers to search the database and download titles and chapters of the U.S.C. and view a list of titles and classification tables containing sections of the U.S.C. affected by recently enacted law.

Another option to locate the rules without a fee is Cornell University Law School's Legal Information Institute (L.I.I.) online site.[6] Using this site, you can search by identifying a publication and specific rule or by browsing a rule publication's table of contents for the topic you are researching. The United States Courts website is another free source on which you can locate specific rules by using the tables of contents of the documents to see the text of the rules.[7] This site provides links to specific federal courts and valuable information on rule-making such as proposed and successful changes to the rules as well as reviews and comments to the rules. Reviews and comments to the rules are written by the Committee on Rules of Practice and Procedure. Judges and lawyers may use these as persuasive authority when determining the meaning of a rule.

---

5. The address is http://uscode.house.gov.
6. The site is found at www.law.cornell.edu/uscode.
7. The address is www.uscourts.gov.

While the free online sites are an easy way to locate the rules, they are not the best places to research unfamiliar rules. In addition to researching print versions of the United States Code, researching on Lexis and Westlaw are efficient ways to research federal rules. These services provide searchable databases focused on federal rules and databases that include the rules with federal statutes.

B. Court-Specific Rules, Including Local Rules

Through the Rules Enabling Act, Congress also authorized courts to "prescribe rules for the conduct of their business."[8] These rules supplement the procedural rules discussed above and often provide more detail about how to proceed in a particular court. They are called *local rules* when they refer to the rules that originate in specific trial and appellate courts and govern filings and appearances in those courts only. Some local rules also address issues such as courtroom decorum and professionalism before the court. Like the federal rules of procedure and evidence, local rules have the force of law.

The United States Supreme Court Rules, for example, dictate the number of copies of documents to be filed with the Court, how those documents should be styled, and the requirements for admission to appear before the Court, among other things. As another example, in addition to dictating procedures in the court, the local rules for the Eastern District of Louisiana include rules addressing professionalism and procedures for disciplining lawyers who may violate the law or rules of professional conduct.[9]

Each of the circuits of the United States Courts of Appeals has a set of local rules that supplements the Federal Rules of Appellate Procedure. Federal district courts also have local rules. When more than one federal district court exists within a state, the different district courts may consolidate their local rules into a set of *uniform local rules*.

---

8. 28 U.S.C. § 2071.
9. Unif. Loc. R.D. La. 83.2.10E.

Additionally, the following rules have been promulgated to govern practice and procedure before the identified courts:

(a) the Rules of the Court of Federal Claims,

(b) the Rules of the United States Court of International Trade,

(c) the Rules of Procedure of the Judicial Panel on Multidistrict Litigation,

(d) the Rules of Practice and Procedure of the United States Tax Court, and

(e) the Rules of the Court of Appeals for the Armed Forces.

Local rules are published on court websites and in West deskbooks, which are updated annually. Consulting the table of contents preceding a set of rules either online or in a deskbook is a simple way to locate relevant rules.[10] Some court websites provide search engines for searching their local rules, and deskbooks include indexes that you can search for local rules. The United States Courts website[11] provides links to all federal court local rules. These rules are also available on Lexis and Westlaw.

Further, the U.S.C.A. and the U.S.C.S. both publish the following rules:

- the Rules of the Supreme Court of the United States,
- the Rules of the Court of Federal Claims,
- the Rules of the United States Court of International Trade,
- the Rules of Procedure of the Judicial Panel on Multidistrict Litigation,
- the Rules of Practice and Procedure of the United States Tax Court,
- the Rules of the Court of Appeals for the Armed Forces, and
- the local rules of each of the United States Courts of Appeals.

---

10. The local rules of the federal district courts use a numbering system that corresponds to the federal rules of procedure, discussed earlier in this chapter, which can make searching for local rules a bit easier. For example, Federal Rule of Civil Procedure 26 addresses discovery; thus, Rule 26 of federal district court local rules will ordinarily address discovery.

11. The home page is www.uscourts.gov.

Each of these sources has a General Index and a Popular Name Table in which one can use search terms or the name of the rules to locate the rules or specific provisions of the rules.

III. Rules of Professional Responsibility

Although rules of professional responsibility are adopted and enforced by states, not the federal government, they are included here because ethical conduct is so important to successful practice.

A. Background

The legal profession is a self-policing and self-regulating profession that is governed by state codes of professional responsibility. The American Bar Association (ABA) publishes the Model Rules of Professional Responsibility. These rules are models because the ABA is a private organization with no law-making power. State legislatures or courts must propose and adopt rules for these rules to govern lawyers in a particular state. All states except California have adopted rules based on the ABA Model Rules.[12]

Ordinarily, the rules of professional responsibility applicable to lawyers practicing in federal and state courts are the rules governing the state bar for the state in which the court sits. Violating a rule may subject the lawyer to discipline by the state bar association; in some states, a violation of a rule may also be used to support allegations in a lawsuit against the lawyer for malpractice. As is noted in the previous section on local rules, some federal courts also supplement the state rules of professional conduct with their own rules of conduct.

Further, some federal rules and statutes address lawyers' obligations more specifically than the rules of professional responsibility, thus also supplementing state rules. For example, Federal Rule of

---

12. California has its own rules of professional responsibility, but they are not modeled after the ABA Rules.

Civil Procedure 11 requires lawyers to sign each pleading and motion filed with the court to certify that the document has been properly researched and that it is not filed for an improper purpose, among other things. The rule addresses the propriety of representations made by lawyers to the court and empowers the court to sanction lawyers for rule violations.

In addition to rules of professionalism governing practicing lawyers, similar rules and codes govern judicial conduct. States have codes of judicial conduct, many of which are modeled after the ABA Model Code of Judicial Conduct. Federal judges must abide by the Code of Conduct for United States Judges, which is a set of principles and guidelines adopted by the Judicial Conference of the United States. Federal law also provides procedures for filing complaints against federal judges in the Judicial Conduct and Disability Act of 1980.[13]

B. Researching Rules of Professional Responsibility

When researching rules of professional responsibility, first identify the state rules applicable to the lawyer or judge as well as any specific federal rules. The state rules of professional responsibility and the state code of judicial conduct are easily located online on state bar association websites and on multiple other free websites. Another helpful site is supported by the ABA's Center for Professional Responsibility.[14] This site provides a list of states with links to each state's professional responsibility rules, codes of judicial conduct, and other materials related to professional responsibility. State rules and codes are usually published with the state statutes.

Once you have identified the applicable code of professional responsibility, the second step is to use your search terms in the appropriate index or database or consult the table of rules that precedes the rules themselves to determine which rules may be relevant to the issue you are researching. Rules and codes of professional responsibility can be lo-

---

13. 28 U.S.C. §§ 351–64 (2006).
14. The address is http://www.americanbar.org/groups/professional_responsibility/resources/links_of_interest.html.

cated by running a search on Lexis or Westlaw in a database for the particular state statute or state court rules. See Table 11-1 for an excerpt from the table of rules for the Model Rules of Professional Responsibility. Notice that the rules are organized by topic, which facilitates locating relevant rules. The code of judicial conduct is similarly organized. More extensive research not restricted by jurisdiction can be done by using the legal ethics and professional responsibility databases.

After locating specific rules, review them to determine if they are relevant to your issue. Review annotations to the rules and commentary about the rules to determine their relevance and meaning. Because most state rules of professional conduct are based on the ABA Model Rules, official comments to the ABA Model Rules may also assist in determining how state rules may be interpreted. The Model Rules and comments are available online on the ABA's website.[15] These rules are also available on Lexis and Westlaw. Official comments to the ABA Model Rules are also often included with the state rules to which they are relevant. Comments to the Model Rules are designed to "explain[] and illustrate[] the meaning and purpose of the Rule[s]"[16] and "are intended as guides to interpretation."[17]

Similarly, because many judicial codes of conduct are based on the ABA Model Code of Judicial Conduct, materials supporting the ABA Code, such as its comments, can be helpful when reviewing and interpreting a similar state provision.

If you are researching the Code of Conduct for United States Judges, a good place to start is the United States Courts website,[18] which provides a link to the text of the Code. The conduct code has a table of canons (rules), which is followed by the canons and commentary to the canons. Additionally, the site provides a link to published advisory opinions regarding the Code, which is preceded by an index to the advisory opinions.

---

15. The address is http://www.americanbar.org/groups/professional_responsibility.html.

16. Model Rules of Prof'l Conduct, Scope 21 (ABA 2004).

17. *Id.*

18. The address is www.uscourts.gov.

**Table 11-1. Excerpt of Table of Rules for the
Model Rules of Professional Responsibility**

Rule 1.0   Terminology

Client-Lawyer Relationship

Rule 1.1   Competence

Rule 1.2   Scope of Representation and Allocation of Authority
             Between Client and Lawyer

Rule 1.3   Diligence

Rule 1.4   Communications

Rule 1.5   Fees

Rule 1.6   Confidentiality of Information

Rule 1.7   Conflict of Interest: Current Clients

Rule 1.8   Conflict of Interest: Current Clients: Specific Rules

Rule 1.9   Duties to Former Clients

Rule 1.10   Imputation of Conflicts of Interest: General Rule

Rule 1.11   Special Conflicts of Interest for Former and Current
             Government Officers and Employees

Rule 1.12   Former Judge, Arbitrator, Mediator or Other Third-
             Party Neutral

Rule 1.13   Organization as Client

Rule 1.14   Client with Diminished Capacity

Rule 1.15   Safekeeping Property

Rule 1.16   Declining or Terminating Representation

Rule 1.17   Sale of Law Practice

Rule 1.18   Duties to Prospective Client

Counselor

Rule 2.1   Advisor

Rule 2.2   (Deleted)

Rule 2.3   Evaluation for Use by Third Persons

Rule 2.4   Lawyer Serving as Third-Party Neutral

Advocate

Rule 3.1   Meritorious Claims and Contentions

Rule 3.2   Expediting Litigation

Rule 3.3   Candor toward the Tribunal

Rule 3.4   Fairness to Opposing Party and Counsel

Rule 3.5   Impartiality and Decorum of the Tribunal

Rule 3.6   Trial Publicity

Rule 3.7   Lawyer as Witness

Rule 3.8   Special Responsibilities of a Prosecutor

Rule 3.9   Advocate in Nonadjudicative Proceedings

Researching the Judicial Conduct and Disability Act of 1980 or other federal rules or statutes on professional conduct is best done by searching the index to the U.S.C.A. or the U.S.C.S. or searching online using Lexis or Westlaw.

Several secondary sources are available to assist with researching rules of professional responsibility. Some sources are jurisdiction specific. Others address professional responsibility in a more general way but are annotated with citations to jurisdiction-specific rules and decisions. One helpful secondary source is the *Restatement of the Law Third: The Law Governing Lawyers* (American Law Institute 2000–2011). This publication addresses ethics issues and applications of rules across the Unites States. The ABA site on professional responsibility noted above offers a link comparing the Model Rules with the *Restatement of the Law Third: The Law Governing Lawyers*. Researching in secondary sources is discussed in Chapter 3.

About the Authors

Mary Garvey Algero is the Warren E. Mouledoux Distinguished Professor of Law, Director of the Legal Research and Writing Program, and Co-Director of the Westerfield Fellows Program at Loyola University New Orleans College of Law. She is the author of *Louisiana Legal Research*.

Spencer Simons is Director of the O'Quinn Law Library and Associate Professor of Law at the University of Houston Law Center. He is the author of *Texas Legal Research*.

Suzanne Rowe is the James L. and Ilene R. Hershner Professor and Director of Legal Research and Writing at the University of Oregon School of Law. She is the author of *Oregon Legal Research* and co-author of several other titles in the Legal Research Series.

Scott Childs is Associate Professor and Associate Dean for Library and Technology Services at the University of Tennessee College of Law. He is the author of *North Carolina Legal Research*.

Sarah Ricks is a Clinical Professor of Law and Co-Director of the Pro Bono Research Project at Rutgers School of Law-Camden. She is the author of *Current Issues in Constitutional Litigation: A Context and Practice Casebook*.

Index